Florence
Shortlist

timeout.com / florence

119

147

2

Contents

857 34186

ABOUT THE GUIDE

The *Time Out Florence Shortlist* is one of a series of pocket guides to cities around the globe. Drawing on the expertise of local authors, it distils their knowledge into a handy, easy-to-use format that ensures you get the most from your trip, whether you're a first-time or a return visitor.

Time Out Florence Shortlist is divided into four sections:

Welcome to Florence introduces the city and provides inspiration for your visit.

Florence Day by Day helps you plan your trip with an events calendar and customised itineraries.

Florence by Area is the main visitor section of the guide. It includes detailed listings and reviews for the very best sights, museums, restaurants and wine bars ⑩, cafés and gelaterie ⑩, shops ⑩ and entertainment venues ⑩, all organised by area with a corresponding street map. To help navigation, each area of Florence has been assigned its own colour.

Florence Essentials provides practical visitor information, including accommodation options and details of public transport.

Shortlists & highlights

We have selected a Shortlist of stand-out venues in each area, which are marked with a heart ♥ in the text. The very best of these appear in the Highlights feature (*see p10*) and receive extended coverage in the guide.

Maps

There's an overview map on *p8* and individual street maps for each area of the city. Venues featured in the guide have been given a grid reference so that you can find them easily on the maps and on the ground.

Prices

All our **restaurant** listings are marked with a euro symbol (€-€€€€) indicating the average price you should expect to pay for a main course (*secondo*): € = under €10; €€ = €10-€25; €€€ = €25-€40; €€€€ = over €40.

A similar system is used in our **Accommodation** chapter, based on the hotel's standard prices for one night in a double room: Budget = under €100; Mid-range = €100-€200; Expensive = €200-€300; Luxury = over €300.

Introduction

Why Florence? 'For the Renaissance' is the obvious answer. But, the City of the Lily is so much more than a place to see Michelangelos and Botticellis. In fact, it boasts two millennia of history layered and merged into one glorious square mile, so easily walkable and convenient to navigate that you may never need to check your bearings on a map. You'll find a variety of world-class cultural events and performing arts venues, and a surprisingly fast-growing contemporary art scene; plus inexpensive food, sublime wine and delicious gelato, which tradition says was invented here. Florence is also one of the world's fashion capitals, with museums celebrating its local designers. It's a cradle of craftsmanship and ingenuity, with shopping opportunities ranging from artisan studios to world-class brands. As a visitor, there are few downsides to Florence, and with the help of our insider tips, even the crowds can be effectively circumvented.

L' AN
D

West arch of piazza della Repubblica

Welcome to Florence

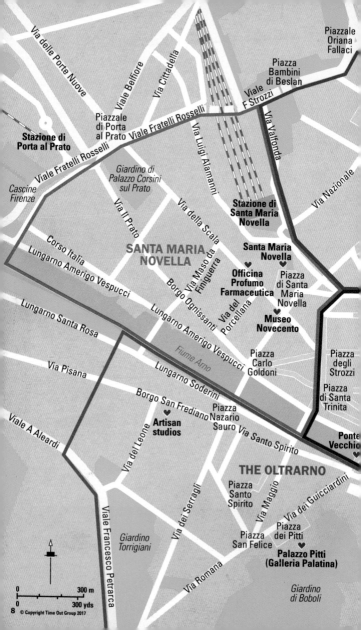

Via delle Porte Nuove

Piazzale Oriana Fallaci

Piazza Bambini di Beslan

Viale Belfiore

Via Cittadella

Viale F Strozzi

Via Valfonda

Piazzale di Porta al Prato

Viale Fratelli Rosselli

Stazione di Porta al Prato

Viale Fratelli Rosselli

Via Luigi Alamanni

Cascine Firenze

Giardino di Palazzo Corsini sul Prato

Via Nazionale

Via II Prato

Via della Scala

Stazione di Santa Maria Novella

Corso Italia

SANTA MARIA NOVELLA

Santa Maria Novella ♥

Lungarno Amerigo Vespucci

Via Maso da Finiguerra

Officina Profumo Farmaceutica ♥

Piazza di Santa Maria Novella

Borgo Ognissanti

Via del Porcellana

Lungarno Santa Rosa

Lungarno Amerigo Vespucci

Museo Novecento ♥

Via Pisana

Fiume Arno

Piazza Carlo Goldoni

Piazza degli Strozzi

Lungarno Soderini

Piazza di Santa Trinita

Viale A Aleardi

Borgo San Frediano

Piazza Nazario Sauro

Via Santo Spirito

Ponte Vecchio ♥

Via dei Leone

Artisan studios ★

Via dei Serragli

THE OLTRARNO

Piazza Santo Spirito

Via Maggio

Via dei Guicciardini

Viale Francesco Petrarca

Giardino Torrigiani

Piazza San Felice

Piazza dei Pitti

Palazzo Pitti (Galleria Palatina) ♥

0   300 m
0   300 yds

Giardino di Boboli

Via Romana

8 © Copyright Time Out Group 2017

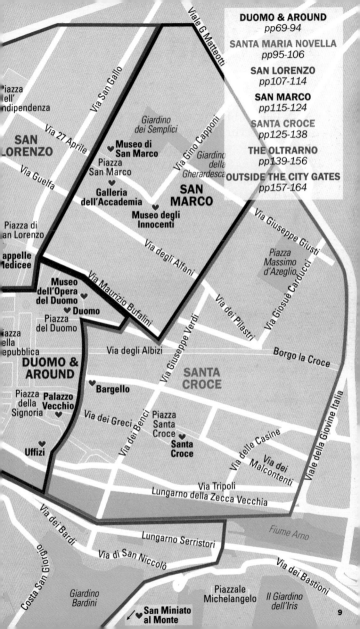

Viale G. Matteotti

Via San Gallo

Piazza dell'Indipendenza

Via 27 Aprile

SAN LORENZO

Via Guelfa

Piazza di San Lorenzo

Cappelle Medicee

Giardino dei Semplici

♥ **Museo di San Marco**

Piazza San Marco

♥ **Galleria dell'Accademia**

♥ **Museo degli Innocenti**

Via degli Alfani

SAN MARCO

Via Gino Capponi

Giardino della Gherardesca

Via Giuseppe Giusti

Piazza Massimo d'Azeglio

Via Giosuè Carducci

Via Maurizio Bufalini

Museo dell'Opera del Duomo ♥

♥ **Duomo**

Piazza del Duomo

Piazza della Repubblica

DUOMO & AROUND

Piazza della Signoria

Palazzo Vecchio ♥

♥ **Uffizi**

Via degli Albizi

Via Giuseppe Verdi

Via dei Pilastri

Borgo la Croce

SANTA CROCE

♥ **Bargello**

Via dei Greci

Via dei Benci

Piazza Santa Croce ♥

Santa Croce

Via delle Casine

Via dei Malcontenti

Viale della Giovine Italia

Via Tripoli

Lungarno della Zecca Vecchia

Via dei Bardi

Lungarno Serristori

Fiume Arno

Via di San Niccolò

Via dei Bastioni

Costa San Giorgio

Giardino Bardini

Piazzale Michelangelo

Il Giardino dell'Iris

♥ **San Miniato al Monte**

9

Highlights

Every part of Florence is packed with artistic and architectural treasures: Brunelleschi's dome and Giotto's campanile, Botticelli's *Birth of Venus* and Michelangelo's *David*, the incomparable Baptistery doors and the gold shops lining the Ponte Vecchio. To stop you getting overwhelmed, here's a rundown of the city's unmissable sights.

01

Uffizi *p88*

If the queues and the two million visitors each year are any indication, this is the art destination to top all Florentine bucket lists. Once the offices of the local magistrates – hence the name 'Uffizi' (offices) – the Vasari-designed building now houses the world's premier collection of Renaissance art, including masterpieces such as Botticelli's *Birth of Venus* and *Primavera*, each of which has its own wall.

02

Galleria dell'Accademia *p118*

This small museum holds numerous noteworthy works, including some lovely examples of Michelangelo's *non finito*, but the main attraction is indisputably his *David*, a statue carrying the technical mastery of the ancient Greeks and all the celebrity power of a rock star.

03

Duomo *p74*

Dominated by Brunelleschi's dome, an engineering feat for the ages, Florence's fairytale-like cathedral complex lives up to its goal. It was commissioned with the aim of proving Florence to be the most important Tuscan city. Built atop the former church of Santa Reparata (the remains of which are in the crypt), the complex also includes Giotto's bell tower. Across from the Duomo (with a Vasari-frescoed dome interior) stands the Romanesque Baptistery and copies of its fabled bronze doors.

04

Museo dell'Opera del Duomo *p80*

This spectacular sculpture museum reopened in late 2015 after a 50 million-euro renovation. Don't let its unassuming entrance deceive you: inside you'll find close to 750 medieval and Renaissance masterpieces, contextualised according to their original roles within the cathedral complex. Heavy hitters include Donatello's *Penitent Magdalene*, Ghiberti's gilded bronze doors (the magnificent Baptistery originals) and a full-scale reconstruction of the original façade by Arnolfo di Cambio.

05

Palazzo Vecchio *p84*

Florence's town hall since medieval times, the imposing Palazzo Vecchio is one of the enduring symbols of the city. Outside, it boasts a 94m (308ft) bell tower; inside are secret passages and the spectacular Salone dei Cinquecento (Hall of the 500) with murals by Vasari and, if rumours are true, Leonardo da Vinci's masterwork *The Battle of Anghiari* hidden beneath.

06

Ponte Vecchio *p90*

The Ponte Vecchio is the city's most iconic bridge, and the only one not destroyed during World War II – legend has it that Hitler was so moved by its beauty, he expressly ordered German troops to leave it untouched. Butcher's shops once lined the walkway, but today, the buildings host fine jewellery shops. Rise extra early to cross the bridge *sans* crowds, or perch next to the central Benvenuto Cellini statue to watch the shopkeepers and street cleaners start their days.

07

San Miniato al Monte *p161*

Conquer the steps above Porta San Niccolò and follow the pathway to the austere San Miniato al Monte. The winding trek to this Romanesque beauty belies its simple interior, where you'll hear monks chanting if you visit in mid-afternoon. Stop at the nearby piazzale Michelangelo at the day's end to take in an unbeatable Tuscan sunset overlooking the city.

08

Bargello *p129*

Once the chief magistrate's headquarters, this building is now home to a wide-ranging sculpture collection. Mystifyingly, it's rarely crowded, despite must-sees such as Michelangelo's *Bacchus*, Donatello's boyish bronze *David* and Brunelleschi's and Ghiberti's bronze panels depicting the *Sacrifice of Isaac*. In summer, the airy courtyard hosts concerts and dance performances – lively and far more palatable than its past function as an exhibition space for executed criminals' bodies.

09

Galleria Palatina *p144*

A showcase of Medici exhibitionism, this grandiose residential palace, which the Medici purchased in the 16th century, is now home to several museums. The highlight is the lavish Galleria Palatina (Palatine Gallery), which leads into the Appartamenti Reali (Royal Apartments) and pristine White Hall. Titian, Peter Paul Rubens and Raphael are all at home here, and the gilded ceilings are dizzying.

10

Santa Croce *p130*

Visiting Santa Croce might inspire an inferiority complex: it's nicknamed the Temple of Italian Glories for a reason. Florence's principal Franciscan church, its 'resting roster' boasts some of the biggest names in the Boot: Michelangelo, Machiavelli and Galileo all have their tombs here. Giotto's floor-to-ceiling frescoes in the Peruzzi and the Bardi chapels are another highlight, but go beyond the basilica: Pazzi Chapel, the complex's hushed former chapter house, is one of the city's most mysterious and architecturally harmonious spaces.

11

Santa Maria Novella *p100*

The Dominican counterpart to Santa Croce, Santa Maria Novella instantly intrigues with its green and white geometric façade, designed by Leon Battista Alberti. More masterpieces include a Giotto crucifix; the *Trinity* by a young Masaccio, and the Strozzi Chapel, frescoed by Filippino Lippi at the end of his career. In recent years: Paolo Uccello's Green Cloister frescoes have been restored and the museum has been expanded with the incorporation of the Caserma Mameli complex.

12

Museo di San Marco *p122*

Set aside some quality time with Fra Angelico: this museum, housed in a monastery, is a testament to the leading 15th-century painter's devotion and talent. The few crowds that come here tend to congregate around his *Annunciation*, a commanding introduction at the top of the complex's first staircase. Other must-sees are the amusingly king-size cell Cosimo de' Medici used on his sporadic spiritual cleanses, as well as the bunk of fire-and-brimstone friar Girolamo Savonarola.

Museo Novecento *p99*

A refreshing ode to 20th-century Italian art – ideal for when Renaissance fatigue rears its head – this modern museum was born from a tragedy. The 1966 Arno flood destroyed or damaged countless Florentine artworks, prompting the formation of a committee tasked with raising global awareness. Hundreds of artists answered their call to donate work to Florence, with local government promising they'd be featured in a future art museum. These donated works are now part of the museum's 300-piece permanent collection.

Officina Profumo-Farmaceutica di Santa Maria Novella *p105*

Antique markets? Check. Scandinavian-inspired concept shops? Check. Flagship boutiques from high fashion's biggest names? Absolutely. Shopping in Florence isn't short on variety: prestigious boutiques from Ferragamo to Pucci line via de' Tornabuoni, while the funkier holes-in-the-wall of via della Spada offer more budget-friendly finds. Save time for a full-blown sensory experience at Officina Profumo-Farmaceutica di Santa Maria Novella, a cosmetic shop with origins dating back to the 13th century, when Dominican friars founded an apothecary in its namesake convent.

15

Museo degli Innocenti *p121*

Designed by Brunelleschi, the 15th-century Ospedale degli Innocenti was a foundling hospital, notably run by laypeople. The museum's focus is threefold: the history of the institute, tales of its children and highlights from its art collection. The latter includes a striking Domenico Ghirlandaio altarpiece and a smattering of Botticelli and Della Robbia works. Yet it's the touching stories of the institute's children, including 20th-century testimonials, that make this a must-stop.

16

The Oltrarno's artisan studios *p179*

Artisan activity has always been concentrated on Florence's south bank, a traditionally poor district that's taken a controversial turn for the trendy in recent years. This long-time mecca for 'Made in Italy' production – leather and paper, painting and sculpture, silver and gold – continues to face challenges. But handmade crafts and design studios doubling as shops are still part of the neighbourhood fabric, from historic, hidden spots like the silk workshop Antico Setificio Fiorentino to dynamic DIY spaces such as Officine Nora.

17

Cappelle Medicee *p112*

To get a true sense of Medici excess, head to their burial site at San Lorenzo. The almost comically opulent Chapel of the Princes is a domed, marbled home to the grand dukes' sarcophagi, while Michelangelo's New Sacristy is comparatively understated. Downstairs, you might accidentally sidestep the modest tomb of final heir Anna Maria Luisa – a minimal acknowledgment of the woman who, by bequeathing her family's art collections to the Tuscan state, is largely responsible for Florence's continued splendour.

Florentine hillside

Sightseeing

UNESCO estimates that Italy is home to around 60 per cent of the world's most important works of art, over half of which are located in Florence, and with the lion's share created in the golden age of Medici patronage. This explosion of artistic invention and architectural brilliance brought to the city the Renaissance masterpieces that still grace its squares and alleyways, museums and churches. Without even setting foot inside those great shrines to art – the Uffizi, Galleria dell'Accademia and the Bargello – the glimpses of Brunelleschi's miraculous dome, Cellini's impossible bronze Perseus and Alberti's faultless façade of Santa Maria Novella are constant reminders that to come to Florence is to enter a honey-stone coloured time-warp.

Past and present

Florence is battling to reconcile its Renaissance legacy
with 21st-century realities – as more citizens are forced
out of the city centre by impossible rents and traffic
restrictions, Florence becomes the domain of wealthy
expats, poor immigrants and tourists. It is also under
pressure to cope with mass tourism while preserving
its unique assets for generations to come. Pollution and
carelessness, not to mention sheer footfall, threaten the
delicate artworks that the crowds flock to admire.

However, although change may be slow, the city
is evolving – new tram lines are being built that will
ease congestion, and the importance of the city's
contemporary art and architecture is gaining recognition.
The Civic Museums finally brought most of the city's
20th-century artworks under one single roof with
the **Museo Novecento** (*see p99*) and designated
the **Forte di Belvedere** (*see p145*) as the venue of
choice for a major yearly contemporary art exhibition.
The Uffizi signed a three-year agreement with Pitti

The Medici Family

The legendary dynasty that helped to shape the Renaissance

The name Medici (pronounced with the stress on the 'e') is all but synonymous with Florence, where the family's largely well-judged patronage funded some of the world's greatest artworks. Many of their bodies are interred in the Cappelle Medicee (*see p112*).

Influential members of the family include **Giovanni di Bicci** (1360-1429), who founded the Medici bank that grew their great wealth; **Cosimo 'il Vecchio'** (1389-1464), who supported Brunelleschi and Donatello and created a wonderful public library (*see p111* Biblioteca Medicea Laurenziana) and had a magnificent town mansion built by Michelozzo (*see p109* Palazzo Medici Riccardi); **Lorenzo 'il Magnifico'** (1449-1492), who ruled Florence during its Renaissance heyday and was influential in the careers of Michelangelo, da Vinci and Botticelli; and **Anna Maria Luisa**, Electress Palatine (1667-1743), to whom every visitor to Florence since the mid-18th century has reason to be thankful.

In her will, she bequeathed all Medici property and treasures to the Grand Duchy in perpetuity, on the sole condition that they never leave the city.

Anna Maria Luisa

Immagine Discovery to turn the old Galleria del Costume into a much more ambitious **Museo della Moda e del Costume** (*see p148*).

It's architecture that Florentines find hard to digest in its latest incarnations. Modernist buildings such as the new Palazzo di Giustizia (law courts) in Novoli are only conceivable well outside the city gates, and controversy still rages over whether the **Teatro dell'Opera** project (*see p164*; expected to swallow up a disproportionate €320 million of public funds by its completion) really was such a good idea.

Uffizi Gallery

Museums and galleries

During the summer, around Easter and on public holidays, Florence spills over with visitors: the sights are crowded and huge queues form at the main museums. The quietest times to visit are from January to March (avoiding Easter), and from October to mid December.

Many of Florence's unrivalled museums have private collections at their core, whether that of a mega-family such as the Medici (**Uffizi**, **Palazzo Pitti**) or of a lone connoisseur (the **Bardini**, **Horne** and **Stibbert**

In the know
They don't like Mondays

It can be a shock to find out that some of Florence's major museums close on Mondays. These include the Uffizi, Galleria dell'Accademia and Galleria Palatina. If it's the first or third Monday of the month, you could go to the Museo di San Marco; on the second or fourth, try the Cappelle Medicee, the Bargello or certain Palazzo Pitti museums. Exceptions apply: when local or national holidays land on a Monday, many of the major museums open for the occasion. Also note that entry to state-run museums is free on the first Sunday of every month for Domenica al Museo.

The Renaissance

The classics that reshaped the world forever

The Renaissance is a massive source of pride for Florence. For centuries, the city has basked in its afterglow, and the world has basked with it.

The guiding doctrine of the Renaissance (*Rinascimento*; literally 'rebirth') was Humanism – the revival of the language, learning and art of the ancient Greeks and Romans, and the reconciliation of this pagan heritage with Christianity. Although the most visible manifestation of the Renaissance in Florence was the astonishing outpouring of art in the 15th century, it was classical studies that sparked the new age.

The groundwork had been done by a handful of men: Dante (1265-1321), Petrarch (1304-74) and Boccaccio (1313-75) all collected Latin manuscripts, which shaped their approach to writing. But it was the mounting Florentine wealth that paid for dedicated manuscript detectives such as Poggio Bracciolini (1380-1459) to dig through neglected monastery libraries across Europe.

A few classical works had never been lost, but those that were known were usually corrupt. The volume of unknown works unearthed during this period was incredible. First came the discovery of Quintilian's *The Training of an Orator*, which detailed Roman education; Columella's *De Re Rustica* on agriculture; key texts on Roman architecture by Vitruvius and Frontinus; and Cicero's *Brutus* (a justification of republicanism). Whereas very few Greek works had been known in Western Europe, suddenly – almost simultaneously – most of Plato,

Homer, Sophocles and many other classics were rediscovered.

The Renaissance focus on a pre-Christian age didn't mean that God was under threat. Just as the Renaissance artists had no compunction about enhancing the beauty of their forms and compositions with classical features and allusions, so Renaissance Humanists sought explanations beyond the scriptures that were complementary to accepted religion rather than a challenge to it. Much effort was made to present the wisdom of the ancients as a precursor to the ultimate wisdom of God.

Nor did the Renaissance fascination with things semi-scientific necessarily mean that this was a scientific age. The 15th century was an era when ideas were still paramount; science, as a process of deduction based on observation and experimentation, didn't really get going until the 17th century. In medicine, the theory of the four humours still held sway. Astronomy and astrology were all but synonymous. Mathematics was an almost mystical art, while alchemy – the attempt to transform base metals into gold – flourished.

It was magnificent while it lasted, but Florence's pre-eminence in art and ideas was abruptly snuffed out on the death of Lorenzo 'il Magnifico' in 1492: the invasion by Charles VIII of France in the 1490s and Savonarola's 'Bonfire of the Vanities' saw to that. The period left Florence with some of the most important masterpieces and artefacts in the world – many of them still in existence, and enjoyed by millions of visitors each year.

museums). Other major museums were founded to preserve treasures too precious to expose to the elements (**Galleria dell'Accademia**, **Bargello** and **Museo dell'Opera del Duomo**).

The main city-run museums are the **Cappella Brancacci**, **Cenacolo di Santo Spirito**, Museo Novecento, **Palazzo Vecchio,** Museo Bardini and Forte di Belvedere, though the latter is open only when hosting exhibitions. State museums are the Pitti museums, Uffizi, Accademia, Bargello, **Museo di San Marco**, **Opificio delle Pietre Dure**, **Cappelle Medicee** and **Museo Archeologico**.

Art lovers should be aware that works of art are often loaned to other museums, and restoration can be carried out with little or no notice, so it's wise to call first if you want to view a specific piece. For details on temporary exhibitions, see events app FirenzeTurismo and local newspapers.

▶ *For information on getting around, public transport and guided tours see Getting Started on p64.*

Tourists on the Ponte Vecchio

Eating & Drinking

When it comes to food, Florentines are creatures of habit. Eating at family-owned, unfussy *trattorie* serving up generations-old recipes of standard Tuscan fare is always an enjoyable experience and a safe bet for both visitors and locals. However, in recent years, the city has undergone a culinary Renaissance: Michelin-starred restaurants are offering a far more adventurous (and expensive) experience than the traditional *trattorie*, whether you're dining at lavish three-star **Enoteca Pinchiorri** or chef Filippo Saporito's **La Leggenda dei Frati**, inside the spectacular Villa Bardini.

Best pizza in town
Caffè Italiano *p132*
Il Pizzaiuolo *p134*
Vico del Carmine *p162*

Contemporary cuisine
Enoteca Pinchiorri *p134*
Ora D'Aria *p85*

Gourmet picnic supplies
Forno Top *p104*
Procacci *p91*
Arà: è Sicilia *p123*

Historic cafés
Caffè Giacosa *p103*
Caffè Giubbe Rosse *p87*
Paszkowski *p89*

Kid-friendly fare
Mercato Centrale First Floor *p114*

Sublime gelato
Badiani *p163*
La Carraia *p152*
Vivoli *p137*

Traditional Italian joints
Alla Vecchia Bettola *p150*
Del Fagioli *p134*
Il Latini *p102*

Wine flights
Casa del Vino *p111*
Fuori Porta *p162*
Le Volpi e l'Uva *p152*

Classics revisited

At mid-level establishments, '*rivisitata*' (revisited) is a word that gets thrown around a lot on menus. Many chefs have their own unique ways of infusing local cuisine with newer elements: witness how young star Simone Cipriani (**Essenziale**, *see p151*) plays with traditional Tuscan soups, creating inventive bites such as the '*pappa al pomodoro* donut' and the '*ribollita* bubble', or how Marco Stabile (**Ora d'Aria**) adds a splash of raspberry ice-cream to game-based risotto. All of this comes without breaking from the principles that keep foodies flocking to Italy: seasonal eating, fresh and locally sourced ingredients, and fair prices.

Restaurants

This guide aims to list the very best eateries in and around town, but it's also worth looking out for windows displaying the recommendation stickers of respected Italian restaurant guides, such as Gambero Rosso's *Ristoranti d'Italia*, *Veronelli*, *L'Espresso*, or Slow Food's

Osterie d'Italia. When in doubt, avoid anywhere that advertises a fixed-price *menù turistico* written in several languages, or places that have staff standing outside trying to reel in passersby. Good restaurants don't need recruiters!

Eating out is a very social affair in Florence, especially in the evenings, and restaurants tend to be informal and lively. You can wear casual dress in all but the very smartest establishments, and children are almost always welcome (it's fairly standard to see children out and about with families long past bedtime hours, which might surprise some visitors). Booking is advisable, especially at weekends or if you want to dine at an outdoor table during the summer months.

Cafés and bars

Florentine café society isn't just about coffee. Cafés and 'bars', as they are known here, are at the centre of social, work and neighbourhood life. Florence is full of simple corner cafés buzzing with local workers throwing back espressos at the bar. There are also genteel, gilded affairs where the cutlery is silver and a table with a view costs more than the barman's hourly wage. And, there are comfy bars populated by students with piles of books

Bistecca alla Fiorentina

In the know
Restaurant price codes

We use the following price codes for restaurant listings throughout the guide; they represent the average cost of one main dish (*secondo*).

€ = under €10

€€ = €10-25

€€€ = €25-40

€€€€ = over €40

and a caffè latte. If it's quality coffee you're after, avoid any place that looks like a second-rate imitation of Starbucks. A typical bar serves coffee all day, inexpensive, simple cocktails and house wine, and makes an easy stop for a snack or a simple, if underwhelming, lunch. Residents are usually on friendly terms with the barista on their home street. Although breakfast is almost always a simple cappuccino and brioche, the 'light lunch' can encompass all manner of buffets, gourmet menus and brunch offerings.

Bear in mind that location is everything when it comes to the bar bill: it usually costs far less if you stand at the bar to drink rather than sit at a table, and you often pay more to sit outside, especially at touristy spots.

Wine bars

Wine bars encompass tiny street booths (known as *fiaschetterie*, *vinerie* or *vinai*) with virtually no seating, serving basic Tuscan wines and rustic snacks, as well as comfortable, traditional drinking holes. They compete with new, upmarket *enoteche* that offer a huge range of labels from all over Italy and beyond, plus something more sophisticated in the way of food. Just be sure, if you're going to a place that's billed as a wine bar, that you order your food as an accessory to the wine, and not the other way around.

Florentine Fast Food

Tripe stands are one of the city's must-try food experiences

Once a dying breed, Florence's *trippai* (tripe vendors) are a new generation of 'offalophiles', proud to be carrying on an ancient Florentine culinary tradition.

When faced with a tripe stand, you would be forgiven for not knowing what was brewing. The mobile stalls are laden with bubbling cauldrons and heated trays, the contents of which are not for the faint-hearted. *Lampredotto* is probably the scariest item: the lining of the last stomach of the cow is simmered for hours in stock and served either in a *panino* with salt, pepper and maybe a lick of garlicky green *salsa verde*, or with its broth in a little dish to be eaten with a plastic fork. Tripe (*trippa*) is served in these parts *alla fiorentina* – in rich tomato sauce topped with a sprinkling of parmesan. It's also eaten cold mixed with pickles and dressed with olive oil,

salt and pepper. Other offerings vary from stall to stall, but watch out for such delights as boiled *nervetti* (tendons), stewed *budelline* (intestines) and *lingua* (tongue).

This Florentine-style fast food is cheap (a *panino con lampredotto* and a plastic cup of plonk will only set you back a few euros), healthy and has a fan base that transcends all social boundaries. You're likely to be munching your cow tummy sarnie in the company of factory workers, builders, shop assistants and slick-suited business types; it's a great way to sample Florentine street life.

Trippai normally open from around 8.30am to 7pm Monday to Friday; some also open on Saturdays. You'll find city-centre stalls under the Loggia del Porcellino; on the corner of via de' Macci and borgo La Croce; in piazza dei Nerli and in Mercato Sant'Ambrogio (see p137).

What to eat

An increasing number of more upmarket restaurants now offer some kind of fixed menu (and we're not talking about the ubiquitous *menù turistico* here). Usually called *menù degustazione*, it consists of a series of courses that allow diners to try the house specialities, or a themed collection of dishes – perhaps a fish-based menu or something more conceptual. Such menus tend to represent the best value at high-end restaurants.

How to eat

Most traditional menus are designed for à la carte ordering, beginning with an *antipasto* (starter). *Primi* are first courses, usually pasta, risotto, soups or salads, and are followed by *secondi* (meat, fish or, now and then, a heartier vegetable dish). *Contorni* are side dishes (vegetables, potatoes, smaller salads, perhaps even chips) and are often brought out separately. *Dolci* are desserts, and it's not uncommon to follow them with a coffee or digestif. You're not obligated to order a dish from every section of the menu, and it's not as if Italians all follow this complete cycle every time they sit down, but in general, when dining out in the evening, it's considered bad form to order only a *primo*.

Kid-friendly fare

Bustling family *trattorie* and *pizzerie* that make dishes to order are the best choices for children. Just ask for *pasta al pomodoro* (with tomato sauce), or a half portion (*mezza porzione*) of what you're ordering. Occasionally you'll see a *menu bambini* (kids' menu) in certain restaurants – don't let it scare you off. It's usually just a selection of smaller-portioned classics for not-so-adventurous palates – think chicken and potatoes or simple pastas. For lunch, instead of heading for the ubiquitous fast-food options, try buying picnic goodies at a market and head for a park. Note: quite a few restaurants offer high chairs (ask for *una seggiolone*).

Special diets

While there are few strictly vegetarian restaurants in Florence, non meat-eaters, particularly those who eat fish, are better off here than in many parts of, say, France or Germany. Most restaurants offer vegetable-based pasta and rice dishes, as well

First floor, Mercato Centrale

as plenty of salads and vegetable side dishes (*contorni*), while an increasing number of more upmarket places serve a specifically vegetarian option. Florence is also quite friendly toward gluten-free diners, with a wide variety of restaurants specialising in dishes *senza glutine* (without the wheat-based protein) or simply offering alternative options. And don't think your choices will be restricted to simple vegetables and flavourless salads: gluten-free pastas and pizzas are prevalent. *Celiaco* is the word for someone with Coeliac disease; your concerns will be taken seriously if you speak to a restaurant staffer about your options.

Wine list

Most budget and moderately priced restaurants offer *vino della casa* (house wine) in quarter-litre, half-litre or litre flasks, which is invariably cheaper than buying by the bottle. If you're in the mood for something more elevated, the *liste dei vini* in Tuscany are unsurprisingly dominated by *vini toscani* (Tuscan wines), but other regional varieties – and even the odd non-Italian label – are now being given more cellar space.

Think Tuscany and you normally think Chianti, Vino Nobile di Montepulciano, Brunello di Montalcino... a rich red swirling in the bottom of your glass, the perfect accompaniment to *bistecca fiorentina*. But there are now plenty of options if you're determined to try a Tuscan white. Late-ripening vermentino varieties present subtle floral perfumes, while Fattoria San Donato's 'Angelica' 2013, an aged-in-oak-barrels Vernaccia, goes best with intense flavours. Even rosé is having a bit of a moment in Tuscany – a frilly, fun-to-drink favourite that makes use of Sangiovese grapes is Bolle di Borro from the Ferragamo family's estate.

Gelato

Florence boasts some top-notch gelaterie, with **Gelateria Badiani** (*see p163*), **Vivoli** (*see p137*) and **La Carraia** (*see p152*) among the best. Between them they produce enough flavours to give a gelato-holic a different flavoured daily dose for several months. Some gelaterie are better than others; always look for a sign saying *produzione propria* or *artigianale* for home-made ice-cream. Too chilly for gelato? Try indulging your sweet tooth with the less familiar semifreddo (literally, half-cold) instead.

Gelato

ACQUA DI
ROSE

MACIS

Shopping

The Florentines' fiercely independent spirit ensures a wonderful array of interesting shops and studios alongside the designer boutiques on via Tornabuoni and the mainstream chains lining via Roma and via Calzaiuoli. From the little leathermakers' ateliers and alternative fashion stores in Santa Croce to the age-old authentic grocers and *salumerie* (delicatessens) around San Lorenzo; from the ancient perfumeries and herbalists of the *centro storico* to the tiny streets across the river that are studded with startlingly original pieces of jewellery, Florence is a shopper's – and browser's – dream.

Where to shop

If the most famous names in **fashion** and Florence's flagship stores are what you're after, head to via Tornabuoni, the Renaissance city's runway for well-heeled residents; you'll spot plenty of visitors balancing multiple shopping bags from the world's biggest labels. Via Roma is another high-rolling street for fashionistas. Veer off onto via del Parione for marbled paper and stationery, Tuscan toys and home bric-a-brac, or via della Spada to find elegant, but hardly bank-breaking, boutiques.

For handmade artisan treasures, the best area to explore is still the Oltrarno – backstreets are a safe bet for stumbling on ateliers and workshops (*see p153*), but you'll also find many enticing spots on more popular drags such as Sdrucciolo de' Pitti, borgo San Frediano and via Santo Spirito.

Vintage bargains pop up sporadically all over the city, but some local favourites lie around Santa Croce and along via dei Fossi (Santa Maria Novella), which also has an array of **antique** shops. As via dei Fossi ends, manoeuvre your way through the roundabout in piazza Carldoni to cross ponte alla Carraia for the **delicatessens** and antique shops of via dei Serragli and surrounding streets. **Leather goods** are famously found in the San Lorenzo area, but avoid buying from street vendors if you're after something high-quality. Cosmetics more your bag? Historic **pharmacies** and **perfumeries** are dotted all around the city, but you'll find an especially high proliferation in the Santa Maria Novella area.

Markets

Markets abound in Florence. They are a shopping staple for its inhabitants and a treasure trove for visitors looking for great photos, mid-morning nibbles and unusual souvenirs. The annual arrival of February's **Fiera del Cioccolato Artigianale** (Craft Chocolate Fair), the **German Christmas market** in piazza Santa Croce and the **autumn farmers' market** in piazza SS Annunziata are eagerly anticipated events on the city's calendar.

Mercato Centrale

Potions, Powders and Perfumes

Don't miss Florence's herbalists and cosmetic shops

Step inside many of Florence's beautiful old perfumeries and you're stepping back in time. As far back as the 11th century, when Benedictine monks began making alcoholic elixirs, the city has been renowned for its knowledge of the therapeutic qualities of herbs. Tuscany's fields of lavender and herbs have helped the region to maintain its reputation as a centre for alternative remedies, and many locals call at an *erboristeria* (herbalist's shop) rather than a chemist for minor ailments.

Some of these stores are joys to behold even if you're not shopping, though their products double as gorgeous gifts. **Officina de' Tornabuoni** (*see p92*), housed in the late Renaissance Palazzo Larderel, sells handmade gifts, textile sprays and perfumes. **Spezieria Erboristeria** (*see p93*), a stone's throw from the Palazzo Vecchio, is an old-fashioned and charming frescoed apothecary that specialises in handmade perfumes and floral *eaux de toilette* with such evocative names as Acqua di Caterina de' Medici.

The **Officina Profumo-Farmaceutica di Santa Maria Novella** (*see p105*), dating back to the thirteenth century, is the most famous Florentine herbalist. Even if you're not usually cosmetic-crazy and herb-happy, the historic venue is worth a visit for its striking structure and old-fashioned elegance.

Another notable shop is **Bizzarri** (Via della Condotta 32r, Duomo & Around, 055 211580, www.bizzarri-fi. biz), a relic that has shelves of jars filled with substances in every colour. Its herbal concoctions are made to secret, generations-old recipes.

Farmacia del Cinghiale (Piazza del Mercato Nuovo 4-5r, Duomo & Around, 055 282128, www. farmaciadelcinghiale.it), named after the famous wild boar statue in the square opposite, was founded in the 1700s and still makes its own herbal remedies and cosmetics.

A newcomer by comparison, the charming **Münstermann** pharmacy (*see p106*) was opened in 1897 and still has its original shop fittings. As well as stocking pharmaceutical and herbal medicines, the mahogany cabinets are filled with unusual hair accessories, jewellery and toiletries.

To go where the locals go, head to **Mercato de Sant'Ambrogio** (*see p137*) – it's a foodie's heaven, with the freshest and cheapest farmers' produce in the city. Meanwhile, the **Mercato di San Lorenzo** (7am-6pm Mon-Sat) covers a cobweb of streets around San Lorenzo church, with stalls selling leather goods, clothes and souvenirs. At its centre is the 19th-century covered **Mercato Centrale** (*see p114*), dedicated to fruit, vegetables, meats, fish and cheeses. The market's vibrant first floor is packed with street-food stands, a Roman-run pizzeria, Chianti wine bar and more. It's

sleek and commercial – much to the chagrin of some local shoppers – but it's quite popular and makes a social spot in the centre.

The **Mercato delle Pulci** flea market (piazzas Annigoni and Ghiberti, 9am-7.30pm Mon-Sat) is a great place to browse bric-a-brac in the hope of finding a tiny piece of the Renaissance to take home with you. Better still for browsers is the **Mercato di Santo Spirito** (8am-2pm Mon-Sat), which becomes an antique and flea market on the second Sunday of the month (8am-6pm). The square is also home to a small daily weekday morning market, and plays host to **Fierucola** on the third Sunday of the month (8am-6pm), a market selling organic foods and wines, handmade clothing, cosmetics and natural medicines.

If it's raining, head for the **Mercato Nuovo** (*see p92*); the alabaster chess sets, stationery, leather goods and scarves make for no-fuss souvenirs and gifts. Rubbing the nose of the bronze boar statue that gives the market its more colloquial name, Mercato del Porcellino, is de rigueur if you want a return visit to Florence.

Opening hours

Supermarkets and larger stores in the city centre tend to stay open throughout the day (*orario continuato*), but most shops still operate standard hours, closing at lunchtime and on Monday mornings. The standard opening times are 3.30pm to 7.30pm on Monday, and 9am to 1pm and 3.30pm to 7.30pm Tuesday to Saturday, with clothes shops sometimes opening closer to 10am. Food shops usually open earlier in the morning (perhaps around 8am), close at 1pm and reopen between 3pm and 5pm, and usually have a *giorno di riposo* (which charmingly translates into 'day of rest'). Many of the central shops stay open for at least part of Sunday; several more open on the last Sunday of the month.

Hours alter slightly from mid June until the end of August, when most shops close on Saturday afternoons. Small shops tend to shut completely at some point during July or August for anything from a week to a month. Opening times listed in this guide apply most of the year, but they can vary, particularly in the case of smaller shops.

Payment and taxes

While credit and debit cards are generally standard in shops now, count on never using them for purchases below €20, and don't be surprised when shop owners ask if you have any smaller change if paying in cash. They're not being rude, but the obsession with *spiccioli* (small change) can be a bit bewildering to first-timers. Visitors from outside the EU are sometimes entitled to a VAT rebate on larger purchases. Look for the 'tax-free' signs in shop windows.

Entertainment

Florence has claimed to be the birthplace of opera since *Euridice* was performed in Giardino di Boboli for the wedding of Henry IV of France and Marie de' Medici in 1600. The city retained its position as a cutting-edge musical centre until the early 17th century when focus shifted to Venice. Although 'cutting edge' can hardly be used to describe the live music or nightlife scene today, there is an astonishing amount going on for a small city, with enough cultural events, bars, and even a few clubs, to satisfy most visitors. The long, hot Florentine summer features a fine al fresco cinema scene and open-air arts venues, some of them free, not to mention the seasonal bars and clubs that set up in streets and squares all over the city.

Film

Romanticised, picture-perfect scenes from *A Room with a View* have burned an image of Florence into the collective psyche of the English-speaking world and beyond. Although Merchant Ivory's adaptation of the Edwardian classic is now three decades old, it still strikes a chord with visitors who, like Lucy Honeychurch, come to Florence to be transfigured by Giotto's frescoes in Santa Croce. Ridley Scott's *Hannibal* represents the polar-opposite, capturing the psychopathic, dark, medieval heart of Florentine history through its allusion to the Pazzi conspiracy.

The apocalyptic plot of *Inferno* (2016) is forgettable, but the breathtaking aerial shots of Florence have likely inspired many flight bookings since the film's release. And, for all its historical inaccuracies and hiccups, the Rai 1 programme *Medici: Masters of Florence* screened on Netflix in 2016-17 has also reignited interest in the Renaissance city.

Most screenings are in Italian (either Italian films or dubbed), but original-language films do pop up year-round, especially at the Odeon Cinema (*see p94*),

Spazio Alfieri and La Compagnia (*see p124*). The latter hosts the annual international film series 50 Giorni di Cinema Internazionale (*see p60*) and Primavera di Cinema Orientale (an Eastern film festival held in spring). English-language magazine *The Florentine* has cinema listings.

Nightlife

The popularity of the *aperitivo* has led to a seismic shift in Florentine nightlife patterns. Although it's still standard practice to go home for dinner directly after work before hitting the town after 10pm, it's now equally commonplace to go straight from the office to one of the many bars serving complimentary, if sometimes underwhelming, buffets with drinks – and then move on to another nightlife spot.

Piazzale Michelangelo at dawn

The late-night club is the loser in this new evening timetable: several historic city-centre clubs have closed, while other nightlife venues tend to close down or change hands as quickly as they crop up. Some spaces have morphed into bar/clubs serving early-evening *aperitivi* in the hope of roping punters in for the night. A much wider choice is available in summer, when al fresco venues pop up all over the city (*see p46* Summer Bars & Clubs). That's not to say clubbing has died a death; it's just treated less as a nightly entertainment and more as a one-off occasion.

Meanwhile, many of the nightlife venues in the suburbs, and some in town, survive on the euros of music junkies. Considering its size, the city has a rich indie music scene, with a smattering of local labels and international musicians of all genres performing in even the smallest venues. One of the best ways to find out about gigs is to pick up *Firenze Spettacolo*, a monthly Italian-language magazine showcasing the city's music scene.

Florence Queer Festival *p61*

The free English-language magazine *The Florentine* also has information on up-coming events. To book tickets for concerts (regardless of genre), call the venue directly or contact the Box Office ticket agency (Via delle Vecchie Carceri 1, ex Murate complex, Sant'Ambrogio, 055 210804, www.boxol.it tickets). Note that the opening times of bars and clubs are notoriously vague and erratic, and phones are rarely answered.

Nightclubs usually charge an admission fee that includes a drink, although some still use the unpopular card system. At these venues, you're given a card that's stamped whenever you buy drinks or use the cloakroom. You then hand the card in at the till and pay before leaving (be warned: don't lose it). Some smaller clubs are members-only, but becoming a member usually just means paying a nominal one-time fee for an annual card.

LGBT Florence

Though Florence has been popular with gay writers, artists and travellers for centuries, it was only in 1970 that the city got its first proper gay disco, **Tabasco**, which sadly closed in 2017.

Orchestra della Toscana

Despite Italy's traditional Roman Catholic culture and Florence's sometimes provincial tendencies, Tuscans tend to be more understanding and progressive towards the LGBT community than some other areas of Italy. In 2004 Tuscany was the first Italian region to ban discrimination against homosexuals in public life. Florence hosted its first Pride parade in 2016, drawing thousands to the streets, including the mayor and regional president, but for the rest of the year, the city's LGBT scene can seem limited and many people prefer to head for Bologna or Rome. However, many venues host one-off events throughout the year, particularly during the **Florence Queer Festival** in November (*see p61*) or Pride season in the spring. In 2016, Pride parties ran at venues such as FLOG (*see p163*) and the Limonaia di Villa Strozzi (via Pisana 77, Oltrarno, www. limonaiastrozzi.it). Limonaia also hosted the first **Toscana**

Pride Park in 2016, which featured a week-long series of LGBT-themed DJ sets and parties, performances, lectures and conferences and concerts. Check local press for what's on while you're in town – magazines such as *Firenze Spettacolo* and *Firenze Urban Lifestyle* have dedicated LGBT sections.

▶ *For other LGBT resources in Florence see p181.*

Performing arts

Florence is home to around 15 professionally run theatres and a fluid number of music venues, with more opening each year as historic spaces are restored and upgraded. However, budget restraints have resulted in short seasons, lower production values and an increasing number of monologues. Most theatre productions are in Italian, but you can find English-language shows and a fair amount of non-verbal theatre, while dance and music performances are, of course, universally enjoyable without proficiency in Italian.

In an attempt to protect themselves from funding cuts, 20 venues in Florence and neighbouring towns have joined forces to form **Firenze dei Teatri** (www.firenzedeiteatri.it). Its most successful scheme is Passteatri, a voucher booklet, costing €48, that allows the holder to pick six performances out of a choice of more than 50. Similarly, the regional network **Fondazione Toscana Spettacolo** (www.toscanaspettacolo.it) co-manages theatre, dance and children's seasons for around 50 venues across Tuscany. The biggest success story brought about by the change in funding, however, is the birth (and prompt rise to National Theatre status) of the **Fondazione della Toscana**, a joint project of **Teatro della Pergola** in Florence (*see p124*) and Pontedera Teatro near Pisa. As a result, the Pergola now produces (or co-produces) several plays each year, enlisting leading directors and encouraging new talent. It also hosts talks

Summer Bars & Clubs

How to enjoy those warm evenings with music alfresco

From the end of May to the beginning of September most Florentine nightlife shifts to outdoor venues – or informal gatherings – in piazze, gardens and villas. Most venues have free admission and stay open until the small hours. Each summer brings new openings to replace previous closures, as well as the return after absence of established venues.

Popular spots in recent years have included OFF Bar, set up in the gardens at the Fortezza da Basso (viale Filippo Strozzi 6, www. facebook.com/off.bar); Tamburello Benci Bar, a collective of via de' Benci venues that combine to form a hub at the Parco delle Cascine; and more culture-focused spaces such as outdoor bar FLOWER in piazzale Michelangelo (www. facebook.com/floweralpiazzale), a literary alternative to the glamorous nearby club Flo (viale Michelangiolo 82, 055650791, www.flofirenze. com), well known for turning away anyone whose summer outfit isn't up to standard.

Piazza del Carmine also plays host to nightly gigs and events through its Di Cultura in Piazza initiative (www.diculturainpiazza.eu), which boasts a seasonal pizzeria to boot. The neighbouring piazza Santo Spirito occasionally hosts special events, too, but the square's church steps, central fountain and cheap bars have a makeshift vibe that's more melting pot-meeting point than true gig venue.

Other one-off events are organised in piazza Pitti, the Boboli Gardens and Forte di Belvedere, as well as at the Stazione Leopolda, particularly during the Fabbrica Europa performing arts festival in June.

Through the music stronghold Visarno Arena, which hosts international giants in the summertime, the Parco delle Cascine is experiencing a revival, although most of the park is still considered dodgy after dark. For riverside fun, head to Fiorino sull'Arno (lungarno Pecori Giraldi, 328 2013217, www.facebook. com/fiorino.sullarno, a sprawling bar-pizzeria-concert venue or the can't-go-wrong seasonal favourite Easy Living .

Bear in mind that the local council grants permission to these summer-only venues on a year-by-year basis, so the situation can change at any time. Check the local press for details.

La Bastarda di Istanbul, Teatro di Rifredi

and readings; runs workshops and tours; maintains a specialist library and a museum; organises events for children, and stages exhibitions. The Foundation also manages the **Teatro Niccolini** (*see p94*) and **Teatro Studio Mila Pieralli** in nearby Scandicci. Meanwhile Stefano Massini, one of Italy's best young playwrights – who honed his craft at the **Teatro di Rifredi** in Florence – has been appointed artistic advisor of Milan's prestigious Piccolo Teatro, and his plays (notably the *Lehman Trilogy*, a five-hour saga about the banking crisis), are being staged across the world.

Despite its financial worries and gargantuan overheads (it sustains a full orchestra, chorus and armies of staff), the **Teatro dell'Opera** (*see p164*) is the hub of classical music in the city and one of Italy's foremost opera houses. If you get the chance to catch an Opera di Firenze production, don't miss it. Also keep an eye open for summer opera shows at **Palazzo Pitti**: the acoustics aren't always perfect, but the setting is superb. The **Orchestra della Toscana** is based at the Teatro Verdi, while the excellent Amici della Musica chamber music programme takes place at the Teatro della Pergola. In the tourist season, Florence is also awash with concerts and small opera stagings, often held in churches or museums, whose standard can sometimes be surprisingly good.

The contemporary dance scene is still lively and Tuscan dance companies have a far more solid international reputation than their theatrical counterparts. Ballet, however, suffered a big blow when MaggioDanza (the dance ensemble of the Teatro dell'Opera) was axed in 2015.

You can buy tickets for most venues and events several months in advance from the Box Office ticket agency in Santa Croce (*see p125*) or from its website www.boxol.it. Unsold seats can also be bought from the theatre's box office from one hour prior to the performance, although smaller or occasional venues may not accept card payments. Many hotels and travel agents also book tickets for major events. Show time is generally at 9pm Tuesday to Saturday, with a Sunday matinee at 4pm. The season runs roughly from October to April; in the summer months performances transfer to open-air venues and festivals.

La Mer – Virgilio Sieni

Florence
Day by Day

Itineraries

Florence's wealth of artistic treasures attracts in excess of 16 million overnight visitors annually. While there's a lot to be said for just taking in gorgeous, art-studded churches, fascinating museums and gelaterie as you find them, for a truly enjoyable experience it pays to be organised. If you have an itinerary planned, know which sights need pre-booking, and quickly gain a basic knowledge of the city centre, you're a step ahead of the rest.

▶ *Budgets include transport, meals and admission prices, but not accommodation or shopping.*

ESSENTIAL WEEKEND

Florence in two days
Budget €100 per person per day
Getting around Walking

DAY 1

Morning

If you haven't done so online, first thing in the morning drop in at one of the Duomo ticket offices and reserve a same-day slot for climbing the Cupola. Then, head to piazza della Repubblica for breakfast at **Gilli's** (*see p87*) before visiting the **Duomo**, **Baptistery**, **Museo dell'Opera del Duomo** and **Santa Reparata Crypt**: they are all included in your 48-hour Duomo ticket. Stop for a breather at **Grom**, right round the corner. Be careful not to be late for your Cupola booking but, if you miss your slot, you still have the option of climbing the Campanile instead.

Lunch

It's now time for a break from art, and the nearby **Mercato Centrale** (*see p114*) can make a fun diversion. While you're at it, grab lunch at **Casa del Vino** (*see p111*). Your next destination is the **Galleria dell'Accademia** (*see p118*) for a date with dashing *David*. Then head to **Santa Croce** (*see p130*) to explore its alternative shopping scene and visit the church that gives the neighbourhood its name.

Evening

The Santa Croce and Sant'Ambrogio areas offer some of the city centre's most attractive dining options, so you'll be spoilt for choice. Wrap up the evening with drinks at **The William** or a stroll around the centre.

Palazzo Vecchio

DAY 2

Morning

Kick off the day in style with breakfast at **Caffè Rivoire** (*see p87*). The **Uffizi** (*see p88*) opens at 8.15am and, as long as you're nifty and have worked out a plan of what you want to see, you can get to the *Birth of Venus* long before the tour groups do. Halfway through your visit, squeeze in a quick espresso or a juice on the terrace of the Uffizi cafeteria to admire the exterior of the 13th-century **Palazzo Vecchio** (*see p84*). For lunch, **All'Antico Vinaio** is almost directly across the road as you exit the gallery.

Afternoon

Now cross the **Ponte Vecchio** (*see p90*) to **Palazzo Pitti**. This sumptuous one-time home of the Medici family is hugely rewarding; topping a long list of must-dos is the **Galleria Palatina** (*see p144*), which houses the world's best collection of Titians and Raphaels. Behind the palace is the **Giardino di Boboli** (*see p147*), one of the city's best-loved green spaces: statues, grottoes and fountains are dotted around the splendidly formal gardens. If you haven't already had lunch this is the perfect stopping-off point for a picnic. Exit the park by the Forte di Belvedere, then use your Boboli ticket to enter the **Giardino Bardini** (*see p146*) across the road for impressive views of the city that beat those from the more celebrated piazzale Michelangelo.

Evening

Exit the gardens on via de' Bardi and browse the amazing jewellery, clothing, shoe and art shops in the narrow streets of the **Oltrarno** (*see p139*), before meandering over to piazza Santo Spirito for drinks and dinner. Lined with bars and restaurants such as **Caffè Ricchi**, this bohemian piazza is pure laidback Italian chic and charm, and guaranteed to make you feel you're living *la dolce vita*.

FAMILY DAY OUT

The Renaissance, the fun way
Budget €180 for a family of four
Getting around Walking, ATAF family ticket (€6)

Morning

Breakfast first at **Ditta Artigianale** (*see p154*), a relaxed spot with excellent coffee. Afterwards, catch a bus to **piazzale Michelangelo** (*see p160*) and pinpoint the main sights on a good map; a child's understanding of the city improves dramatically if they can see how it fits together. Older children could climb the **Cupola** (*see p76*) or the **Campanile** (*see p76*) for an unrivalled view over the rooftops. The **Museo Leonardo da Vinci** in via dei Servi (*see p118*), with its da Vinci machines at work, is great fun if you still have some time before lunch.

Gelato

Afternoon

A five-minute walk from here, the **Caffetteria delle Oblate** (*see p135*), on the roof of the Oblate library, provides a scenic spot for a healthy lunch. The children's section of the library is free to visit and has English-language books and games. The same building is also home to the **Museo Fiorentino di Preistoria** (*see 131*), which will be a hit with any young fossil hunters. Now head to **Palazzo Vecchio** (*see p84*), where family-friendly exhibits will bring the powerful Medici family to life. You can also can hire a Kit for Families for a self-guided visit and take part in activities organised by **Mus.E**. Afterwards, head to **Gelateria dei Neri** (*see 136*).

Evening

It's a ten-minute walk from here to ride the **vintage carousel** in piazza della Repubblica. Opt for supper at an informal spot in the centre such as **Focacceria Bondi** (*see 113*) or catch a minibus (C2 or C3) or tram (T1) to the **Fosso Bandito** (Angolo Viale Fratelli Rosselli and Via del Fosso Macinante, 055365500, www. fossobandito.com), a pizzeria with outdoor play area. It's next to the **Teatro dell'Opera** (*see p164*), where you may be lucky enough to catch a family-friendly performance.

▶ *Palazzo Vecchio is closed on Thursday afternoons*

BUDGET BREAK

Florence on a shoestring
Budget €30
Getting around Walking

Morning

Pastries at **Sieni** (*see p114*) are great for jumpstarting your day. Stroll through San Lorenzo and by the Duomo to **piazza della Signoria** and the **Loggia dei Lanzi** (*see p78*), a free open-air museum. Nearby are lesser-known gems such as **Orsanmichele** (*see p79*) and the church of **Santa Trinita** (*see p100*) with its Ghirlandaio frescoes, both with free admission. Now follow the *lungarni* east to via de' Benci, pass by the church of Santa Croce and peep into the **Scuola del Cuoio** to see the artisans at work.

Afternoon

If you're feeling peckish, head to the **Mercato di Sant'Ambrogio** (*see p137*), where the food stalls offer cheap and hearty sustenance: you could be brave and try a *panino col lampredotto* at **Da Rocco**. Just across the **Ponte Vecchio**, the church of **Santa Felicita** (*see p148*) has more amazing free art, including a chapel with some of Pontormo's and Bronzino's finest mannerist works. If you arrive early (the church opens at 3.30pm), idle the time away by wandering the charming streets and alleys of the **Oltrarno** and peeping into the **artisan workshops** (*see p153*). Afterwards, set out for the hilltop abbey of **San Miniato al Monte** (*see p161*), where at 5.30pm a Gregorian evensong concert awaits you. Then stroll to the **piazzale Michelangelo** (*see p160*) to take in the grand view,

Fountain of Neptune

and to the nearby **Giardino delle Rose** (*see p159*) for some free contemporary art.

Evening

In the summer, check www.estate fiorentina.it for free events across town. Otherwise, a safe bet is spending the evening in the lively literary café of the **Murate** complex, where an affordable *apericena* (aperitif with buffet dinner) is served between 6.30pm and 9.30pm.

▶ *The state museums (Accademia, Bargello, Medici Chapels, Uffizi, all museums at the Pitti Palace and Medici Villas) are free for all on the first Sunday of each month*

FLORENCE FASHION

Designers, boutiques and brands
Budget €100 per person
Getting around Walking

Morning

After breakfast and people-watching in the café of the **Gucci Museo** (*see p78*), begin your tour of the fashionable side of Florence by visiting the collections of Gucci clothing and accessories from the 1950s to 2000s upstairs. Next, make your way across the Arno while peeking at the glitzy displays of the Ponte Vecchio jewellers. Climbing the costa San Giorgio to **Villa Bardini** (*see p149*) and its **Capucci Museum** is something you may need sensible shoes for, but you'll be rewarded with some amazing views and world-class *couture*.

Afternoon

Back at river level in piazza de' Pitti, refuel at the charming **Pitti Gola e Cantina** (*see p151*) before taking in the historic garments and accessories at **Museo della Moda e del Costume** (*see p148*). The same ticket also admits you to the **Tesoro dei Granduchi** (*see p149*), where exhibits include jaw-dropping pieces of jewellery. Now head down via Maggio and across ponte Santa Trinita to the **Museo Ferragamo** (*see p78*); you'll find shoes to die (or kill) for by Italian designer Salvatore Ferragamo, whose flagship store is just round the corner. Stroll down **via dei Tornabuoni** and browse the designer shops of Emilio Pucci, Giorgio Armani, Bulgari, Dior, Fendi, Gucci, Prada, Tiffany, Burberry and Valentino. Thirsty? It's time to order a Negroni cocktail from the Roberto Cavalli-branded **Caffè Giacosa** (*see p103*). You could also squeeze in a visit to the **Museo Novecento** (*see p99*) to learn about the Pitti fashion shows.

Evening

Look for a stylish *aperitivo* spot in the vicinity – perhaps among the fashionable locals at the Ferragamo-owned **La Terrazza Lounge Bar** (*see p94*) in the summer months, or, if it's winter, **Slowly** (*see p94*) is an excellent alternative offering classy cocktails and nibbles.

▶ *On Fridays, the Gucci Museo (all year) and the Museo Novecento (summer only) are open until 11pm. The Pitti fashion shows are held in January and June*

Museo Ferragamo

Scoppio del Carro

Diary

Nothing impresses in Florence quite like its artistic heritage... except perhaps the pageantry of its many annual traditions. Spring brings the bizarre pyrotechnics of the **Scoppio del Carro**, when an antique cart festooned with fireworks is escorted through the streets. *Sbandieratori* (flag-throwers) are spotted year-round, but you'll know summer is near when you see the procession heading toward Santa Croce to perform ahead of the first **calcio storico** match. Crowds stand along the Arno to marvel at the sky during the **San Giovanni** fireworks display, and say goodbye to summer with **La Rificolona** lantern parade through the city. And **Christmas** festivities culminate with an elaborate Magi procession to celebrate the **Epiphany**. These and other traditional festivities are supplemented by a summer-long cultural festival, plus one-off film, food and family events.

Spring

Spring in Florence is one of the liveliest times of the year, with social life setting up in the city's piazzas, and seasonal gardens opening their gates. Easter celebrations include the flag and firework parade known as the **Scoppio del Carro**. April and May can bring spontaneous showers, but tourist crowds and queues are lighter during this lovely shoulder season. Around the end of May, Tuscany's open-air venues emerge from hibernation.

8 Mar Festa della Donna

For International Women's Day, women are traditionally presented with yellow mimosa flowers. Civic museums typically offer free or reduced admission for women and, in the evening, restaurants and clubs get packed with girlie gangs set on having a wild night out.

Mar Taste

www.pittimmagine.com/corporate/fairs/taste.htm)

Festa della Donna

Scoppio del Carro

Held each March in Stazione Leopolda (Outside the City Gates), this food festival, put on by Pitti Immagine, brings together 250 Italian artisanal producers of everything from truffle pâtés, salami, cured lard and chocolate to olive oil, wine, beer and silver-leaf spumante.

Late Mar/Apr Holy Week and Pasquetta

Bakeries around Florence sell traditional Easter rosemary buns called *pan di ramerino*. Pasquetta, on the Monday following Easter, is a holiday in its own right, with many civic and state museums opening their doors for the occasion.

♥ Mar/Apr Scoppio del Carro

At 9.30am on Easter morning, a parade of costumed musicians, flag-throwers and dignitaries escort a wooden cart, the *Brindellone*, laden with fireworks and pulled by four white oxen, from via il Prato (watch from the three-storey wooden doors on the left of the Hotel Villa Medici) to a jam-packed piazza del Duomo. Meanwhile, another parade departs from the church of Santissimi Apostoli with a holy fire kindled with the flints from the Holy Sepulchre. At 11am, during mass, a dove-shaped rocket shoots along a wire from the high altar to the *carro* (wagon) outside, starting the fireworks. If all goes smoothly, it's said that the year's harvest will be good.

Late Apr/early May & early Oct Mostra Mercato di Piante e Fiori

Growers from all over Tuscany proudly exhibit and sell their plants and blooms at these spectacular horticultural shows, which are laid out around a grand 19th-century glasshouse in Giardino dell'Orticoltura.

Late Apr-early July Maggio Musicale Fiorentino

www.maggiofiorentino.com
Founded in 1933 and held at Opera di Firenze, Florence's 'Musical May' is universally acclaimed as one of the best festivals in Italy for opera, concerts and dance performances.

Late Apr/May Festa del Grillo

On the feast of Ascension, a traditional family event held in Parco delle Cascine (entrance nr ponte della Vittoria).

Mid May Artigianato e Palazzo

www.artigianatoepalazzo.
Master artisans from Italy and beyond demonstrate their skills and sell their wares at this upmarket craft show in one of Tuscany's finest Italianate gardens at Corsini Gardens, Santa Maria Novella.

May Amico Museo

www.regione.toscana.it/ amicomuseo
This event held throughout Tuscany means special and late openings, events, concerts and guided visits to familiarise the crowds with the region's lesser-known local museums.

May-June Fabbrica Europa

www.fabbricaeuropa.net
This interdisciplinary, innovative performing arts showcase is anchored at Stazione Leopolda, a former railway station by Porta al Prato, but spin-off events and shows take place throughout Florence and Tuscany.

Late May Mille Miglia

www.millemiglia.it
Vintage car lovers get an eyeful in Florence with a grand spectacle: almost 400 vintage cars take part in this 1,600km (1,000-mile) race, winding their way back from Rome to Brescia, moving through Siena and entering Florence for a jaunt through much of the city, passing Porta Romana on the way to piazza della Signoria and exiting the city via piazzale Michelangelo.

Summer

Minimal air-conditioning and maximum crowds mean the heat can be more stifling inside than out, so, with the temperatures soaring, it's best to embrace the alfresco lifestyle. Grab an Aperol spritz and see an outdoor film, enjoy open-air bars doubling as music venues, catch a classical concert in a cool church cloister or hit the sandy dancefloor on the Arno 'beach'. However, if you should find yourself in Florence, or many other Tuscan towns, on the **Ferragosto** (Feast of the Assumption; 15 August), the chances are that your only

Calcio storico

company will be other tourists wandering the baked streets. The Florentines desert the city, and are likely to stay away for several days either side. The sun sets on the Florentine summer with **La Rificolona**, an early September ritual that sees families crowd the streets with paper lanterns.

June-July Florence Dance Festival

www.florencedancefestival.org
Staged mostly in the courtyard of the Bargello Museum (*see p129*), this festival fuses some of the greatest names in contemporary, traditional and classical dance.

♥ June-Sept Estate Fiorentina

www.estatefiorentina.it
This festival is an ever-expanding and loosely connected series of arts and cultural events, and smaller-scale festivals, that run throughout the summer. However, sporadic events under the Estate Fiorentina umbrella have been known to pop up as early as April and as late as December. Headlining events usually include big-name concerts at the Visarno Arena and Amphitheatre at Le Cascine, while more artsy initiatives run at contemporary hubs such as Le Murate, Palazzo Strozzi and the Museo Novecento. Outdoor cinema, circus shows, electronic music festivals, and elegant outdoor dinners: the programme is as varied as they come.

♥ June Calcio Storico

When an upsurge in violence prompted authorities to crack down on game regulations, the future for Florence's rugby-football-boxing hybrid known as the *calcio storico* seemed uncertain. But it's still going strong and pretty much as it has been since the 16th century. Two preliminary matches are normally played in piazza Santa Croce in early June, while the final is held on 24 June, a city holiday. Teams representing the city's ancient quarters (Santa Croce, Santa Maria Novella, Santo Spirito and San Giovanni) parade through the streets before settling old rivalries in a no-holds-barred 27-a-side match played by bare-chested lads in bright medieval breeches. Yes, really.

Festa di San Giovanni

venues host lantern-decorating competitions and runway-esque *rificolona* shows.

Sept-Oct Intercity Festival
www.teatrodellalimonaia.it
Every year the festival presents emerging playwrights from a different city. From New York (1988) to Bucharest (2016) and many more, over three decades Intercity, held at Teatro della Limonaia (Outside the City Gates), has built a 12,000-strong library of plays and introduced a huge number of authors previously unknown in Italy, notably Sarah Kane.

Autumn
Tourist crowds tend to thin out once the back-to-school season begins, and prices around town reflect this. Summer is slow to let go (locals frequently talk of *rientro*, or the return to regular work schedules, until late September). Far from falling into a post-summer slump, though, Florence becomes more of its authentic self, and autumn events are more targeted at locals. Restaurants stock up with new oil and wine after the harvest season, and hotels slash their prices when November rolls around.

24 June Festa di San Giovanni
A public holiday in Florence. A huge fireworks display takes place at 10pm near piazzale Michelangelo to honour the city's patron saint, John the Baptist. It's best enjoyed from the *lungarni* (just follow the crowds) or on the Arno 'beach'.

10 Aug Festa di San Lorenzo
An annual morning parade and evening party with free watermelon and lasagne honouring San Lorenzo's martyrdom, held in the saint's namesake piazza.

❤ 7 Sept La Rificolona
In the past, country folk used to walk to Florence on the eve of the Nativity of the Virgin Mary, as a pilgrimage as well as for the fair that's still held in piazza SS Annunziata. They carried paper lanterns, or *rificolone*, to light their way. Today, children still parade through the city proudly swaying their colourful candlelit paper lanterns. Smaller neighbourhood versions run across town, and many craft shops and children's

Late Sept-early Oct Tempo Reale Festival
www.temporeale.it
Cult Florentine music organisation Tempo Reale puts together a variety of concerts, events and exhibitions throughout the year, but it is most active during this two week showcase of experimental sounds at Villa Strozzi.

❤ Late Oct-early Dec 50 Days of International Cinema
www.50giornidicinema.it
Founded in 2007 as a way of centralising Florence's

internationally orientated film festivals, this movie marathon is now an established favourite for film buffs, though the venues have shifted through the years. Now screenings take place at the recently restored La Compagnia (*see p124*), converted into a cinema in late 2016. The season traditionally kicks off with France Odeon, spotlighting French cinema, and wraps up with the NICE City of Florence Award, honouring an Italian film selected by American audiences. Films are shown in their original language and subtitles in English are now standard for most.

Late Oct-early Dec Biennale Enogastronomica
www.biennaleenogastronomica.it
Much of the programming at this mega biennial event is geared toward industry insiders. But you can always count on finding temporary food and wine markets set up downtown for the occasion, as well as local restaurants, shops and bars offering themed menus, discounts or special events.

Mid Nov Florence Queer Festival
www.florencequeerfestival.it
A landmark LGBTQ event in Italy, Florence Queer Festival technically forms part of 50 Days of International Cinema (*see left*), but the focus extends beyond film into theatrical performances, exhibitions, parties and conferences. Past editions have included exhibitions of nightclub photography, drag shows and talks on the many shades of identity, sexual and otherwise.

Oct/Nov Florence Tattoo Convention
www.florencetattooconvention.com
Autumn visitors needing a break from Botticelli and Brunelleschi can explore ink artistry at this fascinating event held at Fortezza da Basso.

❤ Late Oct-late Nov Musica dei Popoli
www.musicadeipopoli.com
Starting the first weekend in October and running for about a month, this vibrant and varied

Florence Queer Festival

world music festival held at FLOG (*see p163*) brings together musicians from Senegal to Spain. Genres run the gamut from folk to funk. Not to be missed.

Winter

Winter in Florence lays the Christmas cheer on thick to make up for all the chill: think outdoor markets, concerts, religious rituals and seasonal treats galore. As Christmas approaches, the Italian tradition of Nativity scenes (*presepi*) is embraced. Many churches set up cribs, the main ones in Florence being in the Duomo, at San Lorenzo, Santa Croce, Chiesa di Dante and Santa Maria de' Ricci. Some country villages in Tuscany also stage *presepi viventi* – live re-enactments of the Nativity. Florence sees a spike in visitors as Christmas approaches, but things quieten down again after the Epiphany festivities, making January and February ideal months for museum visits. There's a nip in the air from late November onwards, but temperatures don't typically get too cold until February.

Early Dec **Christmas Market**
This picturesque German-style Weihnachtsmarkt in piazza Santa Croce has become an irresistible destination for Christmas cheer. The shopping isn't usually anything special, but the festive atmosphere is tough to resist, with friends and couples cosying up for mulled wine and holiday treats.

Dec **Natale**
Christmas in Florence is marked by the ice-skating rink set up at the Parterre in piazza della Libertà, while piazza del Duomo hosts a huge Christmas tree; the Uffizi hosts an annual series, I Mai Visti

(never-before-seen), displaying major artworks from the museum's collections and concerts take place throughout the season.

24 Dec **Christmas Concert**
This annual concert by the Orchestra Regionale Toscana at Teatro Verdi (*see p138*) doesn't necessarily include Christmas music, but there is usually something worth checking out.

31 Dec **San Silvestro**
The city puts on a major concert in piazzale Michelangelo and hosts pop-up parties and entertainment in select squares both within and beyond the gates.

6 Jan **Epifania**
In Florence, Epiphany events centre on the Arno river where *La Befana*, a kindly witch, rewards well-behaved children with stockings full of toys and sweets. In the afternoon, the **Cavalcata dei Magi**, or Procession of the Three Kings, runs from piazza Pitti to piazza Duomo.

Cavalcata dei Magi

Loggia dei Lanzi, piazza della Signoria

Florence by Area

Getting Started

With a historic centre roughly a fifth the size of Rome's, Florence is easily navigable. Most major sights are in walking distance of any other central point and, with the dome of the Duomo and the River Arno's four central bridges as reference points, it's practically impossible to get lost. The majority of the main sights cluster north of the two central bridges (Ponte Vecchio and Ponte Santa Trinita), around the **Duomo**. Other important sights are in the areas around this rectangle: **Santa Maria Novella**, **San Lorenzo**, **San Marco**, **Santa Croce** and the **Oltrarno**. We use these neighbourhood designations throughout the guide; attractions that lie beyond the historic centre are included in the chapter **Outside the City Gates**.

Public transport

The pedestrianisation of the Duomo and its surroundings in 2009 and the Oltrarno's piazza del Carmine in 2015 means that buses are next to useless within the city walls. Thankfully, scenic routes outside the gates – Lines 7, 12 and 13 – are unscathed. Line 7's terminus is now in San Marco, and it reaches the quaint hilltop village of Fiesole in less than 30 minutes. Lines 12 and 13 are circular routes, climbing to piazzale Michelangelo (*see p160*) from opposite sides.

The cramped C1 and C2 are the only lines that still cut through the heart of the city (north–south and west–east respectively); D minibuses cover chunks of the *lungarni* and much of the Oltrarno, including Santo Spirito. An extensive tram project is underway, set to add two new lines to the existing Santa Maria Novella–Scandicci route by mid-2018. Line 2 will run from Peretola airport to piazza dell'Unità d'Italia, close to the Santa Maria Novella station, while Line 3 will facilitate movement between the station and Careggi hospital.

A few tips. Fines are steep, so always have a valid ticket (look for the ATAF sticker in shop and bar windows, and don't forget to stamp your ticket in the machine on board). For a map of electric bus routes and timetables, see www.ataf.net.

Pre-booking

Firenze Musei Firenze Musei (the state-run museums of Florence) strongly recommends booking for the Uffizi and the Accademia, as well as, at busy times of year, the Pitti museums; this could save you a two-hour wait. Reserve as soon as you can (www.b-ticket.com/b-ticket/uffizi is the official online vendor for Firenze Musei or call 055 294883). Advance booking costs €4 for the Uffizi and Accademia; tickets are collected from a window beside the normal ticket office. At Palazzo Pitti's various museums, advance booking costs €3 and tickets can be picked up at an office in the right-hand wing before you reach the main entrance. If you're unable to book ahead, last issuing times for tickets vary (we give closing times, not last admission, in our listings), but try to get to the ticket office at least an hour before the museum closes.

Compared to their state-run counterparts, crowds tend to be (slightly) thinner at Florence's civic museums, but pre-booking is still advisable at heavy hitters such as Palazzo Vecchio and Santa Maria Novella. The civic museums (which also include Museo Novecento, Museo Bardini and the Cappella Brancacci) have an online ticketing system at ticketsmuseums.comune.fi.it. For most civic museums, there is a fee of

In the know
In the black or in the red?

The most complex thing about navigating in Florence is the street-numbering system, which has two sets of numbers, in red and black. The red numbers denote a place of business, and run separately from the black, so 16r and 18r may be 100 metres away from each other, separated by a series of black numbers. (Adding to the confusion, red numbers are currently being gradually phased out by local government.)

Piazzale Michelangelo

€0.80 for pre-booking your ticket, and you'll be allowed direct access upon arrival, skipping the queue.

Guided tours

All Florence's tour companies offer a range of itineraries, with English-language options, covering the main monuments and museums on foot or by bus. The highly reputable **AGT Firenze – Florence Associated Tourist Guides** (0574 608254, www.florencetouristguides.com), **Florence Guides** (347 737 8374, www.florenceguides.it) and **ACG Florence & Tuscany** (055 7877744, www.firenze-guide.com) have a big selection of standard tours; **Florencetown** specialises in American tourism (055 281103, www.florencetown.com).

> **In the know**
> **Firenze Card**
>
> If you are planning to visit lots of sights, it's definitely worth investing in a €72 Firenze Card, which lasts 72 hours from first validation and gives you entry to 72 museums in Florence, eliminating the need to queue. The card can be used once in each museum, and on all public transport. Pre-order it at www.firenzecard.it, or buy it at a tourist information office or at one of the museum ticket offices.

If you're after a personal touch and something beyond Brunelleschi, **Context Florence** (0158 977508, www.contextflorence.com) uses tour guides who are also Masters or PhD-level scholars, and limits groups to six; Alexandra Lawrence's **Explore Florence** (exploreflorence@gmail.com, www.exploreflorence. net) is another in-depth option, and **Travelability** (055 4684663, www.travel-ability.com) offers customisable, accessible itineraries for those with special needs. **Tuscany Bike Tours** (055 3860253, www.tuscany-biketours.com) provides leisurely and more energetic explorations of Florence on two wheels. Sightseeing buses are another option: **City Sightseeing Firenze** (piazza Stazione 1, 055 290451, www.firenze.city-sightseeing.it, 8am-6pm daily; €23/1 day, €28/2 days, €33/3 days; €12/1 day, €14/2 days, €17/3 days reductions; no cards for tickets bought on board) runs two lines: Lines A (one hour) and B (two hours). Both depart from Santa Maria Novella train station. Otherwise, the best ways to see the city – besides on your own two feet – are by bike or moped (*see p177* Moped & bike hire).

The Last Judgement (Giorgio Vasari and Federico Zuccari, 1579), Duomo

Duomo & Around

Stretching from the streets just north of the Duomo to the Ponte Vecchio, the compact central area of the city corresponds almost exactly to the ninth-century city walls. As the original nucleus of Florence, it's the ideal place to start your explorations, taking in both the former administrative hub of **piazza della Signoria** and the religious and cultural heartland around the astounding **Cathedral of Santa Maria del Fiore** (known as the **Duomo**) – one of Europe's most recognised landmarks. The cathedral is so huge that there's no spot nearby from which you can see it in its entirety; the cathedral complex is a truly awe-inspiring sight, dominating the city's skyline from all sides, *see p74*.

❤ **Shortlist**

Best galleries
Devotional art at Museo dell'Opera del Duomo (*p80*), open-air sculpture at Loggia dei Lanzi (*p78*) and Renaissance art at the Uffizi (*p88*).

Best restaurant
Head chef Marco Stabile serves up stylish Italian at Ora D'Aria (*p85*).

Best culture
The oldest theatre in Florence, Teatro Niccolini (*p94*).

Best old-fashioned pharmacies
Potions and powders at Officina de' Tornabuoni (*p92*) and Spezierie-Erboristerie Palazzo Vecchio (*p84*).

Best nibbles
Procacci (*p91*) for truffles and prosecco.

Best cafés
Caffè Giubbe Rosse (*p87*), Paszkowski (*p89*) and Caffè Rivoire (*p87*) for a slice of history with your espresso.

Best sights
The iconic Duomo complex (*p74*), impressive Palazzo Vecchio (*p84*) and unmissable Ponte Vecchio (*p84*).

Best nightspots
Cocktails at Slowly (*p94*), La Terrazza Lounge Bar (*p94*) and Mayday Lounge Café (*p94*).

On the north side is the entrance to the 'dome' itself, Brunelleschi's spectacular **Cupola**. The **Campanile**, Giotto's elegant bell tower, is south of the Duomo. Many of the cathedral's artistic treasures can be found in the fascinating **Museo dell'Opera del Duomo**, on the north-east side of piazza del Duomo, while the octagonal, marble-clad **Baptistery** stands facing the Duomo's main doors in tourist-packed **piazza San Giovanni**, also the location of the tiny **Museo del Bigallo**.

West of the Baptistery is via de' Cerretani, home to the 11th-century **Santa Maria Maggiore**. South from the Duomo's façade is via de' Calzaiuoli and the church of **Orsanmichele**, famous for its statue-filled external niches.

South-east is Florence's civic showpiece square, **piazza della Signoria**; a delightful space that has been the focus of civic activity since its creation in the late 13th century. The piazza is dominated by the **Palazzo Vecchio** but also home to several very familiar sculptures, including a copy of Michelangelo's *David* (the original is in the Accademia), Giambologna's equestrian bronze of *Cosimo I*, notable for the horse cast as a single piece, and Ammannati's Neptune fountain, of which Michelangelo is reputed to have wailed, 'Ammannati, what beautiful marble you have ruined!' Beyond the fountain are copies of Donatello's *Marzocco* and *Judith and Holofernes*. Beyond *David* is *Hercules and Cacus* by Bandinelli, described by Benvenuto Cellini as a 'sack of melons'. Cellini himself is represented by a fabulous *Perseus* standing victorious in the adjacent **Loggia dei Lanzi**. Also in the loggia is Giambologna's spiralling marble *Abduction of the Sabine Woman*.

Leading down to the river from piazza della Signoria, the piazzale degli Uffizi is home to the world-renowned **Uffizi**. Head north from here and you'll find the entrance to the **Badia Fiorentina** on via del Proconsolo and its elegant stone tower. This is 'Danteland', with the **Museo Casa di Dante** and the **Chiesa di Dante** – the lovely little church where Dante's beloved Beatrice is buried – a stone's throw away.

Back at the river end of the Uffizi and to the west is the landmark **Ponte Vecchio**, with its rows of gold jewellery shops and the **Corridoio Vasariano**, built by Giorgio Vasari as a private walkway for the Medici family.

In the district's south-west corner, is **Museo Ferragamo**, devoted to shoes, and north of **piazza Santa Trinita** is the designer shopping mecca of **via de' Tornabuoni**, dominated by the gargantuan stones of **Palazzo Strozzi**.

➔ Getting around

This pedestrian area takes no longer than ten minutes to walk from end to end. The main thoroughfares – especially via dei Calzaiuoli between the Duomo and piazza della Signoria – do get overcrowded, but it's a pleasure to get lost in the maze of medieval side streets. Forget your map or GPS and just wander where curiosity takes you: you'll never be more than a couple of turns from the main landmarks anyway.

Sights & museums

Badia Fiorentina

Via Dante Alighieri (055 264402). **Open** *3-6pm Mon. Donations.* **Map** *p73 M8.*

A Benedictine abbey founded in the tenth century by Willa, the mother of Ugo, Margrave of Tuscany, the Badia Fiorentina was the richest religious institution in medieval Florence. Willa had been deeply influenced by Romuald, a monk who travelled around Tuscany denouncing the wickedness of the clergy, flagellating himself and urging the rich to build monasteries; it was Romuald who persuaded Willa to found the Badia in 978.

When Ugo was a child, his exiled father returned to Florence and invented a novel paternity test: asking the boy to recognise the father he'd never seen in a room of men. Happily for his mother, Ugo succeeded. The people decided he must have had divine guidance, and he was considered a visionary leader. Ugo lavished money and land on what was then known as the Badia Fiorentia, and was eventually buried there in a Roman sarcophagus (later replaced by a tomb made by Renaissance sculptor Mino da Fiesole) that's still housed in the abbey.

It was here in 1274, just across the street from his probable birthplace, that the eight-year-old Dante fell in love at first sight with Beatrice Portinari. He was devastated when her family arranged her marriage, at the tender age of 17, to Simone de' Bardi, and absolutely crushed when she died seven years later. Poor Dante attempted to forget his pain and anguish by throwing himself into war.

The Badia has been rebuilt many times since then, but retains a graceful Romanesque campanile and exquisite carved ceiling. The Chiostro degli Aranci dates from 1430 and is frescoed with scenes from the life of San Bernardo. Inside the church, Bernardo is celebrated once again in a Filippino Lippi painting. The Cappella dei Pandolfini is where Boccaccio held the first public reading of the works of Dante.

Corridoio Vasariano

Between Palazzo Vecchio and Palazzo Pitti (www.uffizi.it). **Open** *From May 2018, hours and ticket prices to be confirmed.*

If you look up from the Ponte Vecchio, you'll see a neat row of small round windows running on top of the jewellery shops on the east (upstream) side of the bridge: it's the Corridoio Vasariano (Vasari corridor). Commissioned by Cosimo I de' Medici to court architect Giorgio Vasari and completed in five months in 1565, the corridor was a quick and safe private walkway between the administrative offices at Palazzo Vecchio (*see p84*) north of the river and the new Grand Ducal residence, Palazzo Pitti (*see p144*), on the left bank.

Until recently the corridor housed the Uffizi collection of self-portraits, which are soon to be relocated to the main gallery (*see p88*). At the time of writing, the corridor was closed to the public for the installation of suitable safety measures, air conditioning and improved lighting, but from May 2018 the corridor will display the Uffizi collection of Greek, Roman and Etruscan stone inscriptions, as well as providing an optional direct link for visitors between the Uffizi gallery and the Palazzo Pitti museums. Regardless, you can follow the route of this ingenious passage at street level from Palazzo Vecchio (watch for the little bridge joining Palazzo Vecchio and the Uffizi) to the little door next to Buontalenti's grotto in the Giardino di Boboli (*see p147*).

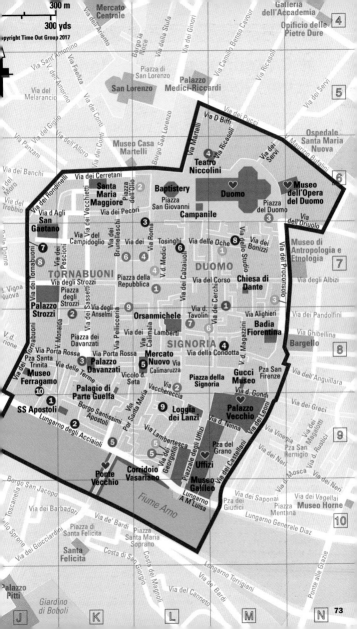

Cattedrale di Santa Maria del Fiore (Duomo)

Piazza del Duomo (055 2302885, www.ilgrandemuseodelduomo.it). **Open** *10am-5pm Mon-Wed, Fri; 10am-4.30pm Thur; 10am-4.45pm Sat; 1.30-3.30pm Sun.* **Admission** *€15, 48-hr ticket incl the Museo dell'Opera del Duomo (see p80).* **Map** *p73 M6.*

The result of work spanning more than six centuries, the Duomo represents the geographical, cultural and historical centre of the city. The building was commissioned by the Florentine Republic as an opportunity to affirm its status as the most important Tuscan city. The competition to find an architect was won by Arnolfo di Cambio and the first stones were laid on 8 September 1296 around the exterior of Santa Reparata. Building continued for the next 170 years – despite the 1348 plague that killed half of Florence's 90,000 population – with guidance and revision from three further architects. When it was finally consecrated in 1436, Santa Maria del Fiore was the largest cathedral in Europe, and it's still the world's third largest after St Peter's in Rome and St Paul's in London.

The rich exterior in white Carrara, green Prato and red Maremma marbles reflects the 170-year-long building period, with a huge variation in styles. In the 19th century, Emilio de Fabris designed a neo-Gothic façade that was added to the Duomo between 1871 and 1887.

The Duomo's bronze doors (1899-1903) are decorated with scenes from the life of the Virgin. Each door is complemented by a mosaic lunette by Barbarino. These represent (right to left): local artists, merchants and Humanists honouring Christ; Christ with Mary and John the Baptist; and Charity among the Florentine noblemen who had established the city's charitable foundations. Above them are the 12 Apostles.

After the splendid exterior, the interior is underwhelming but full of fascinating peculiarities: notably, Paolo Uccello's clock on the inner façade, which marks 24 hours, operates anti-clockwise and starts its days at sunset.

Standing directly underneath the dome, the size is even more breathtaking inside than out. The lantern in the centre is 90m (295ft) above you and the diameter of the inner dome is 43m (141ft) across, housing within it one of the largest frescoed surfaces in the world. Brunelleschi had intended the decoration to be mosaic. However, interior work only began some 125 years after his death in 1572, when Giorgio Vasari and Don Vincenzo Borghini decided to fresco the surface instead.

Vasari was succeeded by Federico Zuccari, who had a much more flamboyant dry-painting style, believing that the viewing distance wasted the delicacy of Vasari's wet fresco technique. Zuccari's most crucial contribution is the rendering of Dante's vision of Hell.

Brunelleschi's Cupola

💛 Cattedrale di Santa Maria del Fiore (Duomo) *continued*

Crypt of Santa Reparata

Open 10am-5pm Mon-Wed, Fri; 10am-4.30pm Thur; 10am-4.45pm Sat; 1.30-3.30pm Sun.

Excavations carried out between 1965 and 1973 unearthed the medieval ruins of Santa Reparata, which are now on view for visitors. The entrance to the crypt is inside the Duomo itself. The church's foundation date is unknown. The intricate mosaic floor was built only 30cm above the Roman remains of houses and shops, some of which are visible. Also here is the tomb of Brunelleschi.

Cupola

Accessed via the Porta della Mandorla on the north side of the cathedral. Open 8.15am-7pm daily.

Containing four million bricks and weighing 37,000 tonnes, the Cupola isn't just visually stunning: as the first octagonal dome built without a wooden supporting frame, it is also an incredible feat of Renaissance engineering.

Filippo Brunelleschi won the commission in 1418 – following two years of fierce debate over his design – together with the more experienced Lorenzo Ghiberti. Brunelleschi first considered designing a classic semi-spherical dome, but the sheer size of the structure precluded the traditional method of laying tree trunks across the diameter in order to build around them. In the end, he made the dome support itself by building two shells, one on top of the other, and by laying the

bricks in herringbone-pattern rings to integrate successive self-supporting layers.

The Cupola provides fantastic views over the city centre and the surrounding hills. And while the 463 steps (about 20 minutes up and down) are not for the faint-hearted or those with limited mobility, climbing the curve between the Cupola's two shells is a truly unforgettable experience.

Campanile

Open 8.30am-7pm Mon-Fri; 8.30am-5pm Sat; 1-4pm Sun. Booking required. Restrictions may apply in adverse weather conditions.

The cathedral's three-floor, 414-step Campanile (bell tower) was designed by Giotto in 1334, though his plans weren't followed faithfully. Andrea Pisano, who continued the work after Giotto's death in 1337, doubled the thickness of the walls, while Francesco Talenti, who saw the building to completion in 1359, inserted the large windows high up the tower. Inlaid with pretty pink, white and green marble, the Campanile is decorated with bas-reliefs by Giotto and 16 sculptures of prophets, patriarchs and pagans (the originals are in the Museo dell'Opera del Duomo, see *p80*). The steps to the top are steep and narrow, but great views await.

Baptistery

Open 8.15-10.15am, 11.15am-7.30pm Mon-Fri; 8.15-6.30 Sat; 8.15am-1.30pm Sun.

The Baptistery of St John the Baptist – the patron saint of Florence – was built to an octagonal design between 1059 and 1128. It also functioned for a period as the cathedral for Florence (then Florentia).

The Renaissance started on this spot when, in 1400, the Calimala guild of cloth merchants held a competition to find an artist to create a pair of bronze doors for the north entrance. Judging works by seven artists, Brunelleschi among them, they gave the commission to the 20-year-old Ghiberti; Brunelleschi later got revenge with superior work on the Cupola, but never sculpted again. The deep pictorial space and emphasis on figures of the 28 relief panels have led many scholars to consider these doors to be the very first signs of Renaissance art.

The Calimala then commissioned Ghiberti to make the even more remarkable east doors – described by Vasari as 'undeniably perfect in every way'. These took the artist and his workshop (including Michelozzo and Benozzo Gozzoli) 27 years to complete. They're known, since Michelangelo coined the phrase, as the 'Gate of Paradise'. The doors you see here are copies (the originals are in the Museo dell'Opera del Duomo; see p80).

The very first set of Baptistery doors were those on the south side, completed by Andrea Pisano in 1336, after only six years of work. The interior of this octagonal building is worth visiting for the dazzling Last Judgement mosaic that lines the vault ceiling: an 8m-high (26ft) mosaic figure of Christ in Judgement dominating the apse (1225), and the mosaics of Hell that are thought to have inspired Dante's Inferno.

La Porta del Paradiso (Lorenzo Ghiberti, 1425–52)

Gucci Museo

Piazza della Signoria 10 (055 75927010, www.guccimuseo.com). **Open** *10am-8pm daily; Fri until 11pm.* **Admission** *€7 (€5 Fri 8-11pm).* **Map** *p73 M8.*

Together with fellow local designers Pucci, Ferragamo, Cavalli, Coveri and up-and-coming Patrizia Pepe, Gucci belongs in the Olympus of fashion megabrands. Located in the 14th-century Palazzo del Tribunale della Mercanzia overlooking piazza della Signoria, the Gucci Museo opened in 2011 to celebrate the 90th anniversary of the company founded by Guccio Gucci in 1921.

Nine rooms over three floors house the permanent exhibits showcasing the signature designs of the Gucci brand including the iconic travel cases, the horse-bit loafer (1952) and bamboo-handle handbags (1947). Fashionistas will swoon before Gucci's evening gowns, worn by the stars on red carpets or featured in the leading fashion glossies. Two more rooms house exhibitions of contemporary art and design.

The bookshop and café-restaurant – both free to visit – display a series of terracotta crests of the historic trade guilds of Florence, formerly on the façade of the building. Visit on a Friday night to take advantage of reduced tickets that are partly devoted to restoring the city's art treasures.

❤ Loggia dei Lanzi

Piazza della Signoria. **Open** *always.* **Admission** *free.* **Map** *p73 L9.*

This 14th-century loggia derives its name from the *lanzichenecchi*, a private army of Cosimo I that used to be stationed here. Built in the late 1300s to shelter civic bigwigs during ceremonies, by the mid 15th century it had become a favourite spot for old men to gossip and shelter from the sun.

Since the late 18th century, the loggia has been used as an open-air museum, best enjoyed at night after the crowds dissolve. Cellini's fabulous *Perseus* stands victorious holding the snaky head of Medusa. The bronze is testament to the artist's pig-headed determination: most considered it impossible to cast, but after several failed attempts, Cellini finally succeeded by burning even his family furniture to fan the furnace. Also in the loggia is Giambologna's spiralling marble *Abduction of a Sabine Woman* (1582), a virtuoso attempt to outdo Cellini, and Agnolo Gaddi's *Seven Virtues*.

Museo Ferragamo

Piazza Santa Trinita 5r (055 3562846, www.museoferragamo. it). **Open** *10am-7.30pm daily.* **Admission** *€6.* **Map** *p73 J8.*

Down some steps from the eponymous shop and into the medieval basement, this corporate museum is as elegant and stylish as the shoes on display. In the first chamber, you can see order forms signed by famous actors and actresses, including John Wayne, and wooden 'lasts' (foot shapes) for Ava Gardner and Drew Barrymore. The rest of the museum is filled with a choice selection of the company's 10,000 shoes. Exhibits change periodically and there are pairs created for Marilyn Monroe, Judy Garland and Audrey Hepburn, affording an opportunity for shoe lovers to drool over some of the world's most beautiful footwear.

Museo Galileo

Piazza dei Giudici 1 (055 265311, www.museogalileo.it). **Open** *9.30am-6pm Mon, Wed-Sun; 9.30am-1pm Tue.* **Admission** *€9. No cards.* **Map** *p73 L10.*

Spanning 18 rooms on two floors, the new exhibition layout presents

Statue of Perseus (Benvenuto Cellini) *p78* and Palazzo Vecchio *p84*

more than 1,000 instruments and devices of major scientific importance and exceptional beauty, placing them in the historical and cultural setting in which the Medici and Lorraine collections were assembled.

The only surviving instruments designed and built by Galileo Galilei are the big draw here, notably two of his original telescopes and the objective lens of the telescope with which he discovered Jupiter's moons. A morbid reliquary in the shape of his middle right finger is also on display, offering unintentionally ironic echoes to the honour more usually bestowed on saints.

In the other rooms are a collection of prisms and optical games, armillary spheres, globes, nautical devices, a selection of electromagnetic and electrostatic instruments and a mix of machines, mechanisms and models including a 19th-century clock (*pianola*) that writes a sentence with a mechanical hand.

Orsanmichele & Museo di Orsanmichele

Via dell'Arte della Lana (church 055 210305, museum 055 284944, www.bargellomusei.beniculturali. it). **Open** *church 10am-5pm daily, museum 10am-5pm Mon.* **Admission** *free.* **Map** *p73 L8.*

Most famous for the statues in the 14 niches that surround the building, Orsanmichele has become a relic of the extreme dedication and pride of Florentine trades, and a reminder that a competitive climate often heralds the greatest art. There's no spire and no overt religious symbols: Orsanmichele may not look much like a church, but it is – although one with a difference, melding as it does the relationship between art, religion and commerce.

In 1290, a loggia intended as a grain store was built to a design by Arnolfo di Cambio, the original architect of the Duomo, in the garden (*orto*) of the Monastery of San Michele

💜 Museo dell'Opera del Duomo

Piazza del Duomo 9 (055 2302885, www.ilgrandemuseodelduomo.it). **Open** *9am-7.30pm daily (or later in summer). Closed 1st Tue of mth.* **Admission** *€15 combined with Duomo (see p74).* **Map** *p73 M6.*

Built on the site of the 15th-century cathedral workshop where Michelangelo carved his famous *David*, the Museum of the Cathedral Works is billed as the second largest collection of devotional art in the world after the Vatican museums in Rome.

Much expanded and imaginatively reorganised between 2012 and 2015 at a cost of €45 million, the museum now showcases over 750 works of art covering 720 years of history in 25 rooms over three floors, making a total display area of about 6,000sq m (almost 65,000sq ft).

Every single piece in its unique collection has some kind of direct link with the Duomo complex; from the early basilica of Santa Reparata to the 19th-century façade, with works by the greatest medieval and Renaissance artists: find their names engraved on the north wall of the museum's entry corridor.

The most impressive room is the skylit **Salone del Paradiso**, spanning three floors. Its highlights include Arnolfo di Cambio's mesmerising *Madonna with the Glass Eyes* and the monumental statue of *Pope Boniface VIII*. A must-see is also the original ten gilt-bronze panels of the recently restored east door of the Baptistery, the so-called *Porta del Paradiso* (Gate of Paradise), sculpted by Lorenzo Ghiberti over 27 years between 1425 and 1452. The realism of its pictorial reliefs and an effective use of perspective mark a clean step into the Renaissance, compared to the two earlier doors to the left and right (Andrea Pisano's 1336 south door and Ghiberti's 1403-24 north door).

Donatello was the first artist to free sculpture from its Gothic limitations. In the **Sala della Maddalena** is an extreme example of the artist's unprecedented use of naturalism: the emotive wooden *Penitent Saint Mary Magdalene*. Dishevelled and ugly, the sculpture provoked a mix of outrage and awe when it was placed in the Baptistery in 1456.

In the **Tribuna di Michelangelo**, the *Pietà Bandini* (c1547-55) is a heart-rending unfinished piece intended by Michelangelo for his own tombstone: he sculpted his own features on the face of elderly Nicodemus. The obviously much inferior and out of proportion Mary Magdalene on the left is the later work of a pupil.

The **Galleria della Cupola** displays models of Brunelleschi's dome, alongside tools and the pulleys and ropes used to winch building materials (and workers) up inside the cupola.

The originals of Donatello's *Prophets* from the exterior of the bell tower are upstairs in the **Galleria del Campanile**, notably *Habakkuk* (affectionately called *Lo Zuccone* by Florentines, meaning 'marrow head'), a work of such realism that Donatello himself is said to have gripped it and screamed, 'Speak, damn you, speak!'. This floor also houses the Sala delle Cantorie with two enormous and joyful choir galleries by Donatello and Luca della Robbia.

The **Sala del Tesoro** contains two stunning silver pieces: a 250kg (550lb) processional cross and a 400kg (880lb) altar front worked on by the likes of Michelozzo, Verrocchio, Antonio del Pollaiolo and Bernardo Cennini. Also on the first floor is a five-room gallery illustrating the façade made for the cathedral in the 19th century Don't miss the panoramic terrace that offers a remarkable view of Brunelleschi's dome.

Habakkuk (Donatello, c.1425)

Reliefs and statues from the Campanile

(hence, 'Orsanmichele'). The loggia burned down in 1304, along with a painting of the Madonna that, from 1292, had been said to perform miracles. Such was the effect of her miracles that people flocked from across Tuscany to worship her. When the building was reconstructed in the mid 1300s by Talenti and Fioravante, the painting was replaced and honoured by the creation of a marvellously elaborate glass and marble tabernacle by Andrea Orcagna. This was replaced in 1347 by Bernardo Daddi's *Coronation of the Madonna with Eight Angels*, which is still here today.

During reconstruction of the building, two upper floors were added for religious services. From the outset, the council intended the building to be a magnificent advertisement for the wealth of the city's guilds, and in 1339 each guild was instructed to fill one of the loggia's 14 niches with a statue of its patron saint. Only the wool guild obliged, so in 1406, after the building's conversion into a church, the council handed the guilds a ten-year deadline.

Six years later, the Calimala cloth importers, the wealthiest of all the guilds, commissioned Ghiberti to create a life-sized bronze of John the Baptist. It was the largest statue ever cast in Florence, and its arrival spurred the other major guilds into action. The guild of armourers was represented by a tense *St George* by Donatello (now in the Bargello; *see p129*), one of the first psychologically realistic sculptures of the Renaissance, while the Parte Guelfa guild had Donatello gild their bronze, a *St Louis of Toulouse* (later removed by the Medici in their drive to expunge all memory of the Guelphs).

All the statues in the external niches today are copies. However, the originals can be found on the first floor of the museum,

displayed on a platform in their original order. And on the second floor is a collection of statues of 14th-century saints and prophets in Arenaria stone. They were on the external façade of the church until the 1950s.

The church and museum do not always stick to the opening hours posted, so it's advisable to phone to check the hours before making a special trip.

Palazzo Strozzi

Piazza Strozzi (055 2645155 info, 055 2469600 bookings, www.palazzostrozzi.org). **Open** *10am-8pm daily; 10am-11pm Thur.* **Admission** *€12. CCC Strozzina exhibitions vary.* **Map** *p73 J7.*

Flanked by Florence's most stylish shopping streets, Palazzo Strozzi is one of the most magnificent of the 100 or so palaces built in the city during the 15th century. In 1489, work began on the construction of the *palazzo* by order of Filippo Strozzi, whose family had been exiled from Florence in 1434 for opposing the Medici. However, they'd made good use of the time, moving south and becoming bankers to the King of Naples; by the time they returned to Florence in 1466, they'd amassed a fortune. Filippo began buying up property in the centre of Florence eight years later, until he had acquired enough real estate to build the biggest palace in the city.

An astrologer was asked to choose an auspicious day to lay the foundation stone; 6 August 1489 tied in nicely with a new law that tax-exempted anyone who built a house on an empty site. When Filippo died in 1491, he left his heirs to complete the project, which eventually bankrupted them, but the palace remained in the family up until 1937, when it became the seat of an insurance company. It was finally handed over to the state in 1999.

Behind the imposing rusticated stone walls lie a few cultural institutions including the *Gabinetto Vieusseux*, the Humanist Institute's Renaissance book and manuscript collection. A pleasant café and a bookshop open onto the *palazzo's* Renaissance courtyard (admission free), which also hosts concerts, contemporary art installations, theatrical performances and events.

For over a decade, the independent public-private *Fondazione Palazzo Strozzi* has been hosting the most important and talked-about exhibitions in Florence in the *piano nobile* of the *palazzo*.

Also managed by the Fondazione Palazzo Strozzi, the Centro di Cultura Contemporanea Strozzina, or **CCC Strozzina** (www.strozzina.org), is a modern space in the *palazzo's* cellar which holds imaginatively curated international contemporary events and shows with works by the likes of Cindy Sherman, Andreas Gursky and Gerhard Richter and emerging artists.

Restaurants & wine bars

Coquinarius €€
Via delle Oche 11r (055 2302153, www.coquinarius.com). **Open** *12.30-3pm, 6.30-10.30pm Mon-Sun.* **Map** *p73 M7* ❶ *Traditional Italian*

Tucked away behind the Duomo, this cosy little restaurant-wine bar is great for a quiet lunch or an informal evening meal. The wine list is ever-changing as the owners discover new producers worth spotlighting. But it's not all about the grapes: mouth-watering first courses are enough to satisfy on their own (go for the *pici*, a thick Sienese pasta, served with roast beef sauce and rosemary), but you'll probably want to save room for seconds like the tuna tartare

with avocado, mango, lime and ginger. Imaginative appetisers are another strength, and for those with a sweet tooth, the home-made cakes are truly divine.

Fiaschetteria-Osteria Nuvoli €
Piazza dell'Olio 15 (055 2396616). **Open** *9.30am-3pm Sun; 8am-9pm Mon-Sat.* **Map** *p73 L6* ❷ *Traditional Italian*

There aren't many spots in Duomo territory where you'll find Florentines in droves, but this delightfully traditional, two-part eatery is one of the few. Grab a hefty sandwich upstairs if you want a satisfying quick bite – the salty *schiacciata* bread topped with any of the cold cuts or *sott'oli* (pickled vegetables) is lovely, and you can people-watch on the wobbly chairs outside or squeeze in at the countertop if it's not too crowded. For a more leisurely meal (and a longer menu), make your way downstairs to dine on no-frills, filling fare (the meatballs and potatoes work wonders when you're weary post-sightseeing).

Fishing Lab Alle Murate €€
Via del Proconsolo 16r (055 240618, www.fishinglab.it/en). **Open** *10am-midnight daily.* **Map** *p73 N8* ❸ *Seafood*

Call it contrived (many have), but this cool concept restaurant has a beguiling mix of old and new, best seen not on its menu, but in its design. Fishing Lab's bar is spacious, its main floor sleek and clean-lined, contrasting with the frescoed ceiling vaults upstairs and Roman Florence ruins on the cosy lower level. The menu offers snack and meal-size portions of street seafood (think mixed fried fish or mini sandwiches), as well as pastas, sampling platters and raw selections. Rather than strictly adhering to a lunch and dinner schedule, the kitchen and bar stay open all day: pop in for

❤ Palazzo Vecchio

Piazza della Signoria, (055 2768325, www.museicivicifiorentini.comune. fi.it). **Open** *Apr-Sept 9am-11pm Mon-Wed, Fri-Sun; 9am-2pm Thur. Oct-Mar 9am-7pm Mon-Wed, Fri-Sun; 9am-1pm Thur. Shorter opening times apply to the tower and ramparts.* **Admission** *€4 to €18 depending on ticket combinations.* **Map** *p73 M9*

Florence's austere and commanding town hall was built to Arnolfo di Cambio's late 13th-century plans to represent the immense strength of the city at the time. Despite the Mannerist makeover of the interior carried out by Vasari between 1555 and 1574, the rustic stone exterior of the building and Arnolfo's tower, the highest in the city at 94m (308ft), remained largely intact. It became known as Palazzo Vecchio ('old') when Cosimo I moved his family to the 'new' Palazzo Pitti (*see p144*) in 1565.

The **Salone dei Cinquecento** (Hall of the Five Hundred) should have been decorated by Michelangelo and Leonardo, not with the zestless scenes of victory over Siena and Pisa by Vasari that cover the walls. Leonardo abandoned the project, while Michelangelo had only finished the cartoon for the Battle of Cascine when he was summoned to Rome by Pope Julius II. Many believe Leonardo's sketches lie beneath the Vasari mural. One of Michelangelo's commissions did end up here, however: *Genius of Victory*, a statue thought to have been carved, along with the

better-known *Slaves*, for the Pope's never-finished tomb.

Off the Salone is the **Studiolo di Francesco I**, the office where Francesco hid away to practise alchemy. Upstairs are the **Quartiere degli Elementi** in the east wing, and the apartments of Cosimo I's wife Eleonora da Toledo on the west side. Bronzino used intense pastel hues to depict a surreal *Crossing the Red Sea* in Eleonora's private chapel off the Green Room. On the outer wall of the same room, a closed door marks the beginning of the Corridoio Vasariano (*see p72*).

Further ahead, the more sedate **Cappella dei Priori** is decorated with fake mosaics and an idealised *Annunciation*. Beyond is the garish Sala dell'Udienza ('Hearing room')

Frescoes (Giorgio Vasari, Sale de Michelozzo

and the **Sala dei Gigli** with its ceiling by Giuliano and Benedetto da Maiano, and some sublime frescoes by Ghirlandaio opposite the door. Donatello's original *Judith and Holofernes*, rich in political significance, is also here. Finally, go through into the **Map Room** for the gigantic 16th-century globe by Egnazio Danti.

Weather permitting, visitors can climb the tower for fabulous views of the city. On the way down, the 30 works of art from the Loeser collection has shorter opening hours. The *Tracce di Firenze* (Traces of Florence) exhibition near the ticket office is free for all. Plus, remains of the Roman theatre of ancient Florentia can be visited separately or by purchasing a joint ticket with the museum.

an afternoon pick-me-up, grab an early lunch before most spots are open or indulge in the four-person raw tasting menu. Wash it all down with a crisp Vermentino or any of the other whites and bubblies on the extensive wine list.

Irene €€€
Piazza della Repubblica 7 (055 2735891, www.roccofortehotels. com/hotels-and-resorts/hotel-savoy/restaurant-and-bar/irene). **Open** *12.30-10.30pm daily.* **Map** *p73 L7* ④ *Contemporary Italian*
The aesthetic at the Hotel Savoy's popular bistro-style eatery and cocktail bar is retro, but the food and service are far from old-fashioned. Steered by food director Fulvio Pierangelini and head chef Giovanni Cosmai, Irene flaunts an eclectic menu inspired – but never inhibited – by the tenets of Tuscan dining. With fresh first courses (try the octopus salad), it'd be easy to stop at a light lunch, but Irene is the kind of place where you'll want to indulge. A tip: the risotto made with San Gimignano saffron, shrimp tartare and pistachio is heavenly.

❤ Ora d'Aria €€€€
Via de' Georgofili 11r (055 2001699, www.oradariaristorante.com). **Open** *12.30-2.30pm Tues-Sat and 7.30-10pm Mon-Sat.* **Map** *p73 L9* ⑤ *Experimental Italian*
Marco Stabile, the young Tuscan chef in charge of the kitchen at this stylish Michelin-starred eatery, has impeccable credentials and his dishes are executed with skill. His changing seasonal menus – usually rife with seafood and game options – are based on fresh, understated ingredients, all carefully researched and winningly assembled. If you're ready to indulge, try one of the pricy but bountiful tasting menus (at €90 per person, plus a €5 cover charge, they deliver). À la carte options are also available. Stabile fuses traditional practices with more

High-tech Hunt for a Lost da Vinci

A wiped-out Leonardo is causing controversy, centuries after its creation

Between 1503 and 1504, the Republic of Florence commissioned two mural paintings that would have had Leonardo da Vinci and Michelangelo Buonarroti working back to back in the Salone dei Cinquecento in Palazzo Vecchio (see p84). Leonardo would portray *The Battle of Anghiari*, while Michelangelo's subject would be the Battle of Cascine.

Michelangelo was summoned to Rome in 1505 by the Pope. Yet Leonardo began his mural and worked on it with several assistants, probably completing 15 to 20sq m (160 to 200sq ft) of the centrepiece, *The Fight for the Standard*. The painting was left unaccomplished when da Vinci relocated to Milan in 1506. The unfinished mural was still visible in 1563 when the reinstated Medici asked Vasari to remodel the hall and wipe out anything celebrating the Republic, including Leonardo's aborted *Battle*.

But Maurizio Seracini, a Florentine biomedical engineer, believes that Vasari was too fine a connoisseur to destroy a masterpiece, and he has been trying to prove the survival of Leonardo's mural since 1975. Funding this quest isn't the only concern, since the debate is fierce: to what lengths should we threaten Vasari's work in order to search for the lost da Vinci, and what to do if faced with one masterpiece topped by another?

At first, Seracini was convinced that Leonardo had worked on the western wall. Then, in 2002, researchers from the University of Florence detected a 2cm gap behind Vasari's *eastern* mural. Maybe – Seracini reasoned – Vasari

had built a new wall parallel to the original, in order to protect Leonardo's work? Seracini also noticed that a green flag in Vasari's *Battle of Marciano* bore two tiny words in white paint: '*Cerca trova*' ('Seek, and you shall find'). Could it be a clue? Since then, all efforts have concentrated on the eastern wall.

Following this, Professor Raymond DuVarney suggested that neutron-activation analysis might reveal traces of paint chemicals by measuring their gamma rays, so in 2011, Seracini and his team were allowed to bore several holes into Vasari's work and insert an endoscopic probe in the gap. The six points were chosen by Florentine restorers to cause the least damage to the Vasari mural and did not match Seracini's desired search areas. However, in a statement issued in March 2012, Seracini and his *National Geographic* backers claimed to have found manganese- and iron-based black pigment compatible with Leonardo's black paint from taken from his other works. The results were certified by two private laboratories – one Seracini's own – and apparently, the samples gathered were too small to allow a third opinion from a public institute.

The latest chapter in the saga dates from August 2012, when a jurisdiction feud broke out between local powers (in the form of the then city Mayor Matteo Renzi) and central government. In the end, permission was denied by the Ministry of Culture to allow further investigation. Is a mystery better marketing material than a flop?

innovative ideas: you'll find beef ragu-topped polenta and Florentine steak alongside game-stuffed tortellini with foie gras and liquorice cream. Everything is beautifully presented, and there's a substantial wine list, though some of the prices per bottle are rather inflated.

Osteria I Buongustai €€
Via dei Cerchi 15r (055 291304, www.facebook.com/ ibuongustaifirenze). **Open** *8am-4pm Mon-Fri; 8am-11pm Sat.* **Map** *p73 M8* ❻ *Traditional Italian*
Just turning around in this tiny lunch favourite can be a challenge: its foyer and main dining room overflow with neighbourhood workers, in-the-know visitors and intrepid staff wriggling their way through narrow spaces. The cheap prices, local crowd and efficient service make all the manoeuvring well worth it. You won't find better prices in the town centre for hearty *primi* such as *spaghetti all'amatriciana* (pasta with a pork cheek-based sauce) and *tagliolini al tartufo* (truffle pasta).

Cafés, bars & gelaterie
❤ Caffè Giubbe Rosse
Piazza della Repubblica 13/14r (055 212280, www.giubberosse.it). **Open** *10am-2am daily.* **Map** *p73 K7* ❶ *Café*
This historic haunt is something of a local legend: once a hub for 20th-century Florentine literati, it's believed to be the birthplace of the Futurist movement. Past regulars included the poet-painter Ardengo Soffici, and the café's intellectual ties are well-documented in its decor today. Food here is rather forgettable, but stopping in for a fairly-priced coffee or Campari-based cocktail, a perusal of the newspaper stack and a lively discussion of current events is a must for all lovers of literary cafés.

❤ Caffè Rivoire
Piazza della Signoria 5r (055 214412, www.rivoire.it). **Open** *Summer 7.30am-midnight Tue-Sun. Winter 7.30am-9pm Tue-Sun.* **Map** *p73 L8* ❷ *Café and chocolatier*
Founded in 1872 as a chocolate factory with ties to the Savoy royals, Rivoire later became a bohemian haunt before morphing into the most famous and best loved of all Florentine cafés. Its chocolates – also available in gift boxes – are divine and its house-brand coffee and seasonal hot chocolate beverage are among the best in the city. The outside tables have unmatched views of Palazzo Vecchio and the Loggia dei Lanzi. One downside: your wallet will be hit hard for the privilege. Knock back an espresso at the bar to sample some of the glamour without the hefty price tag.

Edoardo
Piazza del Duomo 45r (055 281055, www.edoardobio.it). **Open** *11am-11.30pm daily.* **Map** *p73 M7* ❸ *Gelateria*
Hidden in the back corner of Florence's busiest piazza, this organic gelateria offers some of the city's most memorable flavours (the red wine or hazelnut-laden Gianduia varieties are popular choices). Sorbets are made strictly with seasonal fruits, and the homemade cones add another layer of goodness to each treat. There's nowhere to sit inside, and the queue frequently snakes around the street corner, but Edoardo is a reliably good sweet stop, especially on evening strolls.

Gilli
Piazza della Repubblica 36-39r (055 213896, www.gilli.it). **Open** *7.30am-12.30am daily.* **Map** *p73 L7* ❹ *Café*
With the continual closing of many of the city centre's most beloved

♥ Uffizi

*Piazzale degli Uffizi 6 (055 23885, www.uffizi.it). **Open** 8.15am-6.50pm Tue-Sun; June-Sept until 10pm Tue only. Ticket office closes at 6.05pm. **Admission** €8; €4 reductions. Free on 1st Sun of every month. Advance booking B-ticket (www.b-ticket.com/b-ticket/uffizi); booking charge €4. Audio tours €6 (single headset) or €10 (double headset). **Map** p73 L9.*

This temple of Renaissance art is Italy's most visited art gallery by far, receiving over two million visitors yearly, and about 2,000 to 9,000 visitors daily. The building was designed by Vasari in the 16th century as a public administration centre for Cosimo I; hence 'Uffizi' meaning 'offices'.

Since there cannot be more than about 1,000 people in the building at any given time, booking in advance is the best way to skip the ticket lines, but beware of (deceptively official-looking!) secondary ticketing websites and apps reselling tickets with unreasonable markups. The busiest days are weekends and Tuesdays (the gallery is closed on Mondays) and the peak hours are mid morning and early afternoon, so be smart and schedule accordingly, setting aside at least two hours for your visit. In the summer, one pleasant option is to take advantage of the late opening hours on Tuesdays, when free entertainment is on offer.

Since 2015, the Uffizi Galleries, comprising the Uffizi, Corridoio Vasariano (see p72) and Palazzo Pitti (see p144), have been under the single directorship of

German-born art historian Eike Schmidt – the first non-Italian Uffizi director, whose stated aim is to make the collections as widely accessible as possible.

The Uffizi has undergone massive changes in recent years, with cranes and scaffolding blighting the loggiato since 2006 (work is expected to finish in 2022). On the plus side, exhibition space has doubled, with no fewer than 56 new rooms made available between 2011 and 2015.

The Uffizi collections hold a total of around 5,400 artworks, 2,900 of which are currently on display. The return of Leonardo da Vinci's Adoration of the Magi in the spring of 2017 after a five-year restoration, meant that all of the gallery's 'non-lendable and unmovable works' were finally on permanent display again. The list of these 28 masterpieces are the ultimate shortlist of Uffizi artworks that you shouldn't miss.

They include Gentile da Fabriano's *Adoration of the Magi*; Botticelli's *Birth of Venus* and *Allegory of Spring*; Leonardo and Verrocchio's *Annunciation*, Michelangelo's *Doni Tondo*; Raphael's *Madonna of the Goldfinch* and Parmigianino's *Madonna with the Long Neck*.

A curated anthology from the Uffizi's unparalleled collection of self-portraits is taking over a dozen rooms in the west wing on the first floor in November 2017. Formerly housed in the Corridoio Vasariano, the collection was started by Cardinal Leopoldo de' Medici in the mid 18th century and boosted in 2005 with the acquisition of 295 self-portraits by contemporary artists from Raimondo Rezzonico's private collection. The Uffizi self-portraits now consist of almost 1,800 pieces in a variety of techniques; recent additions include a watercolour by Jean Michel Folon and a video self-portrait by Bill Viola.

Allegory of Spring (Sandro Botticelli, c.1482)

shops and bars to make room for international designers and mass-market chains, murmurings abound about the future of the historic Gilli. Its closure would be a blow to its loyal clientele and to its many impressed visitors. Gilli's belle époque interior is original, its seasonally themed sweet window displays are wickedly tempting and its rich, flavoured hot chocolates legendary. Service is hit or miss, but Gilli's institutional status endures. Outside seating year-round.

'Ino
Via de' Georgofili 3r-7r (055 214154, www.inofirenze.com). **Open** *11am-5pm daily.* **Map** *p73 L9* ⑤
Gourmet sandwich bar
At this classy, contemporary sandwich bar and deli – behind the Uffizi, near where the Mafia placed its bomb in 1993 – they've perfected the art of the *panino*, and most choices will set you back around €8. It's higher than the local average for sandwiches, but so is the quality of these ingredients. Fillings are sourced from all over the country by owner Alessandro Frassica. Sandwiches (to be enjoyed seated at a barrel table, perched at the counter, or to take away) are made to order and filled according to seasonal availability, with plenty of vegetarian-friendly options as well as mouth-watering meats. The deli/shop is stocked with tempting goodies, and there's a range of sweets that make excellent gifts (you can't go wrong with *biscotti* by Fratelli Lunardi).

❤ Paszkowski
Piazza della Repubblica 35r (055 210236, www.paszkowski.it). **Open** *7am-2am daily.* **Map** *p73 K7* ⑥
Café
Among Florence's elegant historic cafés, this corner place stands out for its modestly priced and genuinely delicious lunch options.

💙 Ponte Vecchio

Between lungarno Acciaioli and via Guicciardini. **Map** *p73 K9.*

Crossing Florence's oldest bridge must be on any visitor's checklist of things to do in Florence. The 14th-century shop-lined – or rather shop-laden – Ponte Vecchio is the busiest pedestrian thoroughfare between the two banks of the Arno and an apt symbol of this mercantile city. Head for one of the two neighbouring bridges (ponte alle Grazie or ponte Santa Trinita; *see p100*) to take mandatory pictures – with the right light, it's as pretty as they come!

A series of bridges has occupied the narrowest spot on the river for more than 1,000 years, but the builders of the current one remain unknown, although Vasari attributes the project to Taddeo Gaddi.

Bridges with shops on them were common in medieval times, but by 1593 the original tenants of this one, a lively mix of butchers, fishmongers, tanners and blacksmiths, were deemed too smelly and loud to stay, and were evicted on the orders of Ferdinando I. The shops and workshops were given over to the gold- and silversmiths, whose descendants still occupy them. A sharp rise in rents led to many of the 17th-century shopkeepers adding the back shops (*retrobotteghe*) that still hang precariously over the bridge's sides.

This was famously the only bridge in the city to be spared from destruction during the German army's retreat in 1944 – supposedly on Hitler's orders, but certainly thanks to the efforts of Gerhard Wolf, German consul in Florence during World War II. Against all the odds, its low arches also survived the massive impact of water and debris in the catastrophic 1966 flood.

The bust topping the fountain in the centre of the bridge is of Benvenuto Cellini, put up by the goldsmiths of Florence in 1901 to mark the fourth centenary since the birth (3 November 1500) of their illustrious colleague.

Regulars and intrigued passers-by queue up by the glass display in the back, scoping out the daily specials and rhythmically reciting their orders to the expedient staff (he who hesitates is lost). Generally, there's at least one hearty soup and tasty pasta on offer, with a range of roasted veggies and other sides to choose from. By night, the venue regularly hosts live musicians, mini orchestras and DJ sets on its outdoor terrace.

Perchè No!

Via de' Tavolini 19r (055 2398969, www.percheno.firenze.it). **Open** *noon-8pm Wed-Mon.* **No cards**. **Map** *p73 L8* 7 *Gelateria*
This is a favourite with the locals – many have been coming for generations. Not by chance, it is often cited as the best gelateria for the more traditional flavours – *crema* (sweet egg custard), pistachio and chocolate. It's narrow and the one or two benches haphazardly stuck inside are hardly adequate seating, so prepare to take a scenic walk with your ice-cream in hand.

♥ Procacci

Via de' Tornabuoni 64r (055 211656, www.procacci1885.it/en/florence). **Open** *10am-9pm Mon-Sat; 11am-8pm Sun. Closed Aug.* **Map** *p73 J7* 8 *Bar & shop*
One of the few traditional shops to survive the onslaught of international designer names on this thoroughfare, the small wood-lined wine bar and shop is a favourite with nostalgic Florentines and is famous for its truffle-based specialities. In season (Oct-Dec), truffles arrive daily at around 10am, filling the room with their soft musty aroma. Try a melt-in-your-mouth sandwich filled with *prosciutto crudo* and truffled artichoke cream.

La Terrazza

Rinascente, piazza della Repubblica 1 (055 283612, www.rinascente.it/rinascente/it/barcafe/202). **Open** *9am-8.30pm daily.* **Map** *p73 L7* 9 *Café*
The rooftop terrace café at this department store affords some of the most stunning views of the city; the splendour of Brunelleschi's Cupola at such close quarters is unforgettable, especially at sundown, when the city is bathed in pink light. Come for cocktails or coffee rather than the mediocre food; you're paying for the quality of the view, not the menu.

Shops

La Bottega dell'Olio

Piazza del Limbo 4r (055 2670468, www.labottegadelloliofirenze.it). **Open** *Mar-Sept 10am-7pm Mon-Sat. Closed 2wks Jan. Oct-Feb 2.30-6.30pm Mon; 10am-1pm, 2-6.30pm Tue-Sat.* **Map** *p73 J9* 1 *Gifts & souvenirs*
Fans of the 'green gold' will go wild for La Bottega dell'Olio, which stocks all things olive oil, from soaps and delicacies to olive-wood breadboards, oil dispensers and pestles and mortars.

Boutique Nadine

Lungarno degli Acciaiuoli 22r (055 287851, www.boutiquenadine.it). **Open** *2.30-7.30pm Mon; 10am-7.30pm Tue-Sat, noon-7pm Sun* **Map** *p73 K9* 2 *Vintage*
This mood-brightening boutique boasts a varied selection of vintage and lovely contemporary pieces from owner Irene's brand, Orette. Gucci bags, Louis Vuitton trunks, Pucci dresses and Yves Saint Laurent shoes are all standard finds, but the costume jewellery and household knick-knacks are easily as fun to browse through as the illustrious labels. You'll also find plenty of old but unused

stock, probably dug out from dusty storerooms and still in the original packaging. A second shop in via de' Benci 32r (055 2478274) also stocks menswear.

Luisa Via Roma

Via Roma 19-21r (055 217826, www.luisaviaroma.com). **Open** *10am-7.30pm Mon-Sat; 11am-7.30pm Sun.* **Map** *p73 L7* **3** *Fashion*

Renowned for its inventive, multimedia window displays, and now an online shopping giant, this multi-level supershop is almost museum-like, bordering on cartoonish in certain sections. It features the latest from Issey Miyake, Marc Jacobs, Mulberry, Chloé and others. Scoop up a pair of signature sparkly flats by Italian power blogger Chiara Ferragni (The Blonde Salad) or just soak up all the visual stimulation.

Maledetti Toscani

Via della Condotta 36r (055 211981, www.maledettitoscani.com). **Open** *11am-7.30pm Tues-Sun; 1.30-7.30pm Mon.* **Map** *p73 M8* **4** *Leather goods*

Maledetti Toscani ('Damn Tuscans') has longstanding roots in leatherwork, traceable back to Montepulciano in 1848, when the first location opened. This Florence shop is well stocked with fine vegetable-tanned leather goods for men and women, from boots and Oxfords to wallets and jackets. Styles range from classic and refined to wearably edgy (picture zany colours or a strategically placed snakeskin patch).

Mercato Nuovo

Between via Calimala and via Porta Rossa. **Open** *9am-6.30pm daily.* **Map** *p73 L8* **5** *Market*

Often referred to as the *Mercato della Paglia* (straw market), its stalls now sell leather and straw goods and cheap souvenirs, but in the 16th century it was erected for silk and gold merchants. The market is also known as the *Porcellino* (Piglet), after the bronze statue of a boar, a copy of a Pietro Tacca bronze that was, in turn, a copy of an ancient marble now in the Uffizi. It's thought to be good luck to rub the boar's nose and put a coin in its mouth: proceeds go to charity and legend says the donor is assured a return trip.

Migone

Via de' Calzaiuoli 85r (055 214004). **Open** *9am-7.30pm daily.* **Map** *p73 L7* **6** *Food*

Lydia Migone's sweet shop is a delight to spend time in, admiring the lovely cardboard Duomos filled with chocolates or sweets, the pretty cellophane bags of sweets and *biscottini*, the slabs of *torrone*, as well as traditional Tuscan bites such as *panforte* (a sugar-dusted fruit and nut bread) and *ricciarelli* (Siena-style macaroons). Prices aren't cheap but the instant charm of a Baptistery-shaped package is pretty tough to deny.

♥ Officina de' Tornabuoni

Via de' Tornabuoni 19 (055 217481, www.odtskincare.com/en). **Open** *10.30am-8pm daily.* **Map** *p73 J7* **7** *Herbs & perfumes*

Housed in the 15th-century Palazzo Larderel, this is a fragrant wonderland of handmade gifts, perfumes and candles, herbal remedies, intensive facial masks and treatments, toiletries and cosmetics. You can even take a piece of the Palazzo with you: in 2015, Officina de' Tornabuoni created a home fragrance inspired by the building, characterised by notes of rose, Florentine iris and violet, among others. There's no main shop window so look for the raised entrance set off the street.

Il Porcellino, Mercato Nuovo

Paperback Exchange

*Via delle Oche 4r (055 293460,
www.papex.it). **Open** 9am-7.30pm
Mon-Fri; 10.30am-7.30pm Sat.
Closed 2wks Aug. **Map** p73 M7* ⑧
Books

Cross-cultural pair Maurizio and
Emily are the winning twosome
behind this old favourite, which
stocks thousands of new and used
English-language fiction and non-
fiction titles, specialising in art,
art history and Italian culture and
lifestyle, from medieval times up
to Frances Mayes and her myriad
copycats. You'll also find children's
books, buzzed-about bestsellers
and new releases – the team can
usually place an order for you if you
can't find what you're looking for.

♥ Spezierie-Erboristeria Palazzo Vecchio

*Via Vacchereccia 9r (055 2396055,
www.spezieriepalazzovecchio.it).
Open 10am-7.30pm Mon-Sat. **Map**
p73 L9* ⑨ *Herbs & perfumes*

A beautiful frescoed interior selling
herbal products made to centuries-
old recipes and, supposedly,
original Florentine perfumes
commissioned by the Medici
family. Charmingly, many of the
scented products have fragrances
inspired by Florentine locations or
characters from history: dab on a
little perfume and you'll give off the
air of Caterina de' Medici, or buy
an air freshener that'll ensure your
living room evokes the Giardino
di Boboli.

VIAJIYU

*Borgo Santi Apostoli 45r (055
290380, www.viajiyu.com, www.
VIAJIYU.setmore.com for apps).
Open by app. **Map** p73 J8* ⑩
Women's shoes

#NoHighHeels is the official
hashtag and working motto of this
colourful shoe boutique founded
by a globetrotting American
entrepreneur with no patience for
impractical footwear. Catering to
professional, worldly women-on-

93

the-go (AKA 'trailblazers', as the brand puts it), VIAJIYU is a stone's throw from the flagship Ferragamo store and rents its space directly from the legendary family. Shoes are all handmade in Italy and there are countless customisable options: the pointed-toe Milano flat is a bestseller, but you'll also find tasselled loafers and low wedges. Visits are by appointment only and price points are reasonable (starting at about €445) for the level of craftsmanship and personalised customer care involved.

Entertainment

♥ Mayday Lounge Café

*Via Dante Alighieri 16r, Duomo & Around (055 2381290, www. maydayclub.it). **Open** 7pm-2am Tue-Sat. Closed 2wks Aug. **Admission** free, membership required (free). **Map** p73 M8* ① *Bar*
This wacky joint with odd art installations and hundreds of old Marconi radios hanging from the ceilings is dark and edgy and has something of a cult following. There's a diverse programme of events to sample.

Odeon Original Sound

*Piazza Strozzi 2, Duomo & Around (39 055 295051/295331, www. odeonfirenze.com). **Open Box office** times vary. Closed Aug. Tickets €6-8. **No cards**. **Map** p73 K7* ② *Cinema*
Mondays, Tuesdays and Thursdays are big draws for English-speakers at this stunning art nouveau cinema as films on current release in English are screened, usually with Italian subtitles. There's a discount of up to 40% with a club card for eight films from a programme of 13 (€36). Before or after your screening, you can socialise with other English-speakers in the bar and bistro; a

discount is offered on the aperitivo buffet when you show your ticket.

♥ Slowly

*Via Porta Rossa 63r, Duomo & Around (055 0351335, www. slowlycafe.com). **Open** 12pm -2am Mon-Sat. **Map** p73 K8* ③ *Bar*
The ultimate chill-out bohemian-chic bar, Slowly is softly lit by candles in mosaic lanterns, with big soft sofas in alcoves, laidback staff and mellow Buddha Bar sounds when the DJ gets stuck in. Even the inevitable crowds of pretty young things can't break the nice and easy spell. The restaurant overlooking the bar serves imaginative global cuisine.

♥ Teatro Niccolini

*Via Ricasoli 3, Duomo & Around. Information and tickets Teatro della Pergola (see p124). Season Oct-Apr. **Map** p73 M6* ④ *Theatre*
Dating from 1648, Teatro Niccolini is the oldest theatre in Florence. It finally reopened in 2016 after 20 years of neglect thanks to publishing entrepreneur Mauro Pagliai, who restored it to its former glory.

♥ La Terrazza Lounge Bar

*Vicolo dell'Oro 6r, Duomo & Around (055 27265987, www. lungarnocollection.com/ la-terrazza-lounge-bar). **Open** Apr-Oct 2.30-11.30pm daily. **Map** p73 K9* ⑤ *Bar*
In-the-know Florentines mix with hotel guests at sundown for aperitifs at the Hotel Continentale's swanky rooftop bar. The sides of the bar are lined with smart biscuit-coloured upholstered benches, and cocktails are served with crudités and minibrioches. Occasional yoga classes are even held here. The main attraction, though, is the 360-degree bird's-eye view of the city. The bar is open in the warmer months, or as the Florentines term it, 'la bella stagione'.

Santa Maria Novella

Many visitors initially think of this part of the city in functional terms – it is, after all, the location of the main train station and where a bus terminal and most car-hire firms can be found. However, there's another, more tranquil and cultured side to Santa Maria Novella. Artistic treasures to be found here include the exquisite **church of Santa Maria Novella** and 20th-century art hub the **Museo Novecento**, a colourful respite from Renaissance Florence.

The station itself is a glorious example of Italian modernist architecture and the Functionalist style. It was constructed between 1932 and 1935 with the approval of Benito Mussolini, but despite its dubious associations, it

Best wine bar
A passionate selection of wine by the glass at gourmet nook Uva Nera (p103).

Best museums
20th-century art at Museo Novecento (p99), sculptures and contemporary exhibitions at Museo Marino Marini (p100).

Best souvenir shopping
Handmade marbled paper at Alberto Cozzi (p104), homeware at MIO Concept Store (p106) and 13th-century pharmacy Officina Profumo-Farmaceutica di Santa Maria Novella (p105).

Best café
Stylish Roberto Cavalli-connected café and cocktail bar Caffè Giacosa (p103).

Best restaurant
The noisy, meaty and hugely popular Il Latini (p102).

Best nightspot
Art Bar: small, unpretentious and lively (p106).

Best sights
Florence's definitive Dominican structure Santa Maria Novella (p100) and beautiful bridge Ponte Santa Trinita (p98).

looks beautiful. Adjacent to the station stands the sleek, white marble **Palazzina Reale**, originally built to house the royal family on their Florentine visits, and now home to an eatery and chic outdoor venue during the summer months. A short walk south, Leon Battista Alberti's exquisite, precision-built façade for the **church of Santa Maria Novella** looks out onto the increasingly pristine piazza of the same name.

South of here is traffic-heavy via della Scala, home to the famous **Officina Profumo-Farmaceutica di Santa Maria Novella**. The triangle formed by via de' Fossi, via della Spada and via della Vigna Nuova is a friendly, lively area cluttered with antiques emporia, designer clothes shops, cafés and *trattorie*. In the centre of the triangle are fine **Palazzo Rucellai** (not open to the public, but its Colosseum-inspired frontage can still be enjoyed),

➜ **Getting around**
This neighbourhood hosts Florence's transportation hub, so options abound, but most take you *out* of the area rather than through the thick of it. Much of the district is best seen on foot, but bus 23 will take you from the station down via della Scala; it has plenty of interesting stops but is not the most inspiring street for an aimless wander.

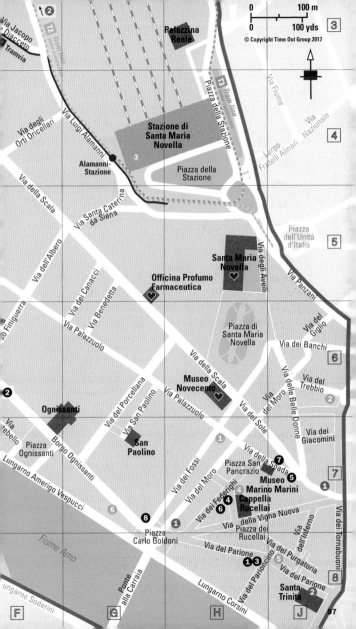

Via Jacopo
Diacceto

Via degli Orti Oricellari

Via Luigi Alamanni

Palazzina Reale

© Copyright Time Out Group 2017

0   100 m

0   100 yds

Via Fiume

Via Nazionale

Piazza della Stazione

Stazione di Santa Maria Novella

Alamanni-Stazione

Piazza della Stazione

Via della Scala

Via Santa Caterina da Siena

Largo Fratelli Alinari

Piazza dell'Unità d'Italia

Via degli Aveli

Via Panzani

Via dell'Albero

Santa Maria Novella ♥

Via Finiguerra

Via dei Canacci

Via Benedetta

Officina Profumo Farmaceutica ♥

Via Palazzuolo

Piazza di Santa Maria Novella

Via dei Banchi

Via del Giglio

Via della Scala

Via del Trebbio

Via del Sole

Via del Moro

Via delle Belle Donne

Museo Novecento ♥

Via dei Giacomini

Via del Porcellana

Via San Paolino

Via Palazzuolo

Ognissanti

Piazza Ognissanti

Borgo Ognissanti

San Paolino

Via dei Fossi

Via della Spada

Piazza San Pancrazio

Museo Marino Marini

Cappella Rucellai

Via del Moro

Via dei Federighi

Via della Vigna Nuova

Via dell'Inferno

Via dei Tornabuoni

Lungarno Amerigo Vespucci

Piazza Carlo Goldoni

Via del Parione

Piazza dei Rucellai

Via del Purgatorio

Fiume Arno

Ponte alla Carraia

Lungarno Corsini

Via del Parione

Via del Parionino

Santa Trinita

Lungarno Soderini

F   G   H   J

97

the **Cappella Rucellai** and the modern art museum, **Museo Marino Marini**.

At the end of via de' Fossi, next to the Arno, is piazza Goldoni. East from here lungarno Corsini leads to **Ponte Santa Trinita**, named after the nearby church and considered by many to be the most beautiful bridge in the world. Following the river west, lungarno Vespucci opens out into **piazza Ognissanti**, a square flanked by swanky hotels and topped by the **church of Ognissanti** – the cloister of which houses the **Cenacolo di Ognissanti**. Further up, elegant residential roads lead towards **Porta al Prato**, part of the old city walls.

Sights & museums

Cappella Rucellai

Via della Spada (055 216912). Open 10am-1pm Wed-Fri; 10am-7pm Sat-Mon. Admission €6 (includes Museo Marino Marini). Map p97 H7.

Once part of the church of San Pancrazio (now the Museo Marino Marini, *see p100*), the chapel retains the church's charming bell tower and contains the tombs of many members of the extended family of 15th-century wool magnate Giovanni Rucellai, including that of his wife Iacopa Strozzi. It's worth a visit to see Alberti's Temple of the Santo Sepolcro: commissioned in 1467 by Giovanni, it was built to the same proportions as the Holy Sepulchre of Jerusalem in an attempt to ensure his salvation. On occasion, it hosts can't-miss concerts.

Cenacolo di Ognissanti

Borgo Ognissanti 42 (055 2398700, 055 2396802). Open 9am-12.30pm, 4-7.30pm daily. Cenacolo and Last Supper 9am-noon Mon, Tue, Sat. Admission free. Map p97 F7.

The church of Ognissanti ('All Saints') was founded in the 13th century by the Umiliati, a group of monks from Lombardy. The monks introduced the wool trade to Florence, bringing with them great prosperity; without them, perhaps, there would have been no Florentine Renaissance. The Umiliati were so rich by the 14th century that they commissioned Giotto to paint the *Maestà* for their high altar; 50 years later, they got Giovanni da Milano to create a flashier altarpiece. Both are now in the Uffizi (*see p88*). Ognissanti was also the parish church of the Vespucci, a family of merchants that included 15th-century navigator Amerigo, who sailed to the Venezuelan coast in 1499 – and had two continents named after him. The church has been rebuilt numerous times and is now visited mainly for paintings by Ghirlandaio. Other frescoes include a *St Augustine* by Botticelli. In the Chapel of St Peter of Alcantara, look for Botticelli's tomb, marked with his family name of Filipepi.

Cenacolo di Ognissanti, the Ognissanti's lovely cloister, accessed via a separate entrance on borgo Ognissanti, is painted with frescoes illustrating the life of St Francis. The cloister's main

❤ Museo Novecento

Piazza Santa Maria Novella 10 (055 286132, www.museonovecento. it). Open 1 Apr-30 Sept 9am-7pm Mon-Wed & Sat, Sun; 9am-2pm Thur; 9am-11pm Fri. 1 Oct-31 Mar 9am-6pm Mon-Wed, Fri-Sun; 9am-2pm Thur. Admission €8.50. Map p97 H6.

Literally translating as the 'Museum of the 1900s', this long-awaited 20th-century art space injected much-needed fresh energy into Florence immediately upon its 2014 opening. The Museo Novecento's story began with a promise made after one of the city's most memorable disasters, the flooding of the Arno river in November 1966. With support from then-mayor Piero Bargellini, art historian Carlo Ludovico Ragghianti appealed to artists all over the world to donate their works to Florence, to replace the thousands of priceless pieces that had been damaged or destroyed by the waters. Those who responded – some 200 do-gooders dubbed the 'Artisti per Firenze' (Artists for Florence) – were told that their work would be displayed in a dedicated space. It took a while, but a promise is a promise: two years shy of the 50th anniversary of the tragedy, the Museo Novecento opened its doors inside the Leopoldine complex.

Italian artworks (around 300 of them, to be exact) are placed in reverse chronological order across 15 rooms, taking you back in time from the 1990s to the beginning of the 20th century. Heavy hitters such as Giorgio de Chirico and still life master Giorgio Morandi

are represented, along with lesser-known figures. The selection is far from comprehensive, but it's impressively varied, vaunting paintings, installations, video work, sound devices and beyond.

The Museo Novecento hosts intriguing temporary exhibitions too (Gaetano Pesce's gaudy *Majesty Betrayed* sculpture caused quite a stir when it was juxtaposed with the basilica façade for several months in late 2016 and early 2017). It is also a popular events venue and concert space, particularly for edgy, experimental 'sound artists'. Numerous collaborations with local arts and entertainment festivals take place throughout the year; check the website for an updated programme ahead of your visit. One thing's for sure: this museum routinely challenges Florence to look beyond its Renaissance glory days.

Superarchitettura (Archizoom and Superstudio, 1966-7), Museo Novecento

point of interest, however, is Ghirlandaio's most famous *Last Supper*, dated 1480.

💜 Museo Marino Marini

Piazza San Pancrazio (055 219432, www.museomarinomarini.it). **Open** *10am-7pm Sat-Mon; 10am-1pm Wed-Fri.* **Admission** *€6 (includes Cappella Rucellai). No cards.* **Map** *p97 J7.*

The original Albertian church on this site, San Pancrazio, was redesigned to accommodate the works of prolific sculptor and painter Marino Marini (1901-80), who hailed from nearby Pistoia. It's now a huge, bright and modern space filled predominantly with sculptures on the theme of horse and rider; the central exhibit is the 6m (20ft) *Composizione Equestre*. The second floor has a series of other bronze and polychrome plaster pieces, including the hypnotic *Nuotatore* (Swimmer) and some fabulous colourful paintings and sculptures of dancers and jugglers created during the early 1950s. The Marini is also a trendy and experimental events venue, frequently hosting public symposiums, concerts and the like, as well as VIP parties now and then. Temporary exhibitions are unlike anything else in Florence: the museum's high-energy administration breathes new life into the space with the annual appointment of a visiting director, Italian or foreign, whose vision shapes the following year's programming.

Santa Trinita

Piazza Santa Trinita (055 216912). **Open** *8am-noon, 4-6pm Mon-Sat; 4-6pm Sun.* **Admission** *free.* **Map** *p97 J8.*

This plain church was built in the 13th century over the ruins of two earlier churches belonging to the Vallombrosans. The order was founded in 1038 by San Giovanni

Highlight

💜 Santa Maria Novella

Piazza Santa Maria Novella (055 219257, www.smn.it). **Open** *Apr-Sept 9am-7pm Mon-Fri. Oct-Mar 9am-5.30pm Mon-Fri. Sept-June 9am-5.30pm Sat; 1-5.30pm Sun. July, August 9am-6.30pm Sat; noon-6.30pm Sun.* **Admission** *€5.* **Map** *p97 H5.*

Called Novella ('New') because it was built on the site of the ninth-century Santa Maria delle Vigne, the church dominates the piazza with its huge, geometrical façade. Santa Maria Novella was the Florentine seat of the Dominicans, an order fond of leading street brawls against suspected heretics.

The pièce de résistance of the church is the magnificent Alberti façade. In 1470, the architect incorporated the Romanesque lower storey into a refined Renaissance scheme. The church interior, however, was designed by the order's monks and is fittingly severe.

The church houses the Crocifisso by Giotto, a simple wooden crucifix that was finally returned to the church in 2001 after a 12-year restoration. It was placed in the centre of the basilica where the Dominicans had originally positioned it in 1290.

Until Vasari had them whitewashed in the mid 16th century, the church walls were covered with frescoes. Fortunately, Masaccio's Trinità of 1427 remains on the left nave, a triumph of trompe l'œil.

In 1485, the Dominicans allowed Ghirlandaio to cover the walls of the Cappella Tornabuoni, behind the altarpiece, with

SANTA MARIA NOVELLA

100

scenes from the life of John the Baptist, featuring a supporting cast from the Tornabuoni family, all wearing beautiful clothes – effectively making the work part-advertisement, as the family were cloth merchants. Ghirlandaio also found time to train a young Michelangelo while working on the chapel. At about the same time, Filippino Lippi was at work next door in the Cappella di Filippo Strozzi, painting scenes from the life of St Philip. A wooden crucifix by Brunelleschi, the envy of Donatello, is to the left of the altarpiece.

To compare Masaccio's easeful use of perspective with the contorted struggles of Paolo Uccello, visit the Chiostro Verde (green cloister) to the left of the church (via a separate entrance). Uccello's lunettes can be considered either visionary experiments of modern art or a complete perspectival mess, depending on your tolerance of artistic licence. Off the Chiostro you'll find the Cappellone (or Cappella) degli Spagnoli, named after the Spanish wife of Cosimo I, Eleonora di Toledo, and decorated with vibrant scenes by Andrea di Bonaiuto. Look out for the odd-looking cupola on the Duomo fresco: it's the artist's own design for the dome, ultimately rejected in favour of Brunelleschi's plan.

Peek inside the Caserma Mameli and its spectacular Grand Cloister, which previously served as a training centre for the Italian military police force but is soon to be incorporated into the museum complex (along with Capella

del Papa and the former dormitories). Its glorious 14th-century arcaded walkway is a real treasure.

Don't skip the upper level: the tiny Cappella del Papa (Pope's Chapel) was designed for Pope Leo X's 1515 visit to Florence – a quiet place for morning reflection and prayer. The captivating Coronation of the Virgin scene on the north wall was painted by Ridolfo del Ghirlandaio.

Crocifisso (Giotto, c1290)

Gualberto Visdomini, who spent much of his life attempting to persuade pious aristocrats to surrender their wealth and live a life of austerity. The order became extremely wealthy and powerful, reaching a peak in the 16th and 17th centuries, when its huge fortress abbey at Vallombrosa, in the Casentino countryside north of Arezzo, was built. Santa Trinita's façade was made at the end of the 16th century by Bernardo Buontalenti (who created the Giardino di Boboli's Grotta Grande), but the church is well worth a visit for the Cappella Sassetti alone. This chapel was luminously frescoed in 1486 by Ghirlandaio with scenes from the life of St Francis: one, set in the piazza della Signoria, features Lorenzo il Magnifico.

Restaurants & wine bars

Buca Mario €€€
Piazza degli Ottaviani 16r (055 214179, www.bucamario.com). **Open** *from 7pm daily.* **Map** *p97 H7* ❶ *Traditional Italian*
Housed in a 16th-century cellar, this traditional Tuscan eatery gets a lot of attention, particularly for its Florentine steak. Apart from said *bistecca*, Buca Mario doesn't prepare many dishes notably better than its competitors, but there's something truly special about its walk-down location and homely ambience (a nice touch is the discreet private dining room, which requires booking three days in advance). The homemade gnocchi are a top choice for a first course.

Cantinetta Antinori
Piazza degli Antinori 3 (055 292234, www.cantinetta-antinori.com). **Open** *noon-2.30pm, 7-10.30 pm Mon-Sat. Closed 3wks Aug.* **Map** *p97 J6* ❷ *Wine bar*

Continuing to attract well-dressed tourists and classy locals since its opening in 1965, this upscale wine bar occupies an elegantly vaulted ground-floor room of the 15th-century Palazzo Antinori, the historic home of one of Tuscany's foremost wine-producing families. Expect a wide variety of wines (including selections from Piedmont, Apulia and Lombardy, as well as Tuscany), plus *grappa* and spirits. The food menu features seasonal, simple items meant to complement the wine, not the other way around.

Fratelli Cuore €
Piazza della Stazione (attached to SMN station) (055 2670264, www.fratellicuore.it). **Open** *24hrs daily.* **Map** *p97 G4* ❸ *Pizzeria, bar & grill*
Quality dining options in the station's immediate vicinity were scarce before Fratelli Cuore entered the scene in 2015. Neapolitan-style pizzas are the speciality here: the five made-fresh varieties are prepared in a wood-fired oven. Simple, classic pastas (*carbonara*, *amatriciana* and so forth), salads (go for the fennel-topped *Cuore*) and burgers (named after major Italian train stations) are also available. Though there's not much ambience to speak of, this place is priceless for those in transit, particularly at odd hours. It's always open, saving the red-eyed train travellers from sloppy chains and offering a safe haven if you're stuck waiting for late-night airport shuttles and the like.

❤ Il Latini €€
Via de' Palchetti 6r (055 210916, www.illatini.com). **Open** *12.30-2pm, 7-10.30pm Tue-Sun. Closed last wk Dec.* **Map** *p97 H7* ❹ *Traditional Italian*
Run by the Latini family since 1950, this rustic eatery has become a Florence classic. Rather hidden,

yet overrun by tourists and the odd Florentine, what keeps people coming back to Latini is the *ciccia* (meat) – and great hunks of it too. Queues are inevitable after 8pm when reservations are no longer taken and, once inside, it'll be noisy and you'll probably be sharing a table with other customers, but that's all part of the fun. Skip the mediocre *primi*, and dive into the hefty *secondi*: this is a good place to order *salsicce e fagioli* (sausage and beans, a Tuscan classic) or, of course, Florentine steak. Il Latini also produces a fine, sludgy-green olive oil, and some decent wines: the house red is very drinkable.

Trattoria Coco Lezzone €€

Via del Parioncino 26r (055 287178, www.cocolezzone.it). Open noon-2.15pm, 7-10.15pm Mon-Sat. Closed 3wks Aug & Tue for dinner. No cards. Map p97 F5 ⑤ *Traditional Italian*

Respect for tradition, hand-selected prime ingredients and a centuries-old wood-burning stove mark out this authentic *trattoria*, in one of Florence's few medieval towers still standing. Open since the 1800s, current owner Gianfranco Paoli has brought this temple of Tuscan tastes back to the limelight, serving simple, well-made classics on the long, family-style tables. Dishes on the menu are thoroughly Tuscan, including traditional soups, home-made pastas and a range of wild game cooked (often for hours on end) in the early 20th-century oven. You'll find a wide variety of roast meats, seafood on Fridays and if you want to try Coco's Florentine steak, you'll have to order it in advance. It's hidden on a backstreet surrounded by parking garages, and you may get lost looking for it. Tip: don't give up.

♥ Uva Nera

Borgo Ognissanti 25r (055 0?. www.uvaneraenoteca.it). Ope. 11.30am-10pm Mon-Sat. Map p. G7 ⑥ *Wine bar*

The wines at this place are never set in stone: 'blame' it on passionate young owner-manager Costanza, who can hardly contain her enthusiasm for researching, then spotlighting, the producers she discovers. She personally visits each of her suppliers before serving their sips or snacks, trusting her own taste and staying firmly committed to small and mid-size companies, with a particular affinity for biodynamic and organic producers. Tuscans are always front and centre, but you'll occasionally find options from Piedmont and further afield. At *aperitivo* time, there's either a generous buffet or a custom-prepared platter, typically filled with scrumptious cold cuts, fresh cheeses with well-matched marmalades and other high quality snacks. The cherry on top is the place's look and feel: retro, but never forced.

Cafés, bars & gelaterie

♥ Caffè Giacosa

Via della Spada 10r (055 2776328, www.caffegiacosa.it). Open 7.45am-8.30pm Mon-Fri; 8.30am-8.30pm Sat; 12.30-8.30pm Sun. Map p97 J7 ① *Café*

Adjacent to Florentine fashion legend Roberto Cavalli's prestigious shop it'd be easy to mistake this café as being strictly for the style set. Don't fall for it: it's chic, but it's hardly snooty, routinely attracting a clientele that defies categorisation by age, nationality or even fashion sense. Staff members are always congenial, particularly the handsome baristas serving up arguably the city's best cappuccino (it's drizzled in chocolate, if you weren't daydreaming about it eady). The tiny space is often packed at peak breakfast hour (around 9am usually), and scoring a seat is next to impossible on weekend afternoons. What keeps the people coming? The flaky pastries, decadent cakes, pralines and cream-filled delights, high fashion portraits and banquette seating (sit down indoors at no extra charge in the mornings) are all solid starts.

Mariano Alimentari

Via del Parione 19r (055 214067). **Open** *8am-3pm, 5-7.30pm Mon-Fri; 8am-3pm Sat. Closed 3wks Aug.* **Map** *p97 J8* ❷ *Sandwich bar*
Tucked out of the way on via del Parione, this walk-in place is tough to beat for a quick sandwich break when you're out exploring. Tuscan bread is filled with delicious ingredients such as marinated aubergines, artichokes or oil-preserved pecorino, and an array of other delicacies. Have a coffee at the bar or in the vaulted wine cellar.

Shops

🖤 Alberto Cozzi

Via del Parione 35r (055 294968, www.facebook.com/AlbertoCozzi1908). Open 3-7pm Mon; 10am-1pm, 3-7pm Tue-Fri; Sat by appt. **Map** *p97 H8* ❶ *Gifts & souvenirs*
Part bookbinder's workshop and showroom, part Florentine gift paradise, this generations-strong shop has been working with libraries to restore books since the turn of the 20th century. If you're lucky, the bookbinders will be at work in the adjacent lab as you shop. Browse through a wonderful selection of marbled stationery, gold-flecked paper and leather-bound journals, which can all be personalised when you purchase.

Baby Bottega

Via il Prato 53-55r (055 286091, www.babybottega.com). Open 10am-1pm, 2.30-7.30pm Mon-Sat. **Map** *p97* ❷ *Children's interiors and toys*
Owner and chief curator Daisy Diaz bridges her identities as an American interior designer and an in-the-know Italian *mamma* at this playful and punchy concept boutique. The focus is on children's interiors, with cool furnishings, light fixtures, accessories and room accents from all the hippest international brands.

Il Bisonte

Via del Parione 31r (055 215722, www.ilbisonte.com). Open 10am-7pm Mon-Sat; 11am-6.30pm Sun. **Map** *p97 H8* ❸ *Leather*
A renowned, long-established outlet for top-tier soft leather bags, accessories and rugged cases.

La Bottega della Frutta

Via de' Federighi 31r (055 2398590, www.facebook.com/La-Bottega-della-Frutta-393945310670529/). Open 8.30am-7.30pm Mon-Sat. Closed Aug. **Map** *p97 H7* ❹ *Groceries*
Your neighbourhood supermarket will never look the same after you see the smörgåsbord of fruits, veggies, and novelty items in this hidden foodie nook. Sift through the wines, vintage balsamic vinegars, truffle-scented oils and speciality sweets, and if you need tips, look to Elisabetta and Francesco, the dynamic duo running the show.

Forno Top

Via della Spada 23r (055 212461, www.fornotop.it). Open 7.30am-7.30pm Mon-Sat. **No cards.** **Map** *p97 J7* ❺ *Bakery*
Delcious sandwiches, hot focaccia and other flatbreads, fabulous carrot or chocolate and pear cakes, and seasonal specialities, including

❤ Officina Profumo-Farmaceutica di Santa Maria Novella

Via della Scala 16 (055 216276, www.smnovella.it). **Open** *9am-8pm daily.* **Admission** *free.* **Map** *p97 G5* ❾ *Herbs & fragrances*

A beautiful 13th-century frescoed chapel in Santa Maria Novella is home to one of the world's oldest herbal pharmacies – now a global brand. The Officina Profumo-Farmaceutica di Santa Maria Novella was officially founded in 1612 by Fra' Angiolo Marchissi, though its origins date back as far as 1221, to the time of the Dominican friars. As you reach the entrance, the scent of the *antica farmacia's* potpourri fills the air.

A domed marble passageway leads to the main hall, which was turned into the shop in 1848. It's lined with mahogany and glass cabinets, and filled with the pharmacy's signature soaps (reputed to be the best in the world), delicate glass bottles of pure oils and perfume essences, and scented paper. Through a gilded archway is the apothecary, a grand antechamber decorated with Medici portraits, where herbal concoctions are still weighed up on brass scales. A back room, dotted with ancient apothecary tools, is where jams, sweets and soaps are packaged in lovely cream, vellum boxes.

The contemporary boom for luxury natural products has transformed the *farmacia* from local icon into internationally coveted brand, with branches in New York, Tokyo, Miami and beyond. The original lavender-smelling salts, 'anti-hysteria' Acqua di Santa Maria Novella, 14th-century Acqua di Rose and powder produced from the ground rhizomes of irises are practically unchanged formulas. Other renowned items include orange-blossom water and pomegranate perfume. However, with globalisation comes the march of modernity: you can now find parabens in the rose cream and tan-prolonging shower gel alongside the medieval ladies' favourite: skin-whitening powder.

History buffs should step inside the dedicated museum space. It offers a look at work tools used in ages past, as well as the collections of copper and bronze objects and Maiolica ceramic pharmaceutical containers.

traditional Tuscan sweets, in this stylish bakery beloved by locals.

Mercatino dei Ninni
Via dei Federighi 11r (055 291604, www.facebook.com/Mercatino-di-Ninni- 1690313241195199). **Open** *10.30am-1pm Tue-Sun; 2:30-7pm daily.* **Map** *p97 H7* ❻ *Vintage & contemporary clothing*
This well-curated vintage and contemporary womenswear shop is run by a former model whose stylish daughter also makes frequent appearances in-house. Items stocked are fairly priced, but hardly inexpensive, since the standard rack on a random day might include a vintage Chanel jacket, Narciso Rodriguez dress, Yves Saint Laurent blouse and other one-of-a-kind finds. Beyond investment pieces for your wardrobe, there are usually a hotchpotch of bags, from boxy Kelly-inspired classics to trendy backpacks, along with shoes from hip contemporary and diffusion lines such as See by Chloe.

♥ MIO Concept Store
Via della Spada 34r (055 2645543, www.mio-concept.com). **Open** *3-7pm Mon; 10am-1.30pm, 2.30-7pm Tue-Sat.* **Map** *p97 J7* ❼ *Design & gifts*
A veritable cabinet of curiosities, this tiny shop teems with design objects for the home and has an ongoing collaboration with Florence's famous French street artist CLET. Finely crafted items, from statement necklaces and mood rings to journals, bric-a-brac, scarves and wall art, are carefully chosen by charismatic German owner-founder Antje d'Almeida, a self-professed globetrotter with a Zen vibe and a knack for pinpointing exactly what her customers want.

Münstermann
Piazza Goldoni 2r (055 210660, www.munstermann.it). **Open** *10am-1pm, 2-7pm Tue-Sat.* **Map** *p97 G7* ❽ *Herbs & perfumes*
This charming shell-shaped corner icon was opened in 1897, a stone's throw from ponte alla Carraia, and still has its original shop fittings. Along with potpourri and perfumes, it stocks pharmaceutical and herbal medicines, toiletries, silver pillboxes, hair accessories, skincare products, sun protection cream and bathroom oddities. The house brand products all use high quality, natural ingredients and follow tried and tested recipes.

Entertainment

♥ Art Bar
Via del Moro 4r, Santa Maria Novella (055 287661, www.facebook.com/pg AnticoCaffeDel MoroArtBarFirenze). **Open** *6.30pm-1am daily. Closed 3wks Aug.* **Map** *p97 H7* ❶ *Bar*
Battered French horns hanging from the ceiling and sepia photos of blues and jazz musicians lend a beatnik air to this tiny but popular bar, best known for its beautiful cocktails adorned with kiwi, strawberry and other eye-catching accents. The ambience is cosy but animated, with student types holed up in the brick cellar sipping their potent piña coladas.

Tender Club
Via Alemanni 4, Santa Maria Novella (www.facebook.com/ tenderclub). **Open** *9.30pm-3.30am Fri & Sat. Tickets prices vary.* **Map** *p97 F2* ❷ *Live music*
While the venue itself isn't particularly memorable, Tender is a great place to hear live music – mainly Italian bands and rock – and people-watch Florentine hipsters.

San Lorenzo

Teeming with life, San Lorenzo is a neighbourhood of contrasts: the incongruously unfinished façade of San Lorenzo church itself and the chapels of the Medici family are rather serious affairs, but the district is also marked out by the fun and frenetic activity generated by its huge market, the high number of tourists, and the plethora of shops, delis, cafés and doughnut stands.

Mercato Centrale, with its upstairs gourmet food-and-drink court that stays open until midnight, constitutes the hub of the area, and spreads its tentacles over a wide swathe of *piazze* that snake north from the church of **San Lorenzo**. The street stalls around here sell cheap clothes, mediocre leather goods and tacky souvenirs.

Best sights
The grand mausoleum, Cappelle
Medicee (p112), the Biblioteca
Mediceo-Laurenziana in
San Lorenzo (p111) and the
Renaissance palace Palazzo
Medici Riccardi (p109).

Best gelateria
Traditional and inventive flavours
at My Sugar (p114).

Best museum
A glimpse into the lives of the
wealthy Martelli family at Museo
Casa Martelli (p109).

Best shop
Sleek boutique Desii Vintage
(p114).

Best cultural experience
Year-round English-language play
'The Medici Dynasty Show' (p114).

Best wine bar
Find bottles for all budgets at Casa
del Vino (p111).

Best lunch
Head upstairs at the Mercato
Centrale (p114).

North-east from **piazza San Lorenzo** (to the east
of the church), on via Cavour, lies the **Palazzo Medici
Riccardi,** with its lovely frescoed chapel painted by
Benozzo Gozzoli, and, further up, is the Chiostro dello
Scalzo, decorated with frescoes by the Mannerist painter
Andrea del Sarto. Right and right again is the Benedictine
refectory of **Cenacolo di Sant'Apollonia.**

Travelling south from the piazza will lead you
past busy shoe and clothes shops in borgo San Lorenzo
directly to the historic house of the wealthy Martelli
family, **Museo Casa Martelli.** North-west you'll find the
spectacular **Cappelle Medicee.** Further up via Faenza lies
the **Cenacolo di Fuligno,** while north-east from here is
piazza dell'Indipendenza, with its grand *palazzi*.

→ Getting around

The main shopping area around the Mercato Centrale, as well as the
pedestrian-packed pockets around the Medici chapels, are best explored
on foot. But as you move west of via Panicale on to the more traffic-heavy
via Nazionale and surrounding areas, you may want to hop on a bus. The 11
and 23 lines stop in piazza dell'Indipendenza, while the 36, 37, 13, 11, 10
and 14B are just a few of the main lines moving up and down via Nazionale.

Sights & museums

❤ Museo Casa Martelli

Via Ferdinando Zannetti 8 (055 216725, www.bargellomusei. beniculturali.it). Open 2-7pm Thur; 9am-2pm Sat; 1st, 3rd & 5th Sun of mth. Free admission and guided visits. Map p110 K6.

One of Florence's hidden gems, this frescoed residential palace turned museum offers a glimpse into the lives of the wealthy Martelli family who lived here from the 15th to the mid 18th century. The family's most prominent members included 18th-century Archbishop of Florence, Giuseppe Maria Martelli, who enlisted the help of architect Bernardino Ciurini, painters Vincenzo Meucci and Bernardo Minozzi and many others in restructuring the palace into what we see today. The family's prolific art collection contains significant pieces that most visitors to Florence don't see: Piero di Cosimo's *Adoration of the Child*, works by Luca Giordano and Salvator Rosa, as well as numerous antique furnishings and decorative elements.

❤ Palazzo Medici Riccardi

Via Cavour 1 (055 2760340, www. palazzo-medici.it). Open 9am-7pm Mon, Tue, Thur -Sun. Admission €4. No cards. Map p110 L5.

In true Medici fashion, the family's 15th-century palace is strategically placed. They bought a string of adjacent houses on via Larga (now via Cavour) in the mid 14th century, when it was a fairly broad road in a peaceful residential area – but in close proximity to the Duomo and merely a few steps from their favoured church, San Lorenzo (*see right*). The Medici thereby made sure their home (until they moved into Palazzo Vecchio in 1540) was in a position of power and would subtly intimidate any opposition with its strongbox-like

appearance. Not wishing to appear too ostentatious, however, Cosimo il Vecchio rejected Brunelleschi's design as too extravagant and plumped for one by Michelozzo, who had recently proved his worth as a heavyweight architect in the rebuilding of the San Marco convent complex. Michelozzo designed a façade with a heavily rusticated lower storey (in the style of many military buildings), but a smoother and more refined first storey and a yet more restrained second storey.

The building was expanded and revamped in the 17th century by the Riccardi, its new owners, but retains Michelozzo's charming chapel, Cappella dei Magi.. Almost entirely covered with frescoes by Benozzo Gozzoli, a student of Fra Angelico, this chapel features a vivid *Procession of the Magi* that is actually a portrait of 15th-century Medici. (In one of the most thoroughly Florentine rituals of the year, an elaborate parade passes from piazza Pitti to piazza del Duomo on Epiphany, re-enacting the wise men's journey to Jesus and costumed as Gozzoli's characters). In another room, off the gallery, is Fra Filippo Lippi's winsome *Madonna and Child*.

❤ San Lorenzo

Piazza San Lorenzo (055 214042, www.operamedicealaurenziana.it). Open Winter 10am-5.30pm Mon-Sat. Summer 10am-5.30pm Mon-Sat; 1.30-5.30pm Sun. Admission €7. No cards. Map p110 L5.

Built where Florence's cathedral stood from the end of the fourth to the ninth century – and thus right on the site of Florence's oldest church – San Lorenzo's sheer size more than compensates for its very plain exterior. San Lorenzo was built between 1419 and 1469 to a design by Brunelleschi (but largely completed by Manetti, his erstwhile assistant, who made

several design alterations), and was the first church to which the architect applied his theory of rational proportion.

Despite the fortune spent on the place, the façade was never finished, hence the digestive biscuit-coloured bricks. In 1518, the Medici Pope Leo X commissioned Michelangelo to design a façade and ordained that the marble should be quarried at Pietrasanta. Michelangelo disagreed, preferring high-quality Carrara marble. In the end, it didn't matter: the scheme was cancelled in 1520.

A couple of artworks in the church merit a closer look. Savonarola snarled his tales of sin and doom from Donatello's bronze pulpits, but the reliefs are also powerful: you can almost hear the crowds scream in the *Deposition*. On the north wall is a *Martyrdom of St Lawrence* by Mannerist painter par excellence Bronzino. In the second chapel on the right is another Mannerist work, a *Marriage of the Virgin* by Rosso Fiorentino, while the north transept holds an *Annunciation* by Filippo Lippi with a clarity of line and a depth of perspective that make it perfect for this interior.

Opening off the north transept is the **Sagrestia Vecchia** (Old Sacristy): another Brunelleschi design, it has a dome segmented like a tangerine and proportions based on cubes and spheres, along with a fabulous painted *tondo* by Donatello. The doors, also by Donatello, feature martyrs, apostles and Church fathers; to the left of the entrance, an elaborate tomb made by Verrocchio out of serpentine, porphyry, marble and bronze contains the remains of Lorenzo il Magnifico's father and uncle.

Reached via the door to the left of the façade is Michelangelo's architectural classic, the **Biblioteca Mediceo-Laurenziana**, built to house the Medici's large library. It still contains priceless volumes, papyri, codices and documents, though not all of them are on permanent display. The entrance corridor has a stunning red and cream inlaid mosaic floor, while the library itself displays Michelangelo's predilection for the human form over any classical architectural norms. However, it's in the vestibule leading into the reading room that the true masterpiece of the library is found. The highly original three-sweep stairwell in *pietra serena* was a ground-breaking design, the first example ever of the expressive Mannerist style in architecture and one of the most elegant staircases ever built. For details of the Cappelle Medicee, *see p112*.

Restaurants & wine bars

For quick lunches and tasty snacks, head to the first floor of the refurbished **Mercato Centrale**, *see p114*.

❤ Casa del Vino €
Via dell'Ariento 16r (055 215609, www.casadelvino.it). **Open** *9.30am-3.30pm Mon-Fri; 9.30am-8pm Sat. Closed Aug.* **Map** *p110 K4* ❶ *Wine bar*

Hidden behind the stalls of the San Lorenzo market, this wine bar has very limited seating on a few benches and stools backed up against the wine cabinets. No matter: punters continue to pile in for a glass of good plonk and some delicious *panini, crostini* and Florentine-style salads (hint: that means tripe) to accompany it. Bottles for all budgets sit on lovely old carved wooden shelves that line the room; you'll find fairly priced wines from all over Italy, plus labels from further afield and plenty of choice by the glass. In addition to the vast selection of wines, you can

❤ Cappelle Medicee

Piazza di Madonna degli Aldobrandini 6 (055 2388602, www.firenzemusei.it). **Open** *8.15am-2pm Tue-Sat; 1st, 3rd, 5th Mon & 2nd, 4th Sun of mth.* **Admission** *€8; free on 1st Sun of every mth. No cards.* **Map** *p110 K5.*

The spectacular Medici mausoleum is the most splendid and fascinating part of the basilica of San Lorenzo. Up the curling stairs at the back of the entrance chamber is the grand **Cappella dei Principi** (Chapel of the Princes), constructed from huge hunks of porphyry and ancient Roman marble hauled into the city by Turkish slaves. The chapel houses six sarcophagi of the Medici Grand Dukes. This mausoleum was commissioned in 1602 but, amazingly, the beautifully intricate inlay of marble and precious stones wasn't completed until 1962, when workers from the Opificio delle Pietre Dure finished the last external pavement; by then, the Medici dynasty had been over for 220 years.

In 1994, the entrance to the **crypt** was discovered beneath a stone under the chapel's altar. This sensational revelation was followed by the exhumation of 49 Medici bodies, and scientists were able to determine the manner in which many of them had died. It was originally thought that Francesco I de' Medici and his mistress Bianca Cappello had suffered from malaria, but tests showed they had in fact been killed by acute arsenic poisoning – probably at the hand of Francesco's jealous brother Ferdinando.

Out of the Cappella dei Principi, a passage to your left leads to Michelangelo's **Sagrestia Nuova** (New Sacristy). This chamber, begun in 1520, is in stark contrast to the excesses of the chapel. It's dominated by the tombs of Lorenzo il Magnifico's relatives: grandson Lorenzo, Duke of Urbino, and his son Giuliano, Duke of Nemours, who grew up alongside Michelangelo. Also here, under the sacristy, is the incomplete tomb of Lorenzo il Magnifico and his brother Giuliano. The Sagrestia Nuova was finished by Giorgio Vasari, after Michelangelo was hauled off to Rome to work on the Sistine Chapel. The great man was furious at having to leave the city – 'I cannot live under pressure from patrons, let alone paint' – but he'd worked long enough on the project to leave it as one of his masterpieces.

purchase Tuscan extra virgin olive oil, balsamic vinegar and Prato's famed Mattei *biscotti*.

La Cucina del Garga €€
Via San Zanobi 33r (055 475286, www.garga.it). Open 7.30-10.30pm Mon-Sat. Map p110 L2 ②
Contemporary Italian

Chef Alessandro Gargani is a bona-fide Florentine who inherited his parents' kitchen prowess. His father, the late Giuliano Gargani, was well known in local art circles and fused his passions for food and painting at the whimsically decorated restaurant he ran with his Canadian wife, Sharon. Sharon's still a big part of proceedings, running cooking classes and picking up ingredients at the market, while Ale oversees kitchen operations, staying faithful to most of his dad's original recipes but also adding his own twists, having lived and cooked in New York City. Think comfort Italian food with a bit of saucy American style thrown in, such as *tagliatelle del magnifico*, a citrus cream pasta with a hint of mint, or the truffle and avocado chicken. Don't skip dessert: Sharon's famous cheesecake won her favour with the Florentines when she first arrived as a young, foreign chef, and the flourless chocolate tart with rosemary and olive oil is unreal.

Sergio Gozzi €
Piazza San Lorenzo 8r (055 281941). Open noon-3.45pm Mon-Sat. Closed Aug. Map p110 L5 ③
Traditional Italian

An authentic, old-fashioned Florentine *trattoria*, this family-run eatery has only hit the tourist radar since the stalls of the San Lorenzo market were cleared out of the church area. Thankfully, its unassuming door still keeps all but the most serious away, making it a less frantic alternative to Trattoria Mario (*see right*) as a

place to sample simple and genuine home cooking. Perhaps begin with *minestrone di verdura, ribollita* or *minestra di farro* (spelt soup), before moving on to a roast or *bistecca alla fiorentina*. On Fridays, you can sample their superb *seppie in inzimino* – sweet tender squid stewed with Swiss chard.

Trattoria Mario €
Via Rosina 2r (055 218550, www. trattoria-mario.com). Open noon-3.30pm Mon-Sat. Closed 3wks Aug. No cards. Map p110 L4 ④
Traditional Italian

Reservations are not taken and the long queue for a table may not seem worth the wait, but you'll be glad you stuck it out. Run by four generations of the Colsi family, you'll be eating elbow-to-elbow with your fellow lunchers on long bare-wood tables inside this chaotic and cramped eatery, which draws an egalitarian mix of people who are all interested in the simple yet excellent Florentine home cooking. Try the earthy *ribollita* (Tuscan vegetable and bread soup), a terrific *bollito misto* (mixed boiled meats) served with a biting garlic and parsley *salsa verde* and, for a supplement, the tasty *bistecca* (steak) or mouth-watering *lombatina* (veal chop). It doesn't get much better for the price.

Cafés, bars & gelaterie

Focacceria Bondi
Via dell'Ariento 85r (055287390). Open 11.30am-12am daily. Map p110 K4 ① *Sandwiches*

By day, this is not just a tasty sandwich shop, but a calm respite from the busy tourist crowds of via dell'Ariento. At lunch, its wooden benches are mostly filled with neighbourhood workers feasting on low cost *focaccine* (triangular *focaccia* bread-based sandwiches). By night, you'll find young

Florentines and internationals squeezing in a post-dinner snack. Best to keep your sandwich simple at a place like this: the fresh mint, goat's cheese and tomato combo is heavenly..

❤ My Sugar
Via de' Ginori 49r (393 0696042).
Open *1-9pm daily.* **Map** *p110 L4* ❷
Gelateria
Run by charming young couple Alberto and Julia, this hole in the wall doesn't look like much from the outside, but it's one of the most buzzed-about gelaterie in Florence, offering a mix of inventive and traditional flavours, including some that show up for a limited time only.

Sieni
Via Sant'Antonino 54r (055 213830, www.pasticceriasieni.it).
Open *7.30am-7.30pm daily.* **No cards.** **Map** *p110 K4* ❸ *Café*
With its turn-of-the-century decor, this 1909 café and *pasticceria* is the real deal, serving up a great range of sweet and savoury breakfast pastries and snacks to a very local crowd, some of them taking a coffee break from their market shopping. Try yours with a hefty slice of perfect polenta cake.

Shops

❤ Desii Vintage
Via dei Conti 17 (055 2302817).
Open *10.30am-1pm, 2.30-7.30pm Mon-Sat.* **Map** *p110 K6* ❶ *Vintage fashion*
This sleek, well-curated boutique carries a large variety of vintage items, from Chanel suits to Louis Vuitton luggage to more affordable finds such as Salvatore Ferragamo flats. With all the combat boots and catchy window displays, it tends to draw trendsetters, particularly during the Pitti Immagine trade show season.

❤ Mercato Centrale
Piazzale Mercato Centrale (055 2399798, www.mercatocentrale. it). **Ground floor** *7am-2pm Mon-Fri; 7am-5pm Sat.* **First floor** *10am-midnight daily.* **Map** *p110 K4* ❷ *Market*
The Mercato Centrale has undergone quite a makeover in recent years – and there's debate over whether or not it's changed for the better. The traditional produce, meat, cheese and fish market on the ground floor is worth exploring for the colours, sights and scents, but if it's a 'local' shopping experience you're looking for, you'll find more Florentines at the less tourist-tracked Mercato Sant'Ambrogio (*see p137*). Upstairs, the chic 'first floor' has become a popular pit stop for both travellers and locals. It's a dynamite dining option if you're wandering in a group and can't all agree on what to eat, or if you're itching for a sit-down snack. The *pizzeria* is particularly noteworthy, if not Florentine: it's run by Roman *pizzaiuolo*, Stefano Callegari, and features a short menu of standard classics, as well as seasonal and Rome-inspired options.

Entertainment

❤ The Medici Dynasty Show
Il Fulgino, via Faenza 48, San Lorenzo (349 1310441, www. medicidynasty.com). Date year-round with more shows in summer. **Map** *p110 J3* ❶ *Theatre show*
This entertaining and original play is performed in English. A concise introduction to Medici history, the show centres on the family's final two heirs; the flamboyant Gian Gastone and future-oriented Anna Maria Luisa, who ensured that the family's art collections would remain in Florence.

San Marco

When it comes to famous attractions, San Marco wins hands-down over all the other districts of Florence, since in the **Accademia** it houses Michelangelo's iconic *David*, perhaps the most famous statue in the world. However, there are plenty of other museums in the neighbourhood to divert you, containing fascinating, family friendly displays of weird and wonderful things.

Head to the nigh-on perfect **piazza della Santissima Annunziata** with its crowds of artsy students and occasional markets and it's apparent that the area is far more than a tourist centre. The square is dominated by its equestrian statue of **Grand Duke Ferdinando I** by Giambologna. The church of **Santissima Annunziata** is to the north.

Best art gallery
Galleria dell'Accademia (*p118*),
home to Michelangelo's David.

Best restaurant
Osteria de L'Ortolano (*p123*), deli
and restaurant in one.

Best museums
The world's earliest institution for
children, Museo degli Innocenti
(*p121*), mystical paintings by
Fra'Angelico at Museo di San
Marco (*p122*).

Best shopping
Vintage couture for fashionistas at
Street Doing (*p123*).

Best cultural venues
Italy's oldest working theatre
Teatro della Pergola (*p124*),
arthouse cinema La Compagnia
(*p124*).

Best nibbles
First-rate Sicilian street food at
Arà: è Sicilia (*p123*).

SAN MARCO

On the eastern side of the square is the **Spedale degli Innocenti**; opened in 1445 as the first foundling hospital in Europe and designed by Filippo Brunelleschi. The building houses an impressive collection of artworks in the revamped **Museo degli Innocenti**.

Heading southeast under the northernmost arch of the Spedale is via della Colonna, flanked by the **Museo Archeologico**. Alternatively, walking south down via de' Servi towards the Duomo will bring you to **Museo Leonardo da Vinci**.

Passing the **Opificio delle Pietre Dure** and the **Accademia**, at the end of via Ricasoli, is piazza di San Marco, home to both the eponymous **church** and the **Museo di San Marco**, filled with works by Fra Angelico. Venture outside the via Ricasoli–San Marco–Santissima Annunziata–via dei Servi quadrangle to find historic opera house **Teatro della Pergola** and the reinvented **Cinema La Compagnia**.

➔ **Getting around**
San Marco is most easily explored on foot. Piazza San Marco is the city's second largest bus hub. The 7 bus to Fiesole leaves from via Giorgio La Pira around the corner.

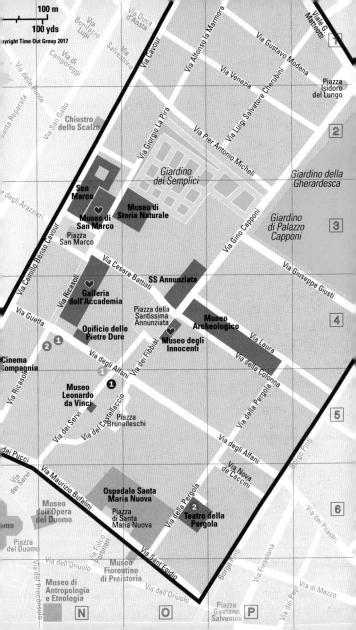

Sights & museums

Museo Archeologico & Museo Egizio

Piazza della SS Annunziata 9b (055 23575, www.archeotoscana. beniculturali.it). **Open** *8.30am-2pm Sat-Mon; 8.30am-7pm Tue-Fri.* **Admission** *€4; €2 reductions. No cards.* **Map** *p117 P4.*

It's easy to come to Florence and get completely submerged in the Renaissance, but the archaeological museum, housed in Palazzo della Crocetta, explains what happened before the Golden Age. The museum has an impressive entrance hall, an enormous temporary exhibition space and the largest collection anywhere of Etruscan coins. Exhibits include jewellery, funerary sculpture, urns and bronzes dating from the fifth century BC, as well as the fabulous *Chimera*, a mythical beast that's part lion, part goat and part snake. Also present is the first-century BC Etruscan bronze *Orator*, famous and historically important because the speaker in question is wearing a Roman toga. The first rooms house Egyptian artefacts (including sarcophagi complete with creepy shrivelled bodies) from prehistoric eras through to AD 310. Outside, the beautiful garden lined with Etruscan tombs and monuments opens only on Saturday mornings, weather conditions allowing.

Museo Leonardo da Vinci

Via de' Servi 66-68r (055 282966, www.mostredileonardo.com). **Open** *Apr-Oct 10am-7pm daily. Nov-Mar 10am-6pm daily.* **Admission** *€7; €5 reductions.* **Map** *p117 N5.*

The painter, sculptor, musician, engineer, inventor, scientist and all-round genius Leonardo da Vinci justly has a museum to himself. The museum offers an attractive, interactive insight into the machines that featured in da Vinci's codes. Several of his most

❤ Galleria dell'Accademia

Via Ricasoli 58-60 (055 294883, www.accademia.org (unofficial info site), www.firenzemusei.it (official ticket booking). **Open** *8.15am-6.50pm Tue-Sun.* **Admission** *€8 (€12.50 with special exhibitions); €6.25 reductions. Free on 1st Sun of every mth No cards.* **Map** *p117 N4.*

Galleria dell'Accademia first became a public museum when Florence was capital of Italy (1865-1871). Then, in 1872, a crucial decision was reached: the original *David* by Michelangelo would be moved here from piazza della Signoria where it had been since 1504. It took several days and a purpose-built cart on tracks to move *David*, which remained hidden from view while the neoclassical *tribuna* (alcove), surmounted by a glass dome created by architect Emilio De Fabris (who also designed the Duomo façade, *see p74*), was completed. The Museo Michelangiolesco, as it became known, opened in July 1882.

Today, Galleria dell'Accademia is Italy's second most-visited museum after the Uffizi (*see p88*), with over 1.4 million visitors yearly. Despite the fact that it contains a huge number of magnificent and historic works in its 11 rooms over two floors, the queue snaking around the block is usually here for one attraction only: Michelangelo's monumental *David*.

The biblical story of David and Goliath had long been a popular theme in Florentine art, but Michelangelo's innovative take on the subject marked a clean break from the tradition exemplified by Donatello's and Verrocchio's graceful bronzes (now both in the Bargello; *see p129*). Michelangelo's *David* is no longer a boy, but a youth on the verge of manhood; and he is portrayed in the tense, purposeful, defiant pose of a hero ready for combat. His deliberately oversized head and hands are the symbols of his deadly weapons: reason and strength. Michelangelo was commissioned to make the statue in 1501, when he was 26, and worked frantically and secretively at it for nearly three years. He achieved the enormous feat of creating a seemingly perfect figure from an unusually tall, impossibly shallow, dangerously fractured and – worse still – previously hacked-at block of Carrara marble, which had lain abandoned for nearly 25 years in a courtyard of the Opera del Duomo.

Other Michelangelo works line the walls of the long hall leading to the *David* salon; among them are four slaves, formerly in Buontalenti's Grotto in Boboli (*see p147*). They were intended for Pope Julius II's tomb in Rome, a project that Michelangelo was forced to abandon in order to paint the Sistine Chapel. They are masterly but unfinished sculptures, called *schiavi* (slaves) or *prigioni* (prisoners) because it seems as if the figures are struggling to escape from their marble constraints. As such, they provide a precious insight into the Master's *non*

finito (unfinished) sculpting technique. Michelangelo was convinced that figures were encased by God inside the stone, and that it was the artist's task to let them emerge.

Highlights of the Accademia collections also include Michelangelo's bronze bust by his pupil Daniele da Volterra; a remarkable anthology of Florentine late Gothic paintings; the elegant bridal scene depicted by Masaccio's brother Lo Scheggia on a wedding chest for the Adimari family (c1450), and some fine Renaissance paintings, such as Botticelli's *Madonna of the Sea* (c1477; attributed by some to Filippino Lippi).

Finally, music lovers should not overlook the fabulous collection of around 50 musical instruments on permanent loan here from the **Luigi Cherubini Music Conservatory** next door.

David (Michaelangelo, 1501–4)

extraordinary inventions have been built from studies taken from his drawings: flying machines, a hydraulic saw, a printing machine and even a massive tank – it measures 5.3m by 3m (17ft by 10ft) and weighs two tonnes. Most of the exhibits can be touched, moved and even dangled from, making this place immensely popular with kids.

Opificio delle Pietre Dure
Via degli Alfani 78 (055 26511, www.opificiodellepietredure. it). Open 8.15am-2pm Mon-Sat. Admission €4; €2 reductions. No cards. Map p117 N4.
In all the grandest palaces and most expensive shops in town, you'll see fine examples of the Florentine craft of inlaying *pietre dure* (semi-precious stones) in intricate mosaics. The Opificio (workshop) was founded by Grand Duke Ferdinando I in 1588. It's now an important restoration centre, but also provides a fascinating insight into this typically Florentine art, with its mezzanine exhibitions of tools and stones, and its displays of the methods used for cutting and polishing the stones, through to inlaying and mosaic techniques.

San Marco
Piazza San Marco (055 2388608). Open 8.15am-1.50pm Mon-Fri; 8.15am-4.50pm Sat, Sun. Closed 2nd, 4th Mon and 1st, 3rd, 5th Sun each mth. Admission €4; €2 reductions. Map p117 N3.
The amount of money lavished by the Medici family on San Lorenzo (*see p109*) is nothing compared with that spent on the church and convent of San Marco. After Cosimo il Vecchio returned from exile in 1434, he organised the transfer of San Marco from the Silvestrine monks to the Dominican friars from Fiesole. Cosimo went on to fund the renovation of the decaying

church and convent by Michelozzo, and also founded a public library that greatly influenced Florentine Humanists; Florentine Humanist Academy meetings were held in the gardens. Ironically, later in the 15th century San Marco became the base of religious fundamentalist Fra Girolamo Savonarola, who burned countless Humanist treasures in his notorious 'Bonfire of the Vanities'.

Inside the church, see Giambologna's 16th-century nave with side chapels. In 1589, he completed the Cappella di Sant'Antonino, where you can now, creepily, see the whole dried body of the saint.

The altarpiece *Madonna and Child* (1440s) is by Fra Angelico, whose other more famous works can be seen next door in the Museo di San Marco (*see opposite*). Two missing panels from the painting were discovered, curiously enough, in Oxford, behind the door of an elderly Englishwoman's house in 2006.

Santissima Annunziata
Piazza della SS Annunziata (055 266181). Open 7.30am-12.30pm, 4-6.30pm daily. Admission free. Map p117 O4.
Despite Brunelleschi's perfectionist ambitions for the square it crowns, Santissima Annunziata – the church of the Servite order – is a place of popular worship rather than perfect proportion. Highlights include a frescoed Baroque ceiling and an opulent shrine built around a miraculous Madonna, purportedly painted by a monk in 1252 and, as the story goes, finished overnight by angels. Surrounding the icon are flowers, silver lamps and pewter body parts, ex-votos left in the hope that the Madonna will cure the dicky heart or gammy leg of a loved one.

Michelozzo was the directing architect and built the Villani

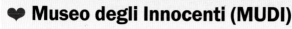

💜 Museo degli Innocenti (MUDI)

Piazza della SS Annunziata 12 (055 2037308, www. istitutodeglinnocenti.it). **Open** *10am-7pm daily.* **Admission** *€5. No cards.* **Map** *p117 O4.*

Europe's first foundling hospital opened here in 1445 thanks to a 1,000-florin bequest by Francesco Datini, a rich merchant from Prato. Although it no longer operates as an orphanage, the Istituto degli Innocenti continues to pursue its mission to care for the well-being of children, and hosts an important UNICEF research centre. However, to the visitor its importance lies first and foremost in the artistic value of the building itself and in the artworks it contains.

Following a €12.8 million, three-year overhaul, the thoroughly redesigned museum opened in June 2016 and is now one of the city's most innovative exhibition spaces, deserving to attract more visitors than ever before. Andrea della Robbia's powder-blue medallions, each featuring a white glazed terracotta Swaddled Baby, grace the elegant Brunelleschi façade and were restored as part of the renovation project. On the flip side, two ultra-modern brass doors have been added, sparking fierce debate.

The museum aims to be child-friendly and fully accessible for disabled visitors, and the new set-up certainly fulfils this promise: there are plenty of engaging multimedia displays, the captions are positioned at a child-friendly eye level, and La Bottega dei Ragazzi – the Institute's own children's workshop and recreational area, providing activities for schools and families – has teamed up with Associazione MUSE to offer a free Family Tour kit (and matching app), available in Italian and English from the reception desk.

The visit spans three different sections and starts from the newly reclaimed basement, where documents and objects recount the history of the institution and the stories of some of the children it saved and raised over the centuries. The second section showcases the building's architectural features, while the second-floor gallery displays the Institute's art collection, which – although it suffered a substantial blow in 1853, when several important works were auctioned off to raise money for the hospital – includes outstanding pieces such as Domenico Ghirlandaio's *Adoration of the Magi*, commissioned for the main altar of the hospital's church.

SAN MARCO

Adoration of the Magi (Domenico Ghirlandaio, c. 1485)

❤ Museo di San Marco

Piazza San Marco 1 (055 2388608, www.polomuseale.firenze.it).
Open *8.15am-1.50pm Tue-Fri, 1st, 3rd & 5th Mon of mth; 8.15am-4.50pm Sat, 2nd & 4th Sun of mth.*
Admission *€4; €2 reductions; free on 1st Sun of every mth. No cards.*
Map *p117 N2.*

The Museo di San Marco is not only a fascinating coming-together of religion and history, but a wonderful place to rest and take in the general splendour. Housed in the Dominican monastery where he worked, the museum is largely dedicated to the ethereal paintings of Fra Angelico (aka Beato Angelico), one of the most important spiritual artists of the 15th century, a man who would never lift a brush without a prayer and who wept whenever he painted a crucifixion.

You're greeted on the first floor by one of the most famous images in Christendom: an other-worldly *Annunciation*, but the images Fra Angelico and his assistants frescoed on the walls of the monks' white-vaulted cells are almost as impressive. Particularly outstanding are the lyrical *Noli Me Tangere*, which depicts Christ appearing to Mary Magdalene in a field of flowers, and the surreal *Mocking of Christ*, in which Christ's torturers are represented simply by relevant fragments of their anatomy (a hand holding a whip, a face spitting).

The cell that was later occupied by Fra Girolamo Savonarola is adorned with portraits of the rabid reformer by Fra Bartolomeo. You can also see his black wool cloak and his cilice, which was tied around the thigh to cause constant pain in reminder of the suffering of Christ. Near the cells reserved specially for Cosimo the Elder is the beautiful library designed by his favourite architect, Michelozzo, in 1441.

On the ground floor, in the Ospizio dei Pellegrini (pilgrims' hospice), are more works by Fra Angelico. The recently restored *Tabernacle of the Madonna dei Linaiuoli*, his first commission from 1433 for the guild of linen makers, is here – painted on wood carved by Ghiberti – and contains some of his best-known images: the multi-coloured musical angels. You can also see a superb *Deposition* and a *Last Judgement*. The Small Refectory (or Guest Refectory) is dominated by a Ghirlandaio *Last Supper* (1486) in which the disciples pick at a repast of bread, wine and cherries against a symbolic background of orange trees, a peacock, a Burmese cat and flying ducks. You may want to compare this with Ghirlandaio's earlier fresco of the same subject in the Cenacolo di Ognissanti.

Library (Michelozzo, 1442-4)

and Madonna chapels, and the oratory on the left side of the church. In 1453, after almost ten years of work and not much progress, directorship was handed to Antonio Manetti. When Manetti ran into financial difficulty, the governing priests ceded the venture to the Gonzaga family. Finally, in 1477, Leon Battista Alberti completed the church with slight modifications. The atrium was frescoed early the following century by Pontormo, Rosso Fiorentino and, most strikingly, Andrea del Sarto, whose *Birth of the Virgin* is set within the walls of a Renaissance palazzo that has cherubs perched on a mantelpiece.

Restaurants & wine bars

♥ Osteria de L'Ortolano €€
Via degli Alfani 91r, (055 2396466, www.osteriafirenze.com). Open 10am-3pm Mon-Sat, 6-10pm Wed-Sat. Closed Aug. Map p117 N4 ❶ *Osteria*

In an area historically devoid of great dining options, Osteria de L'Ortolano (deli by day, restaurant by night) is a refreshingly fair-priced spot for a sit-down dinner, managed by a lovely couple serving seasonal, often unexpectedly rich dishes, from guinea fowl to bitter chicory. There's a thoroughly Tuscan vin santo risotto (made with the region's famous dessert wine), as well as inventive seconds like the beer-based veal meatballs with sweet potatoes. Simpler, kid-friendly fare such as chicken and chips ensures no one in the family will go hungry.

Cafés, bars & gelaterie

♥ Arà: è Sicilia
Via degli Alfani 127r (328 6117029, www.araesicilia.it). Open 10am-10pm daily. Map p117 N4 ❶ *Café*

Specialising in tasty Sicilian street food and desserts, this simple café attracts local workers and students and makes for a welcome break from Florentine staples. Apart from gelato, Tuscany isn't exactly known for its desserts, but here you can indulge in Sicilian sweets: think *cannoli, granite, cassate* (cream gelato pyramid blocks with candied fruit) and praline-based treats, as well as savoury snacks including popular *arancini*, the region's lip-smacking stuffed rice balls.

Carabè
Via Ricasoli 60r (055 289476, www.parcocarabe.it). Open Summer 9am-1am daily. Winter 9am-8pm daily. Closed mid Dec-mid Jan. No cards. Map p117 N4 ❷ *Gelateria*

The Sicilian owners of this gelateria near the Accademia are third-generation ice-cream makers and proud of their heritage. They excel in the island's specialities – one crunchy granita is flavoured with almond milk, fresh lemons are brought in weekly from Sicily to make a tangy ice-cream/sorbet crossbreed and the *cremolata* is made with the pulp of seasonal soft fruits. Along with Arà: è Sicilia (*see left*), it's one of the few places in the city to offer authentic *cassate* and *cannoli* (the round ricotta-filled snaps immortalised as weapons in *The Godfather III*).

Shops

♥ Street Doing
Via de' Servi 88r (055 5381334, www.streetdoingvintage.it). Open 10.30am-7.30pm Mon-Sat, 2.30-7.30pm Sun. Map p117 N5 ❶ *Vintage fashion*

With multiple rooms and an impressive collection of designers, from Florentine favourites to the biggest names in the fashion business, Street Doing requires the most serious vintage shoppers to set aside some time for it. The front room contains artfully arranged accessories and most of the prime stock, but venture toward the back for winter coats, bargain-bin finds and even a full gallery of ballgowns.

Entertainment

❤ La Compagnia

Via Camillo Cavour, 50/R, 50121, San Marco (39 055 268451, www. cinemalacompagnia. it). **Open Box office** *1hr before start of film. Tickets €5-€8; cinema & aperitivo €10; cinema & dinner €15.* **Map** *p117 M4* ❶ *Cinema*

A historic theatre recently converted into a cinema, La Compagnia has given the Odeon some local competition, hosting an impressive range of events, including lectures and meet-and-greets. In addition to its regular line-up of Italian and international films, the theatre is also the headquarters for Florence's annual 50 Days of International Cinema showcase and Primavera di Cinema Orientale, a springtime series of Eastern film festivals (regulars include Middle East Now, Florence Korea Film Fest, Dragon Film Festival and Wa! Japan Film Festival).

❤ Teatro della Pergola

Via della Pergola 18-32, San Marco (055 22641 information, 055 0763333 tickets, www. teatrodellapergola.com). **Box office** *9.30am-6.30pm Mon-Sat. Season Oct-Apr.* **Map** *p117 O6* ❷ *Theatre*

Inaugurated in 1661, the exquisite Pergola is one of Italy's oldest theatres. Shakespeare, Pirandello and Goldoni feature regularly in the programme of old and modern classics presented by this historic theatre, which is now part of the Teatro della Toscana National Theatre. Watch out for behind-the-scene guided visits on Sunday mornings (advance booking necessary). Richly decorated in red and gold and with three layers of boxes, La Pergola is ideal for chamber music and small-scale operas. The excellent series of chamber music concerts promoted by the Amici della Musica is held here, usually on Saturday afternoons and on Monday evenings when there are no theatre shows.

Restoration of the double portrait of the dwarf morgante by Bronzino, Opificio delle Pietro Dure *p120.*

Santa Croce

Like much of the city centre, Santa Croce has a heady air of history and learning. Here you'll find the city's synagogue, the national library and fascinating art: the **Bargello** museum contains a wealth of incredible Renaissance pieces, while the church of **Santa Croce** itself has some of the finest 14th-century frescoes in Florence. But it's not hard to have fun here too, with a lively market and excellent shopping. With its general feeling of buzziness, Santa Croce comes in a close second to the boho-chic Oltrarno for the title of Florence's most exciting area.

Central **piazza Santa Croce** is a natural meeting spot, and home to the imposing Gothic church and attached museum and cloisters. On the south side is the frescoed sepia façade of **Palazzo d'Antella**, decorated in 1620. Outside the church is Enrico Pazzi's 1865 statue

Best art galleries
Renaissance sculpture at Bargello (*p129*). A remarkable art collection at Museo Horne (*p131*).

Best cultural venue
Catch a headline musical or theatre production at Teatro Verdi (*p138*).

Best gelateria
Rich chocolate orange and rice pudding flavours at Vivoli (*p137*).

Best lunch spot
Florentine specialities and a local vibe at Mercato di Sant'Ambrogio (*p137*). Perfect pizzas at Caffe Italiano (*p132*) and Il Pizzaiuolo (*p134*).

Best nightspots
Big beats, plus blues, funk and jazz at Rex Café (*p138*). Late-night live sets from local and international bands at Jazz Club (*p138*).

Best restaurant
Once-in-a-lifetime splurge at Enoteca Pinchiorri (*p134*).

Best sight
Temple of Italian glories Santa Croce (*p130*).

Best shopping
Murano glass inkwells and pens at Signum (*p137*), Euro contemporary fashion at Société Anonyme (*p137*).

of Dante. But it's not always so relaxing: the suicidal/homicidal team sport of *calcio storico* is played here every June and from the end of November there's a vibrant Christmas market.

South-west from the piazza, via de' Benci is dotted with crafts shops and bohemian restaurants running down towards the Arno past the **Museo Horne** to the **ponte alle Grazie**. The bridge was blown up just before the Germans' retreat at the end of World War II and was rebuilt in 1957. Heading east from here, you'll find the **Biblioteca Nazionale**, built to house the three million books and two million documents that were held in the Uffizi until 1935.

→ **Getting around**
The neighbourhood is best explored on foot, but a few bus routes cross it on their way between piazza della Stazione and piazza Beccaria, either through San Marco and piazza d'Azeglio (bus 14, 23) or via the old centre (minibus C1, C2, D).

West of the parish square are myriad winding streets, mostly given over to leather factories and tiny souvenir shops. Via del Proconsolo houses the Bargello at its piazza San Firenze end, while further north towards the Duomo is the **Museo di Antropologia e Etnologia**. Nearby are also the **Museo Fiorentino di Preistoria** and **Casa Buonarroti** on via Ghibellina.

Not so long ago, the area north of Santa Croce church stretching up to piazza de' Ciompi, was the rough-and-ready home to gangs of bored Florentine youths. Increasingly yuppified, it now yields trendy *trattorie* and wine bars. Piazza de' Ciompi was named after the dyers' and wool workers' revolt of 1378. It's dominated by the **Loggia del Pesce**, built by Vasari in 1568 for the Mercato Vecchio, previously in piazza della Repubblica. It was taken apart in the 19th century and re-erected here.

Further east is **Mercato di Sant'Ambrogio**, the world-famous **Cibrèo** restaurant and the shops, bars, *pizzerie* and restaurants of borgo La Croce.

The **Sinagoga & Museo di Arte e Storia Ebraica** lies in Sant Ambrogio, in northern Santa Croce, just south of the elegant piazza Massimo d'Azeglio. To the west of here is borgo Pinti – watch out for the hard-to-find entrance to the church of **Santa Maria Maddalena dei Pazzi** (no.58).

Sights & museums

Casa Buonarroti
Via Ghibellina 70 (055 241752, www.casabuonarroti.it). **Open** *Mar-Oct 10am-5pm Mon, Wed-Sun. Nov-Feb 10am-4pm Mon, Wed-Sun.* **Admission** *€6.50; €4.50 reductions. No cards.* **Map** *p128 P8.*
In 1612, Michelangelo Buonarroti the Younger took the decision to create a building in order to honour the memory of his rather more famous great-uncle. Although Michelangelo (1475-1564) never actually lived here, this 17th-century house, owned by his descendants until 1858, has a collection of memorabilia that gives an insight into Florence's most famous artistic son. On the walls are scenes from the painter's life, while the pieces collected by the artist's great-nephew Filippo include a magnificent wooden model for the façade of San Lorenzo (*see p109*) and two important original works: a bas-relief *Madonna of the Stairs* breastfeeding at the foot of a flight of stairs, and an unfinished *Battle of the Centaurs*.

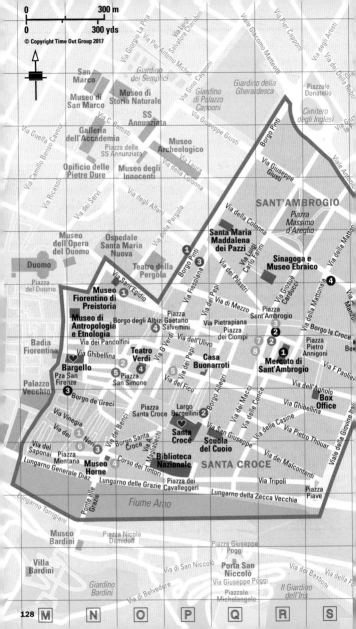

Map Labels

San Marco

Museo di San Marco

Museo di Storia Naturale

SS Annunziata

Galleria dell'Accademia

Opificio delle Pietre Dure

Museo degli Innocenti

Giardino dei Semplici

Giardino di Palazzo Capponi

Piazza della SS Annunziata

Museo Archeologico

Giardino della Gherardesca

Piazzale Donatello

Cimitero degli Inglesi

SANT'AMBROGIO

Piazza Massimo d'Azeglio

Museo dell'Opera del Duomo

Ospedale Santa Maria Nuova

Teatro della Pergola

Santa Maria Maddalena dei Pazzi

Sinagoga e Museo Ebraico

Duomo

Piazza del Duomo

Museo Fiorentino di Preistoria

Museo di Antropologia e Etnologia

Badia Fiorentina

Palazzo Vecchio

Bargello

Pza San Firenze

Borgo degli Albizi

Gaetano Salvemini

Piazza Sant'Ambrogio

Teatro Verdi

Piazza San Simone

Piazza dei Ciompi

Piazza Pietro Annigoni

Casa Buonarroti

Mercato di Sant'Ambrogio

Box Office

Santa Croce

Scuola del Cuoio

Museo Horne

Piazza Santa Croce

Biblioteca Nazionale

SANTA CROCE

Piazza dei Cavalleggeri

Fiume Arno

Museo Bardini

Piazza Nicola Demidoff

Piazza Giuseppe Poggi

Villa Bardini

Porta San Niccolò

Giardino Bardini

Piazzale Michelangelo

Il Giardino dell'Iris

M N O P Q R S

© Copyright Time Out Group 2017

0   300 m
0   300 yds

🖤 Bargello

Via del Proconsolo 4 (055 2388606, www.bargellomusei.beniculturali. it). **Open** *8.15am-5pm daily. Closed 1st, 3rd & 5th Mon of mth, 2nd & 4th Sun of mth.* **Admission** *€8; €4 reductions. Free on the 1st Sun of every month. No cards.* **Map** *p128 N8.*

This imposing, fortified structure has had so many functions over the years that, although it now contains Florence's most important sculpture collection, the history of the building itself is as fascinating as the exhibits. The Bargello started life as the Palazzo del Popolo in 1250 and soon became the mainstay of the chief magistrate, or *podestà*. The bodies of executed criminals were displayed in the courtyard during the 14th century; in the 15th century, law courts, prisons and torture chambers were set up inside. The Medici made it the seat of the *bargello* (chief of police) in the 16th century.

Officially called Museo Nazionale del Bargello, the museum opened in 1865 to celebrate Florence becoming the capital of Italy. It now holds the city's most eclectic and prestigious collection of sculpture.

Upon entering, the first room you enter on the ground floor is the Sala di Michelangelo with such famous pieces as his *Drunken Bacchus* and *Brutus* (the only bust he ever sculpted), and Giambologna's fleet-footed *Mercury*. Works by Andrea Sansovino, Baccio Bandinelli, Bartolomeo Ammannati, Benvenuto Cellini and Giambologna are also in this room.

The Salone Donatello on the first floor contains the artist's two triumphant *Davids* and a tense *St George*, the original of which once stood outside the Orsanmichele church. Also fascinating are the two bronze panels of the *Sacrifice of Isaac*, sculpted by Brunelleschi and Lorenzo Ghiberti for a competition to design the north doors of the Duomo's Baptistery. Back out on the grand loggia you can see Giambologna's bronze birds – they used to spout water in the grotto of the Medici Villa di Castello, and include a madly exaggerated turkey. On this floor, you can also find the little frescoed Magdalen Chapel, which contains the oldest confirmed portrait of Dante, painted by Giotto.

The easily missed second floor has a fascinating selection of bronze statuettes and a fine collection of Florentine busts, including Andrea del Verrocchio's elegant *Lady with Primroses* (1474), perhaps carved in collaboration with his student Leonardo da Vinci.

The rest of the museum contains a variety of collections, including Della Robbia glazed terracottas, Scandinavian chess sets and Egyptian ivories, European clocks, reliquary caskets, Islamic art, Medici arms and armours and a huge collection of medals. There is also a ground-floor wing reserved for temporary exhibitions, while in the summer, the Bargello courtyard provides a striking backdrop for a much-loved evening festival unimaginatively called *Estate al Bargello*.

💜 Santa Croce

Largo Bargellini (left side of the church) (055 2466105, www. santacroceopera.it). **Open** *9.30am-5.30pm Mon-Sat; 1-5.30pm Sun.* **Admission** *€8; €4 reductions (incl museum & chapel); free for under 11s.* **Map** *p128 P9.*

The richest medieval church in the city, Santa Croce has a great deal to offer, even to visitors long tired of church-hopping. Although impressive, the white, pink and green marble façade was only created between 1853 and 1863 by architect Niccolò Matas in the neo-Gothic style. Before that, the façade had been a bare stone front not unlike today's San Lorenzo (*see p109*).

At first sight the interior seems big and gloomy, with overbearing marble tombs clogging the walls. Not all of them contain bodies: Dante's, for example, is simply a memorial to the poet, who is buried in Ravenna. Next to this is the tomb of Michelangelo, by Vasari. The artist had insisted on burial here when the time came, as he wanted 'a view towards the cupola of the Duomo for all eternity'.

It may seem something of a paradox that, while the church is filled with the tombs of the great and the grand, it belongs to the Franciscans, the least worldly of the religious orders. They founded it in 1228, ten years after arriving in the city. But by the late 13th century, their vow of poverty eroded, a new building was planned: intended to be one of the largest in Christendom, it was designed by Arnolfo di Cambio, architect of the Duomo and Palazzo Vecchio.

At the eastern end of the church, the **Bardi and Peruzzi chapels**, which were completely frescoed by Giotto, are masterpieces. That said, the condition of the frescoes is not brilliant – a result of Giotto painting on dry instead of wet plaster and daubing them with whitewash – and were only rediscovered in the mid 18th century. The most striking of the two chapels is the **Bardi**, with scenes from the life of St Francis in haunting, virtual monotone. On the far side of the high altar is the **Cappella Bardi di Vernio**, frescoed by one of Giotto's most interesting followers, Maso di Banco, in vibrant colours.

Brunelleschi's geometric tour de force, the **Cappella dei Pazzi**, was planned in the

Cappella dei Pazzi (The Pazzi Chapel), Basili

1430s and completed almost 40 years later, long after the architect's death. The pure lines of the interior alternate white plaster and grey sandstone and are decorated with Luca della Robbia's painted ceramic roundels of the 12 Apostles, while the four Evangelists are also considered Brunelleschi's.

Across the courtyard is a small **Museo dell'Opera di Santa Croce**; the collection includes Donatello's pious *St Louis of Toulouse* from Orsanmichele (see p78). The backbone of the collection is in the former refectory, with Taddeo Gaddi's imposing yet poetic *Tree of Life* above his *Last Supper* (unfortunately, in very bad condition). Also here is Giorgio Vasari's monumental *Last Supper* and Cimabue's *Crucifixion*.

Museo di Antropologia e Etnologia

Via del Proconsolo 12 (055 2756444, www.msn.unifi.it). **Open** *Oct-May 9.30am-4.30pm Mon, Tue, Thur, Fri; 10am-4.30pm Sat, Sun. June-Sept 10.30am-5.30pm daily.* **Admission** *€6 €3 (€10 combined for University Science museums). No cards.* **Map** *p128 N7.*

Among the mix of artefacts from all over the world on display here are a collection of Peruvian mummies, an Ostyak harp from Lapland, an engraved trumpet from the former Belgian Congo made out of an elephant tusk, Ecuadorian shrunken heads alongside a specially designed skull-beating club, and a Marini-meets-Picasso equestrian monument.

Museo Fiorentino di Preistoria

Via Sant'Egidio 21 (055 295159, www.museofiorentinopreistoria. it). **Open** *3.30-6.30pm Mon; 9.30am-12.30pm, 3.30-6.30pm Tue, Thur; 9.30am-12.30pm Wed, Fri, Sat; guided tours by appointment.* **Admission** *€3. No cards.* **Map** *p128 O6.*

Florence's Museum of Prehistory traces humanity's development from the Paleolithic to the Bronze Age. The first floor contains interesting displays of illustrations following hominid physical changes, and also examines Italy's prehistoric art. The second floor includes a fascinating collection of stone implements.

❤ Museo Horne

Via de' Benci 6 (055 244661, www.museohorne. it). **Open** *9am-1pm Mon-Sat.* **Admission** *€7; €5 reductions. No cards.* **Map** *p128 N10.*

The 15th-century Palazzo Corsi-Alberti was purchased in the 1800s by English architect and art historian Herbert Percy Horne, who restored it to its Renaissance

SANTA CROCE

splendour. Formerly thought to be the work of Giuliano da Sangallo, the building is now generally attributed to Il Cronaca. When he died in 1916, Horne left his *palazzo* and vast collection to the state. Objects range from Renaissance paintings and sculptures to furniture and ceramics, but there are also everyday items such as Florentine coins, a coffee grinder and a pair of spectacles. Upstairs is a damaged wooden panel from a triptych attributed to Masaccio. Also, here is an *Exorcism* by the Maestro di San Severino and, the pride of the collection, a gold-back *Santo Stefano* by Giotto.

Sinagoga & Museo di Arte e Storia Ebraica
Via Farini 4 (055 2346654, www.jewishflorence.it). **Open** *June-Sept 10am-6.30pm Sun-Thur; 10am-5pm Fri. Oct-May 10am-5.30pm Sun-Thur; 10am-3pm Fri.* **Admission** *€6.50; €5 reductions. No cards.* **Map** *p128 R6.*

This 19th-century synagogue is an extraordinarily ornate mix of Moorish, Byzantine and Eastern influences, with its walls and ceilings covered in polychrome arabesques. The Museum of Jewish Art and History holds a collection tracing the history of Jews in Florence, from their supposed arrival as Roman slaves to their official introduction into the city as money-lenders in 1430. Exhibits include documented stories, jewellery, ceremonial objects and furniture, photos and drawings, many of which depict the ghetto that once occupied the area just north of piazza della Repubblica.

Restaurants & wine bars

Beijing8 €€
Via dei Neri 46r (380 7968093, www.beijing8.com). **Open**
11am-10pm daily. **Map** *p128 N9* ❶
Asian fusion

Opened in December 2016, Beijing8 is quite an anomaly: a Scandinavian 'slow fast food' Asian fusion chain just a short walk from the Uffizi. Dig into dumplings in ginger or chilli sauces and warm up with serve-yourself tea. The chic minimalist aesthetic, friendly service and tasty, well-priced bites (try the satisfying lunch-box offer) make this a worthy stop for when you need a break from *pappa al pomodoro*.

♥ Caffè Italiano €€
Via Isola delle Stinche 13r (055 289080, www.caffeitaliano.it). **Open** *12.30-3pm, 7-11pm Tue-Sun. Closed 3wks Aug.* **Map** *p128 O8* ❷
Pizzeria

This tiny venue with a wood-burning oven and just four bare tables has minimal choice – marinara, margherita or Napoli –

but it's a good sign when a pizzeria sticks to the basics, despite growing attention and tourist traffic. The pizzas' light and puffy bases are topped with San Marzano tomatoes and proper *mozzarella di bufala* shipped fresh from Campania. After 10.30pm, the overflow is seated at the adjacent restaurant, Osteria del Caffè Italiano.

Cibrèo €€€€
Via Andrea del Verrocchio 8r (055 2341100, www. edizioniteatrodelsalecibreofirenze. it). **Open** *1-2.30pm, 7-11.15pm Tue-Sat. Closed Aug.* **Map** *p128 R7* ❸
High-end gastronomy

Cibrèo is a must-stop on any Florence foodie's hit list. Located in the heart of the Sant'Ambrogio market area, this is the flaghip of Fabio Picchi's little gastronomic empire (which also includes a bar, a *trattoria*, a theatre with buffet-style food, multiple cookbooks and a clothing and accessories line).

It serves a modern interpretation of Florence's traditional *cucina povera* (peasant's food), with fresh prime ingredients and heavy use of fresh herbs and spices to create intense flavours (they're particularly proud of the oregano). There's no menu, but a chummy waiter will sit at your table in the elegant, wood-panelled room to take you through the options. Dishes change daily, but you can count on a series of delicious *antipasti* arriving automatically, followed by *primi* with no pasta in sight. *Secondi* are divided between meat and particularly good fish. Desserts are fabulous (Bavarian cream and flourless chocolate cake are favourites), and the wine list is everything you might expect. Cibrèo provokes extreme opinions: some think it's the best restaurant in Florence, while others claim that it's overrated, overpriced and overcrowded with tourists.

SANTA CROCE

Del Fagioli *p134*

Del Fagioli €€

Corso de' Tintori 47r (055 244285).
Open *12.30-2.30pm, 7.30-10.30pm
Mon-Sat.* **Map** *p128 O10* ④
Trattoria

This is one of those unpretentious
time-worn places where little has
changed over the years. Opened
by Luigi ('Gigi') Zucchini just
after the flood in 1966, it offers
traditional Florentine cooking and
such standards as *ribollita, pappa
al pomodoro* and *bollito misto con
salsa verde* (mixed boiled meats
served with a bright green parsley
sauce). Del Fagioli is a family
business: Gigi and his son-in-law
Maurizio are in charge of the
kitchen, while sons Antonio and
Simone work in the restaurant.
Gigi's *involtini* (thin rolls of beef
stuffed with cheese, ham and
artichokes) are delicious. There's
warm apple cake to finish.

❤ Enoteca Pinchiorri €€€€

*Via Ghibellina 87 (055 242757,
www.enotecapinchiorri.com).*
Open *7.30-10pm Tue-Sat.* **Map** *p128
P8* ⑤ *High-end gastronomy*

One of the most expensive
restaurants in Florence (and Italy),
Enoteca Pinchiorri is considered
one of Italy's great temples to
gastronomic excellence. Although
French co-owner Annie Féolde
(along with Giorgio Pinchiorri)
no longer does any cooking (the
executive chef is creative Milanese
Riccardo Monco), she oversees the
kitchen and runs front-of-house,
where the atmosphere is of the
formal, luxuriously old-fashioned
kind. You can opt for à la carte or
choose from two tasting menus
(which represent the best value),
each featuring four (€150 per
person) or seven (€225 per person)
tiny but superbly executed courses
(such as John Dory bites in squid
ink, sprouts of spinach, Béarnaise
sauce and lemon chamomile jelly).
Then there's the stellar cellar:

Pinchiorri has amassed a collection
of wines that's second to none and
offers one of the world's great wine
lists. Wherever you eat – inside
the *palazzo* or in the gorgeous,
jasmine-scented courtyard – it all
looks fabulous; service is elegant
and prices are sky high. This place
is so classy that men are required to
wear jackets.

Libreria Brac €€

*Via de' Vagellai 18r (055 0944877,
www.libreriabrac.net).* **Open**
*10am-midnight Mon-Sat; noon-
midnight Sun (brunch until 4pm).
Closed 1wk Aug; Sun in June-Sept.*
Map *p128 N10* ⑥ *Vegetarian*

This contemporary art bookshop
has one important novelty: a
kitchen. Its minimalist, stark white
interior with exciting splashes
of colour gives a nice ambience,
while the charming outdoor
courtyard makes it a great place
to read the morning news over a
soy cappuccino or to enjoy one
of the rich pastas or salads on its
vegetarian and vegan-friendly
menu (there are also several gluten-
free options). Try the Sicilian
salad with fennel, olives, oranges,
almonds and raisins, or opt for the
potato *tortellini* with rocket pesto,
which has hints of ginger. Libreria
Brac also serves as a contemporary
art space. Reservations
recommended.

❤ Il Pizzaiuolo €€

*Via de' Macci 113r (055 241171,
www.ilpizzaiuolo.it).* **Open** *12.30-
3pm, 5pm-midnight Mon-Sat.
Closed Aug.* **Map** *p128 R8* ⑦
Pizzeria

If you're looking to sink your teeth
into a delicious Neapolitan-style
pizza, then Il Pizzaiuolo is the place
to get it. Long considered the go-to
place for the best pizza in Florence,
it has the crowds to match, but
the melt-in-your-mouth burrata
cheese will make it all worthwhile.
Il Pizzaiuolo also serves Neapolitan

pasta dishes, which include spaghetti with tomato, olives and capers from Gaeta, or *trofie* (a kind of pasta) with pesto and cherry tomatoes. Finish the meal off with a *babà al rhum* (a rum-flavoured Neopolitan dessert). The small, white-tiled room is always packed (and often very noisy), so booking is a must here, and be prepared to find yourself sharing a table with strangers.

Teatro del Sale €€€
Via de' Macci 111r (055 2001492, www. edizioniteatrodelsalecibreofirenze. it). Open times vary. Closed Sun evening, Mon all day & Aug. Map p128 Q8 ⑧ *Traditional Italian*
A sister of the Cibrèo restaurants, Teatro del Sale is the most innovative creation of the eccentric Florentine chef Fabio Picchi, and it continues to grow: plans are in the works for the venue to host a full academic programme on the 'theatre of cooking'. The Teatro

sets itself apart on the Florentine culinary scene as a top-notch eatery that also has entertainment, giving its members a theatrical or musical bonus après dinner. At lunch and dinner the kitchen offers Tuscan-centred yet internationally inspired seasonal buffets that change daily.

Cafés, bars & gelaterie

Caffetteria delle Oblate
Via dell'Oriuolo 26 (055 2639685, www.caffetteriadelleoblate.it). Open 2-7pm Mon; 9am-midnight Tue-Sat. Map p128 O7 ① *Café*
With a straight-on view of Brunelleschi's dome from its lovely outdoor terrace and indoor café – a delight that won't cost you a pretty penny – this hangout inside the Oblate Library is a real gem amid the tourist traps around the Duomo. On the second floor, the bright, light-filled space, popular with Italian students, offers gorgeous views over the rooftops of the *centro storico*, and serves

Société Anonyme p137

everything from breakfasts to cocktails and late-night suppers, with occasional concerts, readings and performances.

Caffè Cibrèo
Via Andrea del Verrocchio 5r (055 2345853, www. edizioniteatrodelsalecibreofirenze. it). **Open** *8am-1am Tue-Sat. Closed 2wks Aug.* **No cards. Map** *p128 R8* ❷ *Café*

This delightful café, another of Fabio Picchi's Cibrèo (*see p133*) outposts, is worth visiting for ambience alone: it has exquisite carved wood ceilings, retro poster art that feels more refined than kitschy, antique furniture, a candlelit mosaic and outside tables, but also a knack for making everything it presents look as beautiful as the bar itself (fresh flowers on each table here are standard). It's a relaxing stop where no one will give you the stink-eye for drinking a cappuccino mid-afternoon, and you'll feel perfectly in place scrawling in a notebook or partaking in any particularly literary activity.

Gelateria dei Neri
Via dei Neri 22r (055 210034). **Open** *10am-midnight daily.* **No cards. Map** *p128 N10* ❸ *Gelateria*

A gem for those who want to sample the Florentine frozen assets but have an intolerance to milk – it's one of the few parlours to serve soya ice-cream alongside the classic creamy gelati (go for the buttery salted caramel).

La Loggia degli Albizi
Borgo degli Albizi 39r (055 2479574,www.facebook. com/laloggiadeglialbizi produzionepropria). **Open** *7am-9pm daily. Closed Aug.* **Map** *p128 O7* ❹ *Café*

With some of the best pastries and cakes in town, La Loggia degli Albizi is the perfect stop-off after some hard shopping. Try the *torta della nonna* (crumbly pastry filled with baked pâtisserie cream) or the warm *bomboloni* (fried doughnuts), served after 5pm. They also have a reasonably priced lunch menu with tasty *primi* served by friendly staff.

Mercato di Sant' Ambrogio

❤ Vivoli

Via Isola delle Stinche 7r (055 292334, www.vivoli.it). **Open** *Summer 7.30am-midnight Tue-Sat, 9am-midnight Sun. Winter 7.30am-9pm Tue-Fri, 9am-9pm Sun. Closed mid Aug.* **No cards.** **Map** *p128 O8* **5** *Gelateria*

Local institution Vivoli has clung on jealously to its long-standing but increasingly threatened reputation as the best gelateria in Florence (they've even taken their Tuscan flair to Florida). The wickedly rich chocolate orange and divine *riso* (rice pudding) are still up there with the best of them. So too are its famous *semifreddi* – which are creamier and softer than ordinary gelato. Increasingly appreciated as the years wear on and the brand gets bigger is its ample seating area, where you can indulge leisurely at no extra charge – a rarity at joints this famous.

Shops

❤ Mercato di Sant'Ambrogio

Piazza Ghiberti 45 (www.mercato santambrogio.it). **Open** *7am-2pm Mon-Sat.* **Map** *p128* **1** *R8.*

The glass and cast iron structure of Florence's oldest operating market was designed by Giuseppe Mengoni and opened in 1873. Meat and fish, fruit and vegetables, bread and fresh pasta, herbs and spices, olive oil and Chianti wine, pecorino cheese: a heady mix of flavours fill the air: Sant'Ambrogio still retains the easygoing character and quaintness of an authentic local market. With its 20 stalls, this is a foodie's heaven and the perfect spot to shop for a picnic or grab a quick lunch. Trattoria Da Rocco inside the market is a food kiosk where you can try local classics at steal prices, but the most adventurous should really sample the braised tripe or

boiled *lampredotto*. The adjoining outdoor market features 60-plus stalls, while a flea market can also be found across the square in neighbouring piazza Pietro Annigoni (map *p128 S8*).

Sandra Dori

Via de' Macci 103r (348 3574726, www.sandradori.com). **Open** *10am-1pm Tue-Sat; afternoon by appt.* **Map** *p128 R7* **2** *Gifts & souvenirs*

Sandra Dori is mostly in the business of unusual lamps and candelabras, but her shop intersperses her unusual designs with sweet paintings, handmade chunky plastic and fabric jewellery, fans and all manner of oddities. It's a pleasure to browse.

❤ Signum

Borgo de' Greci 40r (055 280621, www.signumfirenze.it). **Open** *9am-7.30pm Mon-Sat; 10am-7pm Sun.* **Map** *p128 N9* **3** *Gifts & souvenirs*

This delightful shop, housed in an ancient wine cellar, stocks an appealingly wide range of gifts, among them miniature models of shop windows and bookcases, and Murano glass inkwells and pens. **Other locations** Lungarno degli Archibusieri 14r, Duomo & Around (055 289393); via de' Benci 29r, Santa Croce (055 244590).

❤ Société Anonyme

Via de' Niccolini 3f (corner of via della Mattonaia) (055 3860084, www.societeanonyme.it). **Open** *Winter 3.30-7.30pm Mon; 10am-2pm, 3.30-7.30pm Tue-Sun. Summer 4-8pm Mon; 10am-2pm, 4-8pm Tue-Sun.* **Map** *p128 S6* **4** *Boutique fashion*

With its list of avant-garde men's, women's and androgynous brands chalked on to a blackboard at the entrance, Société Anonyme screams 'trendy', and it is. Inside, a deftly styled space filled with art and architectural oddities houses international brands (McQ by Alexander McQueen, Helmut Lang), but also fashion and accessories by up-and-coming Italian designers (local fashion institutes have frequently hosted events and shows inside the boutique). You could spend hours just poking around and trying things on, and prices are on the right side of reasonable for the design calibre offered.

Entertainment

♥ Jazz Club
Via Nuova de' Caccini 3, Santa Croce (055 2479700, www. facebook.com/ jazzclubfirenze.it). **Open** *11pm-3am Tue-Thu, Sun; 11pm-4am Fri-Sat. Closed July, Aug.* **Admission** €6. **No cards.** **Map** *p128 P6* **①** *Live music*
One of the few places in Florence where you can hear live jazz almost nightly, this hard-to find club is worth searching out. It hosts an array of popular local jazz bands, and it has also welcomed notable international acts.

Queer
Borgo Allegri, 9, Santa Croce (366 275 9210, www.bargayfirenze. it). **Open** *8.30pm-3am daily.* **Admission** *free.* **Map** *p8 Q9* **②** *LGBT bar*
A small space with billiard hall games and friendly bartenders, Queer is newish on the LGBT scene and brings together a range of ages and gender identities. Staff are sociable, seating is comfy, cocktails are inexpensive and the mood is light and cheery.

♥ Rex Café
Via Fiesolana 25r, Santa Croce (055 2480331, www.rexfirenze.com). **Open** *6pm-2.30am daily. Closed June-Aug.* **Map** *p128 P6* **③** *Bar*

Clubby Rex is more than a quarter century old and still king of the east of the city, filling up with loyal subjects who sashay to the sounds of the session DJs playing bassy beats and jungle rhythms. Gaudí-esque mosaics decorate the central bar, wrought-iron lamps shed a soft light, while a luscious red antechamber creates welcome seclusion for more intimate gatherings. Tapas are served during the *aperitivo* happy hour (5-9.30 pm), and there are blues, funk and jazz nights, as well as the famed 'Venus' evenings spotlighting local women DJs.

♥ Teatro Verdi
Via Ghibellina 99, Santa Croce (055 212320, www.teatroverdionline. it). **Box office** *10am-1pm, 4-7pm Mon-Fri. Season Oct-Mar.* **Map** *p128 O8* **④** *Theatre*
The city's largest theatre at just over 1,500 seats, Teatro Verdi hosts all the top-notch light comedies, musicals and dance shows whose lavish sets and elaborate choreography would not fit in any of the smaller venues in town. The theatre is also home to the 45-element Orchestra della Toscana, with midweek concerts between October and May.

In the know
Box Office

Via delle Vecchie Carceri 1, ex Murate complex, Sant'Ambrogio, (055 210804, www. boxofficetoscana.it information, www.boxol.it tickets). **Open** *10am-7pm Mon-Fri; 10am-2pm Sat.* **Map** *p128 S9.*

Central ticket agency for concerts, plays, sports events, festivals and exhibitions in Florence, across Italy and abroad.

The Oltrarno

Spanning the width of the city centre along the southern banks of the Arno and extending down to Porta Romana in an oblique triangle is the Oltrarno (literally, 'beyond the Arno'). This eclectic area is a beguiling, contradictory world of ornate *palazzi* with splendid gardens, church squares and tumbledown artisan workshops.

To the west are the salt-of-the-earth parishes of San Frediano and Santo Spirito. **San Frediano** is dominated by piazza del Carmine, a social hub by night and home to the church of **Santa Maria del Carmine** and the **Cappella Brancacci**. This area still very much belongs to the locals.

Santo Spirito's piazza Santo Spirito is the heart of its bohemian neighbourhood, bustling with the comings and goings of locals. A morning market is held in the square from Monday to Saturday, with a flea market on the second

❤ Shortlist

Best cultural venues
Film nights and Italian art and culture courses at British Institute of Florence (*p156*). Literary and musical events at St Mark's English Church (*p156*).

Best green space
Florence's most beloved green oasis Giardino di Boboli (*p147*).

Best museums
A glorious art and antiques collection at Museo Bardini (*p147*), 6,000 costumes at Museo della Moda e del Costume (*p148*).

Best nightspots
Caffé Notte (*p156*): hip artsy café by day, cool hangout by night. NOF (*p156*): small and sweaty but a great spot for live music.

Best shopping
Watch local craftspeople at work in the Oltrarno's artisan studios (*p153*).

Best sights
Baroque and Renaissance masterpieces and sumptuous Royal Apartments at Gallerina Palatina (*p144*). Spend time with Masaccio at Santa Maria del Carmine & Cappella Brancacci (*p148*). Fragments of a 14th-century *Last Supper* by Orcagna in Cenacolo di Santo Spirito (*p145*).

Best winebar
Organic and biodynamic wines, craft beers at Vivanda (*p152*), extensive wine list and nibbles at Le Volpi e l'Uva (*p152*).

Best gelatarie
Stunning riverside views at La Carraia (*p152*). Try salted caramel or lemon and sage at La Sorbettiera (*p154*).

Best restaurant
Boisterous, well-priced trattoria Alla Vecchia Bettola (*p150*).

Sunday of every month and an organic food market every third Sunday.

Between Santo Spirito and a maze of narrow streets to the east is the grand **via Maggio** and its fabulous antiques shops. At its river end the street meets borgo San Jacopo, with its mix of medieval towers, hip clothes shops and 1960s monstrosities. San Jacopo leads east to the southern end of the **Ponte Vecchio**. Heading south-

→ Getting around
In a neighbourhood where nearly every shop window commands attention and business owners wander in and out of each other's doors, the only way to have the 'full experience' is to move by foot. If you don't fancy the trek down the lengthy via dei Serragli, you can take buses 11, 36 or 37 from piazza Ottaviani (Santa Maria Novella) towards the street's southern tip facing Porta Romana.

west down from the bridge is via de' Guicciardini, with its expensive paper, crafts and jewellery shops and the little **Santa Felicita** church. Passing the grandeur of the Medici's **Palazzo Pitti**, it ends in a square dominated by Palazzo Guidi, housing **Casa Guidi**. Here via Maggio and via de' Guicciardini join to become via Romana, a long thoroughfare that leads to **Porta Romana**, lined with picture framers and antiques shops and home to the gory **La Specola** museum and the second entrance to **Giardino di Boboli**.

South-east of the Ponte Vecchio are the *costas* (meaning 'ribs'). These pretty, narrow lanes snake steeply uphill towards the **Forte di Belvedere**, now used for summertime cultural events. Halfway up costa San Giorgio is one of the two entrances to the spectacular, **Giardino Bardini**, while the other is in via de' Bardi, which leads into lungarno Serristori and the **Casa Museo Rodolfo Siviero**. Behind lies the parish of **San Niccolò**, a sleepy area with a village feel until the evening, when the wine bars and *osterie* along via de' Renai open up, overlooking the riverside piazza Demidoff. Here too you'll find the quiet **Museo Bardini** and its glorious collection of antiques. Before you leave the district, note that San Niccolò is also the gateway to **piazzale Michelangelo** and unmissable **San Miniato al Monte** (for both, *see p161*).

Sights & museums

Basilica di Santo Spirito

Piazza Santo Spirito (055 210030, www.basilicasantospirito.it). **Open** 9.30am-12.30pm, 4-5.30pm Mon, Tue, Thur, Fri. **Admission** free. **Map** p142 H10.

Behind the exquisitely simple 18th-century cream façade is one of Brunelleschi's most extraordinary works. In 1397, the resident Augustinian monks decided to replace the church that had been on this site from 1250, eventually commissioning Brunelleschi to design it. Work started in 1444, two years before the great master died, and the façade and exterior walls were never finished. Vasari wrote that if the church had been completed as planned, it would have been 'the most perfect temple of Christianity' and it's easy to see why. Santo Spirito's structure is a beautifully proportioned Latin-cross church, lined with a colonnade of dove-grey *pietra serena* pilasters that shelter 38 chapels. The church is open at

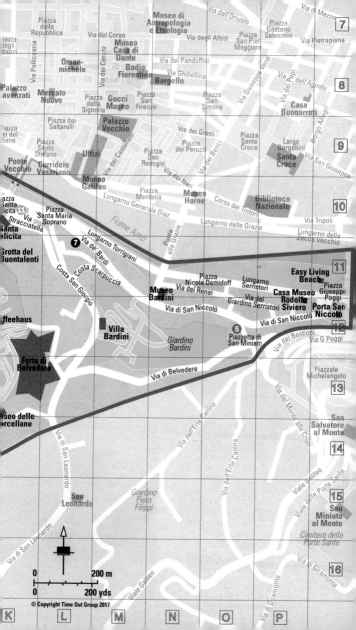

💙 Galleria Palatina

Palazzo Pitti (055 2388614, www.polomuseale.firenze.it). **Open** *8.15am-6.50pm Tue-Sun.* **Admission** *€8.50, €4.25 reductions, combined ticket with the Galleria d'Arte Moderna. Free on the first Sun of every month. No cards.* **Map** *p142 J11.*

This opulent gallery has 28 rooms of paintings, which are hung four- or five-high on its damask walls. From its grand staircase, the Scalone del Moro, to its final exit, it's section after section of unabashed overgilding and visual stimulation, so be sure you're always looking upward. You'll want to linger longest in the five planet rooms, named after Venus, Mercury (Apollo), Mars, Jupiter and Saturn. The **Sala di Venere** (Venus), crowned by a gilded stucco ceiling, is dominated by a statue of Venus by Canova, but also contains Titian's regal *La Bella*. The **Sala di Apollo** houses the nine Muses and is crowded with works by Rosso Fiorentino and Andrea del Sarto. The restored **Sala di Marte** (Mars) glimmers with the Baroque splendour of Pietro da Cortona's vault and is home to Anthony van Dyck's celebrated *Portrait of Cardinal Bentivoglio*; Rubens's *Four Philosophers* and the other works from this room are on show in the **Sala delle Nicchi**. In the **Sala di Giove** (Jupiter) look up to admire the lofty depiction of Jupiter with his eagle and lightning. Look too for Raphael's lover, so-called 'baker girl' Margherita Luti, in his *La Velata*. Finally, the **Sala di Saturno** (Saturn) contains some of Raphael's best-known works: among them the *Madonna of the Grand Duke*, which shows a distinct Leonardo influence, and his last painting, *Holy Family*, seemingly inspired by Michelangelo.

As if the gallery weren't already extravagant enough, a three-year collaboration between the Pitti museums and the Uffizi by the fashion tastemakers at Pitti Immagine Discovery means temporary style-themed exhibitions have been infiltrating this and other spaces; so far, the results have been riveting, if not without controversy. Why not gild the lily, right?

Also occupying the piano nobile (noble floor) of the Palazzo Pitti are the glorious **Appartamenti Reali**. The sumptuous Royal Apartments were the private residence of several ruling families in Florence, including the Medici and, briefly from 1866-1870, King Vittorio Emanuele II of Savoy, when Florence ruled as capital of Italy. Within the 14 rooms you can find period furniture and accessories from the 16th to the 19th century.

Sala di Giove (Jupiter Room)

weekends to worshippers, but it's worth calling ahead to make sure the official opening hours are being kept to.

Casa Guidi

*Piazza San Felice 8 (055 354457, www.browningsociety.org/casa_guidi.html). **Open** Apr-Nov 3-6pm Mon, Wed, Fri. **Admission** by donation. **Map** p142 H11.*
English poets Robert Browning and Elizabeth Barrett Browning came to Florence in April 1847 after a clandestine marriage, and for 14 years an apartment in this house was their home. Now owned by the Landmark Trust and partly rented out as a holiday home, key rooms of the apartment where they lived and wrote are open for visits during certain months. A few pieces in the flat are originals, including the piano used by their son, Pen.

Casa Museo Rodolfo Siviero

*Lungarno Serristori 1-3 (055 2345219, www.museocasasiviero.it). **Open** Sept-June 10am-1pm Mon, Sun; 10am-6pm Sat. July, Aug 10am-1pm Mon, Sun; 10am-2pm, 3-7pm Sat. **Admission** free. **Map** p142 P12.*
This was previously the house of government minister Rodolfo Siviero, dubbed the 'James Bond of art' for his efforts to prevent the Nazis plundering Italian masters. The pieces he saved were returned to their owners, but Siviero left his own private collection to the Regione Toscana on condition it would be open to the public. Among the 500 pieces on display are paintings and sculptures by friends of Siviero, including de Chirico, Annigoni and da Messina.

♥ Cenacolo di Santo Spirito

*Piazza Santo Spirito 29 (055 287043, www.museicivicifiorentini. comune.fi.it). **Open** 10am-4pm Mon, Sat, Sun. **Admission** €4. **No cards. Map** p142 H10.*

Interior of Santo Spirito

Orcagna's 14th-century fresco *The Last Supper*, housed in a former Augustinian refectory, was butchered by an 18th-century architect commissioned to build some doors into it. Only the fringes of the fresco remain, though there's a more complete (albeit heavily restored) *Crucifixion* above it. The small **Museo della Fondazione Romano** here houses an eclectic collection of sculptures given to the state in 1946 on the death of sailor Salvatore Romano.

Forte di Belvedere

*Via San Leonardo (055 27681). **Open** phone for details. **Admission** free. **Map** p142 L13.*
This star-shaped fortress was built in 1590 by Bernardo Buontalenti to protect the city from insurgents. It was then used as a strong room for

Forte di Belvedere

the Medici Grand Dukes' treasures. After a painfully drawn-out restoration, the fort is open once again for temporary art exhibitions, shows and events. (When nothing is running, the fortress is closed to the public.)

Galleria d'Arte Moderna
Palazzo Pitti (055 2388616, www.polomuseale.firenze. it). **Open** *8.15am-6.50pm Tue-Sun.* **Admission** *€8.50; €4.25 reductions (combined ticket with the Galleria Palatina). Free on the first Sun of every mth. No cards.* **Map** *p142 J11.*
The 30 second-floor rooms of the Pitti Palace were royal apartments until 1920; today they're given over to Florence's modern art museum. The collection covers neoclassical to early 20th-century art, with highlights including Giovanni Dupré's bronze sculptures of Cain and Abel and Ottone Rosai's simple *Piazza del Carmine*. Also showcased here is the work of the Macchiaioli school, the early Italian Impressionist group who were ridiculed for painting-by-dots (*macchie*), and works by Giovanni Fattori and Telemaco Signorini.

Giardino Bardini
Via de' Bardi 1r, costa di San Giorgio 2 (055 290112, www. bardinipeyron.it). **Open** *Nov-Feb 8.15am-4.30pm daily. Mar 8.15am-5.30pm daily. Apr, May, Sept, Oct 8.15am-6.30pm daily. June-Aug 8.15am-7.30pm daily. Closed first & last Mon of mth.* **Admission** *€7 (incl Tesoro dei Granduchi, Museo dell Moda e Del Costume, Museo delle Porcellane & Giardino di Boboli). No cards.* **Map** *p142 M12.*
First created in the 1200s by the Mozzi family, this intriguing garden underwent five years of painstaking restoration recently, and is a delight. The garden is divided into three distinct areas: the Baroque steps, leading to a terrace with amazing views; the English wood, a

shady haven of evergreens; and the farm park, with a dwarf orchard, rhododendrons and a 'tunnel' of wisteria and hydrangea.

💗 Giardino di Boboli

Entrances via Romana, the central door of Pitti Palace, Porta Romana and Forte Belvedere (055 2388786/2651838). **Open** *Nov-Feb 8.15am-4.30pm daily. Mar 8.15am-5.30pm daily. June-Aug 8.15am-7.30pm daily. Apr, May, Sept, Oct 8.15am-6.30pm daily. Closed 1st and last Mon in mth.* **Admission** *€7; €3.30 reductions (incl Tesoro dei Granduchi, Museo della Moda e Del Costume, Museo delle Porcellane & Giardino Bardini). Free on the first Sun of every mth. No cards.* **Map** *p142 J12 (main entrance).*

Boboli is the best loved of the few green spaces and parks in the city centre, and is a popular

Giardino Bardini

oasis, particularly on hot summer days. Far to the left of the main entrance is a fountain showing Cosimo I's obese dwarf as a nude *Bacchus*, heralding the walkway that leads to Buontalenti's grotto with Bandinelli's statues of *Ceres* and *Apollo*, casts of Michelangelo's *Slaves*, and a second grotto adorned with frescoes of classical Greek and Roman myths and encrusted with shells. The ramps take you to the amphitheatre, where Jacopo Peri and Giulio Caccini's *Euridice* was staged for the Medici in 1600. At the top of the hill is the **Museo delle Porcellane** *(see below)*, entered through the Giardino dei Cavalieri.

💗 Museo Bardini

Via de' Renai 37 (055 2342427, www.museicivicifiorentini. comune.fi.it/en/bardini/). **Open** *11am-5pm Fri-Mon.* **Admission** *€6.* **Map** *p142 N11.*

Named after its creator, antiquarian Stefano Bardini (1854-1922), this 2,000-strong collection includes sculpture, paintings and applied art from the Middle Ages and Renaissance. Brought together over decades, it was housed here by Bardini, who renovated the former church and convent of San Gregorio della Pace in 1881 into the elegant Renaissance-style structure it is today. Stand-out pieces include the *Madonna della Mela*, the *Madonna dei Cordai* by Donatello and *Atlas* by Guercino, as well as a gorgeous collection of oriental rugs and 15th-century chests. But the museum is as much about the collector as his collection, with the work still exhibited in a layout designed by Bardini.

Museo delle Porcellane

Casino del Cavaliere, Giardino di Boboli, Palazzo Pitti (055 2388709, www.polomuseale.firenze.it). **Open** *Nov-Feb 8.15am-4.30pm daily. Mar 8.15am-5.30pm daily. June-*

Aug 8.15am-7.30pm daily. Apr, May, Sept, Oct 8.15am-6.30pm daily. Closed 1st & last Mon of mth. **Admission** €7; reductions €3.50 (incl Tesoro dei Granduchi, Museo dell Moda e Del Costume, Giardino di Boboli & Giardino Bardini). Free on the first Sun of every mth. No cards. **Map** p142 K13.

Built by Leopoldo de' Medici, this outhouse at the top of the Giardino di Boboli was once a reception room for artists. The museum has ceramics used by the various occupants of Palazzo Pitti and includes the largest selection of Viennese china outside Vienna. Most visitors are more interested in the views.

♥ Museo della Moda e del Costume (Galleria del Costume)

Palazzo Pitti (055 2388713, www. polomuseale.firenze.it). **Open** Nov-Feb 8.15am-4.30pm daily. Mar 8.15am-5.30pm daily. June-Aug 8.15am-7.30pm daily. Apr, May, Sept, Oct 8.15am-6.30pm daily. Closed 1st and last Mon in mth. **Admission** €7 (incl Tesoro dei Granduchi, Museo delle Porcellane, Giardino di Boboli and Giardino Bardini). Free on the first Sun of every mth. No cards. **Map** p142 H12.

The sumptuous Costume Museum is in the Pitti's Palazzina della Meridiana, which periodically served as residence to the Lorraine family and the House of Savoy. Formal, theatrical and everyday outfits from the museum's collection of 6,000 pieces spanning five centuries are shown in rotation, changing every two years. Some more important get-ups are permanently on display, among them Cosimo I's and Eleonora di Toledo's clothes, including her grand velvet creation from Bronzino's portrait.

Santa Felicita

Piazza Santa Felicita 3 (055 213018, www.santafelicitafirenze.it). **Open** 9.30am-12.30, 3.30-5pm Mon-Sat. **Admission** free. **Map** p142 K10.

This church occupies the site of the first church in Florence, founded in the second century AD by Syrian Greek tradesmen. The oldest surviving part is the portico, built in 1564; the interior mainly dates to the 18th century. Most who come here do so to see Pontormo's striking Mannerist Deposition altarpiece in the Cappella Barbadori-Capponi.

♥ Santa Maria del Carmine & Cappella Brancacci

Piazza del Carmine (055 2768224, www.museicivicifiorentini.comune. fi.it). **Open** Chapel 10am-5pm Mon, Wed-Sat; 1-5pm Sun. Phone ahead to book. **Admission** €4. No cards. **Map** p142 E9.

This blowsy Baroque church is dominated by a huge single nave, with pilasters and pious sculptures overlooked by a ceiling fresco of the Ascension. This isn't what visitors queue for, however: they're here for the Cappella Brancacci (Brancacci Chapel). Frescoed in the 15th century by Masaccio and Masolino, it is one of the city's greatest art treasures. Masaccio, who died aged 27, reached his peak with this cycle of paintings, especially the tangibly grief-stricken Adam and Eve in the Expulsion from Paradise, a work that entranced Michelangelo.

La Specola

Via Romana 17 (055 2756444, www.msn.unifi.it). **Open** Tue-Sun 10.30am-5.30pm, closed Mon. **Admission** €6; €3 reductions. No cards. **Map** p142 G12.

A dream day out for older kids with horror fixations, La Specola is the zoology department of the Natural History Museum. The first 23 rooms are crammed with stuffed and pickled animals, including many famously extinct species, and up to here the museum can also be fun for younger children. From Room 24 onwards, however, exhibits are more gruesome. A *Frankenstein*-esque laboratory is filled with wax corpses on satin beds, each a little more dissected than the last, and walls are covered with realistic body parts crafted as teaching aids in the 18th and 19th centuries.

Tesoro dei Granduchi (Museo degli Argenti)

Palazzo Pitti (055 2388709, www. polomuseale.firenze.it). **Open** *Nov-Feb 8.15am-4.30pm daily.*

Resurrection of the son of Theophilus (detail) (Masaccio, 1425), Cappella Brancacci, Santa Maria del Carmine.

Mar 8.15am-5.30pm daily. June-Aug 8.15am-7.30pm daily. Apr, May, Sept, Oct 8.15am-6.30pm daily. Closed 1st & last Mon of mth. *Admission* €7; reductions €3.50 (incl Museo delle Porcellane, Museo della Moda e Del Costume , Giardino di Boboli & Giardino Bardini). Free on the first Sun of every mth. No cards. *Map* p142 J11.
This extravagant two-tier museum section of the Pitti Palace houses an astonishing hoard of treasures amassed by the Medici: not just silver, but everything from tapestries and rock crystal vases to breathtakingly banal miniature animals.

Villa Bardini

Costa di San Giorgio 2 (055 2638599, www.bardinipeyron. it). **Open** *10am-7pm Tue-Sun. Admission €8. No cards. Map p142 M12.*
The restored Villa Bardini is home to a permanent exhibition of the fabulously extravagant creations of couturier Roberto Capucci. The villa also contains a newer museum dedicated to the works of Italian artist Pietro Annigoni, and regularly hosts high calibre exhibitions that are rarely, if ever, crowded.

Restaurants & wine bars

Al Tranvai €€

Piazza Tasso 14r (055 225197, www. altranvai.it). **Open** *12.30-2.30pm, 7.30-10.30pm Tue-Sat; 7-10.30pm Mon. Map p142 D10* ❶ *Traditional Italian*
A favourite among local artisans, Al Tranvai is especially busy at lunch, attracting crowds for the wholesome, down-to-earth cooking and great prices. Dishes hail from the *cucina popolare* tradition: *ribollita*, a hearty Tuscan bread and vegetable soup (or summery bread salad *panzanella* when in season),

lesso rifatto con le cipolle (a tasty beef and onion stew) and simple tagliatelle with leeks. Top off your feasting with a slice of homemade fig and nut cake. The house plonk is just fine.

❤ Alla Vecchia Bettola €€
Viale Ariosto 32-34r (055 224158). **Open** *noon-2.30pm, 7.30-10.30pm Tue-Sat. Closed 3wks Aug.* **Map** *p142 C10* ❷ *Italian*

Still very popular among area residents, this lively *trattoria*, situated on a busy ring road behind piazza Tasso, serves up some of the city's best traditional Florentine fare. The menu of hearty, rustic dishes includes daily specials alongside such regulars as *penne alla Bettola* (with tomato, chilli pepper, vodka and a dash of cream) and a superb beef carpaccio topped with artichoke hearts and shaved parmesan, while offal fans can enjoy tripe and *lampredotto*. The Chianina steak is truly succulent.

Borgo San Jacopo €€€€
Borgo San Jacopo 62r (055 281661, www.lungarnocollection.com/ borgo-san-jacopo). **Open** *12.30-2.30pm, 7-10pm daily.* **Map** *p142 J10* ❸ *Gastronomy*

This posh eatery on the Arno wins the Oscar for the finest seats in Florence: the mini-terrace facing the Ponte Vecchio is as dramatic as an opera stage. Indoors, too, is a 'room with a view' to rival all others. Serving creative takes on Italian cuisine, Trentino-born chef Peter Brunel earned the restaurant's first Michelin star in December 2015. The à la carte menu features heavenly main dishes, such as veal prepared with cheek stew, chicory, Jerusalem artichoke, plum, chestnuts and Vin Santo; there are also two themed tasting menus priced at €105 and €115 each. The staggeringly long wine list includes about 800 varieties; by-the-glass options average around €20. Through the restaurant's popular 'Spoon' series, a rotating rota of Michelin-starred chefs make monthly appearances here, each teaming up with Brunel to create a one-night-only menu.

I Brindellone €€
Piazza Piattellina 10 (055 217879). **Open** *noon-2pm, 7.30-10pm Tue-Sun.* **Map** *p142 E9* ❹ *Traditional Italian*

Tuscan comfort food in all its simple glory. This inexpensive, rough-and-tumble *trattoria* between piazzas Carmine and Tasso still has the blue-collar soul of old San Frediano, serving up simple *primi*, hearty steak and house wine to boisterous crowds of Florentines. It's named after the fancy cart paraded through town during the annual Scoppio del Carro tradition (*see p57*), and old photos of that ritual and other events line the walls in the front room. A particularly good stop for Florentine steak and the lunchtime deals, perhaps after visiting the nearby Brancacci Chapel (Cappella Brancacci) (*see p148*).

Culinaria Bistrot €
Piazza Tasso 13r (055 229494, www.facebook.com/culinaria. degustibus.bistro). **Open** *noon-3pm, 6.45-11pm daily.* **Map** *p142 D10* ❺ *Organic bistro*

Prices are on point at this cosy 'indoor garden' of sorts, where everything on the menu is made using ingredients sourced from the De Gustibus network of farmers. There are scrumptious soups of the day, starting at just €6; inventive starters such as sweet corn pancakes with duck breast; house-made houmous, not easy to find elsewhere in Florence; and, of course, the satisfaction of knowing you're directly supporting a grassroots group of producers.

Essenziale €€

Piazza di Cestello 3r (055 2476956, www.essenziale.me). **Open** *7-10pm Tues-Sat; 11am-4pm Sun. Closed Dec, Jan.* **Map** *p142 E8* ⑥
Experimental Italian

Spearheaded by the talented Simone Cipriani, this concept restaurant makes its principles clear: here, it's about the essentials, stripping away everything that's extraneous and focusing on crafting creative dishes that taste good. The design is chic but the vibe is laid-back, with surprisingly fair prices, nothing marked up for meaningless exclusivity. The tasting menus deliver excellent value: the 'Conoscersi' option offers three courses for €35, including Cipriani's succulent Comfort Spaghetti, while a Salvator Dali-inspired set costs €55 for five dishes. For lighter, but no less flavour-packing options, look to the 'Fast and Casual' section of the menu, which features a Tuscan club sandwich made with guinea fowl and pork cheek and a taco lasagna made with Sriracha sauce, Bechamel, meat ragu, Parmesan cheese and lettuce. A prizeworthy three-course Sunday brunch is served for a modest cost of €28, unlimited coffee and water included.

Langolino

Via delle Caldaie 8r (055 294690, www.facebook.com/langolinofirenze). **Open** *11am-2am Tue-Sat; 11am-midnight Sun.* **Map** *p142 G11* ⑦ *Wine bar*

This intimate corner haunt serves high-quality cold cuts (try the *soprassata*, an Italian dry salami) and heavenly cheeses in varying combinations, paired with a range of excellent wines. It's clear from the furnishings that this place could be nowhere but the Oltrarno: beautifully hand-crafted chairs shaped like the façade of Santo Spirito line the bar. Perfect for *aperitivo* and a lovely late-night (for Florence) drink locale.

Pitti Gola e Cantina

Piazza Pitti 16 (055 212704, www.pittigolaecantina.com). **Open** *1pm-midnight Wed-Mon. Closed on occasions in winter.* **Map** *p142 J11* ⑧ *Wine bar*

Wine and dine in the shadow of Palazzo Pitti at this small, charming *enoteca*. Its popularity means it's often packed with a heavy tourist flow (prompting staff to post a tongue-in-cheek sign declaring 'No water, only wine'). Prices are on the high side, but many locals still swear by this place. The atmosphere is very pleasant, and the staff, though knowledgeable, aren't plagued by the preciousness often seen among wine enthusiasts. Wines are heavily weighted towards Tuscany, and Sangiovese reigns supreme, since the owner is a self-described single-grape purist. Snacks include cured meats and cheeses.

Il Santo Bevitore €€

Via Santo Spirito 64-66r (055 211264, www.ilsantobevitore.com). **Open** *12.30-3pm, 7.30-11.30pm Mon-Sat; 7.30-11.30pm Sun. Closed 3wks Aug.* **Map** *p142 G9* ⑨
Gastronomy

Attracting a diverse clientele of young and trendy locals, off-duty food journalists and discerning travellers, this restaurant is one of the best in the Oltrarno. Occupying a large, vaulted room and adjacent tower just south of the river, it's busy at lunch and especially crowded in the evenings. Menus change every month to stay in line with the seasons and the prime ingredients are all top quality. The prices are honest as is the varied and nicely priced wine list. As well as the ever-present wooden platters laden with selections of cheeses and cold meats, try the fresh *garagnelli* pasta with Calabrian hot sauce Nduija, and the tartar of *chianina*. The owners also run tiny but top-notch wine bar Il Santino a few steps away and bakery shop S. Forno (*see p155*).

❤ Vivanda
Via Santa Monaca 7r (055 2381208, www.vivandafirenze.it). Open 11am-3pm, 6pm- midnight daily. Map p142 F10 ❿ *Wine bar*

Florence's first *enoteca* dedicated to organic wines, Vivanda opened in 2010 and still has a big local fan base. Located between piazza Santo Spirito and piazza del Carmine, Vivanda boasts an extensive wine list of around 100 organic and biodynamic labels from across Italy and the world. They also produce their own label, Dalle Nostre Mani, which has a food and wine shop of the same name around the corner. The kitchen offers a good assortment of antipasti, *primi* and *secondi* including fresh pasta and a variety of vegetable choices. All prime ingredients are locally sourced and seasonal. You can eat here and not worry about your carbon footprint: plates and cutlery are all biodegradable.

❤ Le Volpi e l'Uva
Piazza de' Rossi 1r (055 2398132, www.levolpieluva.com). Open 11am-9pm Mon-Sat. Map p142 K10 ⓫ *Wine bar*

Attracting a diverse range of local wine lovers, this wine bar is a great place for a glass of plonk and a snack. It can get cramped in winter with seats only at the bar, but there's more room in summer thanks to the terrace (reservations are still recommended for outdoor seating). Much of what's on offer will be unfamiliar to all but the most clued-up oenophiles: owners Riccardo and Emilio seek out small, little-known producers from all over Italy, with an eye on value for money. A delicious selection of

snacks includes tasting plates of Italian and French cheeses, cured meats, a range of *crostoni*, crudités, fish carpaccios and rich duck foie gras.

Cafés, bars & gelaterie

❤ La Carraia
Piazza N. Sauro 25r (055 280965, www.lacarraiagroup.eu). Open Winter 11am-10pm daily; Summer 11am–midnight daily. Closed Jan. Map p142 G8 ❶ *Gelateria*

Head honcho Signora Eleanora's modest gelato business has grown into an international franchise with a Florida location opening in 2017. Carraia's queues are crazy in the summer, but it shouldn't be skipped if you're doing the gelato grand tour. You can't really go wrong with a €1 tasting cone, which is a pretty sizeable serving for the price. The crème caramel is lush.

Caffè degli Artigiani
Via dello Sprone 16r (055 291882 caffedegliartigiani.wordpress. com). Open 8am-1am daily. Map p142 J10 ❷ *Bar*

Caffè degli Artigiani is easily one of the Oltrarno's most charming neighbourhood bars: it's the kind of local go-to where friends' paths cross unplanned, but no one is ever surprised to see each other. In winter, the upstairs room, complete with a piano, board games and twinkly lights, is the Oltrarno's sweetest spot for winding down with a glass of wine; warmer weather brings coveted green tables set up outdoors on the adjacent side street. There's light local fare, including *crostini*, salads, *panini* and *carpacci*, plus a modest *aperitivo* buffet, but this place is better suited for a coffee and snack or after-dinner drinks. The memorably medieval-esque toilet is the café's only 'pitfall', pun intended.

💜 Explore the Oltrarno's artisan studios

*Start **Map** p142 D8.*

Few visitors to Florence are aware of the artisan community that has existed in the city for some 500 years. When the Medici moved into the Pitti Palace in the mid 16th century, Florentine bigwigs began to move in. With them came the attendant cabinet-makers and restorers, wood-carvers, dressmakers and cobblers, metal workers and gilders that, added to the *botteghe* (workshops) already established in the area, made for a rich and varied pool of artisan talent that thrived for centuries.

Begin your explorations by crossing over into the Oltrarno via ponte Amerigo Vespucci. First up is **Antico Setificio Fiorentino** (via Lorenzo Bartolini 4, 055 213861, www.anticosetificiofiorentino. com). The only artisan silk workshop left in Florence, it's a must for anyone interested in fabric and interior design – just be sure to book before you go.

Move through the small piazza di Verzaia to reach the nearby via San Giovanni, where you'll find experienced *corniciaio* (framer) Pierluigi Franceschi (no.11, 055 220642, www. franceschicornici.com).

Take a detour through via dell'Orto to piazza Piattellina, where you can stop off for a traditional lunch at I Brindellone (*see p150*); or pass through piazza dei Nerli instead, stopping off at the tiny *trippaio* stand for the ultimate workers' lunch, a *lampredotto panino*.

Next, find your way to the quintessential workshops concentrated in the rough-hewn side streets running off borgo San Frediano. Follow the splendidly named 'Street of the Golden Dragon' until you reach the **Ugolini brothers'** bronze workshop (via del Drago d'Oro 25r, 055 215 343, www.bronzistiugolini. com). Founded in 1800, this family firm still uses traditional methods of casting, engraving and polishing bronze to produce exquisite home accessories.

Inch your way back inward and upward toward piazza Santo Spirito, where you'll find metalworkers **Giuliano Ricchi** and **Gianni Bricci**. Their workspace is hidden within the walls of a residential *palazzo* (piazza Santo Spirito 12).

If talk of the Oltrarno's 'glory days' has you wondering who will keep this district alive, swing south of the *piazza* toward borgo Tegolaio and then turn down via dei Preti, where an innovative workspace of new-generation artisans will give you faith in the future. Margherita de Martino Norante steers the ship at **Officine Nora** (Via dei Preti 4, 055 975 8930, www.officinenora.it), a collective workspace of Italian and international jewellery designers.

Finally, turn back down borgo Tegolaio, take a right on via Sant'Agostino and pass through piazza San Felice. Right at the beginning of via Romana you'll find **Anita Russo** (*see p155*), another young, inspiring artisan honing her ceramic craft in the heart of the city.

Ditta Artigianale Oltrarno

Via dello Sprone 5r (055 0457163, www.dittaartigianale.it).
Open *8am-midnight Mon-Fri; 9am-midnight Sat, Sun.* **Map** *p142 J10* ❸ *Coffee bar/fusion food*

Francesco Sanapo's oft-cited coffee revolution began at the original Ditta Artigianale, and a year later the brand opened this bold Oltrarno offshoot, stylish and surpassing its predecessor in popularity. Ditta Artigianale – particularly at this location – is a place that generates strong opinions: some say it's the best thing to ever happen to Florentine coffee culture, while naysayers cry that it's a pretentious sham built for Instagram likes and bearded hipsters. Truthfully? It's a touch of both. Structurally, it's striking, housed in a revamped building originally designed by the late Giovanni Michelucci, the architect behind Santa Maria Novella station. Coffee-wise, it's of the same calibre and has the same variety you'd find in the via dei Neri location – from flat whites to drip coffee to the 'Big Cappuccio,' a colossal-sized cappuccino that manages to not be overwhelmed by milk. The main difference is that this location offers a full restaurant menu designed by Arturo Dori, who takes the same eclectic, international approach to food as Sanapo does to coffee.

❤ La Sorbettiera

Piazza Tasso 11 (055 5120336, www.lasorbettiera.com. **Open** *12.30-11.30pm Mon-Sat; 11am-1pm, 3-11.30pm Sun.* **Map** *p142 D10* ❹ *Gelateria*

This humble hut in the heart of piazza Tasso is where you'll find arguably the neighbourhood's tastiest, freshest gelato, often served by its friendly southern owner, Antonio. The salted caramel option is divine, and when you order in a cup, always say 'yes' to the thin biscuit topper they offer, which somehow tastes better here than anywhere else, and makes a great edible utensil. Who needs spoons?

Zeb

Via San Miniato 2r (055 2342864, www.zebgastronomia.com). **Open** *Apr-Oct 7.30-10.30pm Mon, Tue; noon-3.30pm, 7.30-10.30pm Thur-Sat. Nov-Mar noon-3.30pm, 7.30-10.30pm Thur-Sat.* **Map** *p142 O12* ❺ *Bistro-deli*

There's no outdoor seating at Zeb, but don't let that put you off; grab a stool at the central bar or in the window of the bright and pretty interior and enjoy an excellent selection of home-style small plates, always served with seasonal ingredients. As is evident from the freshly handwritten menu hanging outside each day, the options are always shifting, but you can generally count on finding outrageously good pastas and salads with creatively tossed fresh ingredients. It's all carried out under the watchful eye of owner Alberto Navari who serves dishes designed by his mother, Giuseppina, in a space that formerly housed their family grocery store.

Shops

And Company

Via Maggio 51r (055 219973, www.andcompanyshop.com). **Map** *p142 H11* ❶ *Gifts & souvenirs*

Walking by Anglo-Italian Betty Soldi's eclectic shop and studio, you might recognise the playful squiggly writing on the windows: the creative calligrapher's work has appeared in prestigious publications and collaborations with brands the world over. And Company is packed with cosmopolitan Betty's charming bric-a-brac, from Florentine monument-themed mugs and espresso cups to tote bags, notebooks, decorative marble slabs, holiday ornaments and much more. The magic happens in her hidden workspace in the back of the shop. Hours can be erratic: pop by if you're in the area, but call ahead if you're heading across town specifically for the visit.

Angela Caputi
Via Santo Spirito 58r (055 212 972, www.angelacaputi.com). **Open** *10am-1pm, 3.30-7.30pm Tue-Sat.* **Map** *p142 G9* ❷ *Jewellery*
Colourful costume jewellery in plastics, resin and crystal from this legendary Florentine designer. Styles are exuberant, with ethnic, art deco and psychedelic patterns. Much of Caputi's inspiration comes from the golden age of Hollywood. **Other locations** Borgo SS Apostoli, Duomo & Around (055 292993).

Anita Russo Ceramic Studio
Via Romana 11r (055 9063823, www.facebook.com/pg/Anita-Russo-Ceramic-Studio-Firenze-479169925458813). Variable hours. **Map** *p142 G12* ❸ *Ceramics*
Anita Russo's inviting space at the foot of via Romana is framed by a cheery blue-green door that sets the tone for the colourful space you'll find inside. The stock is heavy on

In the know
Beach life

Map *p142 Q11.* On a raised stretch of the river at lungarno Serristori, city beach Easy Living and its wood-decked restaurant just above 'sea level' are open day and night to sun seekers between June and September. (Just don't attempt to swim in the Arno river.) Chill on a lounger under a parasol by day, drink a toast to summer on the restaurant terrace by night.

beautifully made kitchenware and accessories for bed and bath: think serving platters, salt and pepper shakers, salad bowls, toothbrush holders, little trays for keys or jewellery. Jewellery isn't as much of a speciality but you'll still find a few well-priced statement rings. Everything is made in Russo's workspace just behind the counter, where she often teaches courses to the cerami-curious.

Giulio Giannini e Figlio
Piazza Pitti 37r (055 212621, www.giuliogiannini.it). **Open** *10am-7pm Mon-Sat; 11am-6.30pm Sun.* **Map** *p142 J11* ❹ *Gifts & souvenirs*
Family-run firm stocking marbled paper, leather desk accessories and greetings cards.

S. Forno
Via Santa Monaca 3 (055 2398580, www.ilsantobevitore.com). **Open** *7.30am-7.30pm daily.* **Map** *p142 F10* ❺ *Bakery*
A boutique bakery if there ever was one, this stylish shop completes the 'Santo' holy trinity – Il Santo Bevitore restaurant (*see p151*) and its spinoffs. There is a plethora of jams, craft beers, juices and pastas up for sale, as well as fresh bread, sweet treats and traditional bakery favourites. *Panini* are served up fresh for a high-quality quick bite at lunchtime.

Sara Amrhein & Scicc, Art
Via dello Sprone 9 (392 9613197, www.sara-amrhein.com). **Open** *11am-7.30pm Mon-Fri.* **Map** *p142 J10* ❻ *Statement jewellery & Tuscan crafts*
This delightful space is shared between American jewellery designer Sara Amrhein, who makes bold polymer clay pieces (necklaces, earrings and bracelets in cheery colours), and crafty Tiziani Salvi, who curates a selection of made-in-Tuscany goods by handpicked artisans.

Il Torchio

Via de' Bardi 17 (055 2342862, www.legatoriailtorchio.com). **Open** *10am-1.30pm, 2.30-7pm Mon-Fri; 10am-1pm Sat.* **Map** *p142 L11* **7** *Gifts & souvenirs*

Young Canadian transplant Erin Ciulla took over this spot to carry on the bookbinding tradition passed down to her by Anna Anichini, with whom she apprenticed. Watch her work in action, and stock up on handmade notebooks, paper boxes, stationery and albums.

Entertainment

💙 British Institute of Florence

Harold Acton Library, Lungarno Guicciardini 9, Oltrarno (39 055 267781, www.britishinstitute.it). **Open** *Wed Lectures from 6pm; screenings from 8pm. Tickets €6.* **No cards.** **Map** *p142 H9* **1** *Cinema*

The British Institute runs a Talking Pictures programme on Wednesday evenings, always preceded by a 6pm lecture – sometimes related to the film, other times as a separate event. Films, which are always either in English or subtitled in English, are sandwiched between an introduction and a discussion. The institute also runs courses in Italian language, complemented by cinema screenings and events.

💙 Caffe' Notte

Via delle Caldaie 18, Oltrarno (055 223067, www.facebook.com/caffenotte). **Open** *7.30am-midnight Mon-Wed; 7.30am-2.30am Thu-Sun.* **Map** *p142 G11* **2** *Café-bar*

A cute hole-in-the-wall on an unsuspecting corner of the Oltrarno, not five minutes' walk from piazza Santo Spirito, this charming spot keeps Christmas lights up year-round and attracts a mixed-age crowd of local residents, international students and resident neighbourhood 'characters'. It's open all day for coffee and food but the night-time is the right time to go here, hence its name.

Mad Souls & Spirits

Borgo S. Frediano 36-38r, Oltrarno (055 627 1621, www.facebook.com/madsoulsandspirits). **Open** *6pm-2am daily.* **Map** *p142 F9* **3** *Bar*

Craft cocktails are the bread and butter of this Borgo San Frediano haunt. Here it's more about the art of a stiff drink than socialising with strangers: expect expert descriptions from the bar staff, who will guide you to a choice of cocktail based on the classics you tell them you like. Although you're welcome to order an old-fashioned standard, you should never ask for a Vodka Red Bull. As the detailed cocktail menu states: 'Drink like a serious person'.

💙 NOF

Borgo S. Frediano, 17/19r, Oltrarno (333 6145376, www.nofclub.it). **Open** *6.30pm-2.30am Mon-Sat. Tickets prices vary.* **Map** *p142 F9* **4** *Live music*

This Oltrarno hideaway makes an easy watering hole for anyone passing through the area, but it's more famous for its gigs, which attracts a sweaty, dancing, mixed-age crowd. Its music schedule is very sporadic but worth checking out.

💙 St Mark's English Church

Via Maggio 16, Santa Spirito, Oltrarno (340 811 9192, www.concertoclassico.info). Tickets €15-€45 opera, €10-€30 concerts. **Map** *p142 H10* **5** *Concert hall*

Apart from one or two slight adaptations to suit the intimate setting, the performances for Opera at St Marks are complete operas with professional singers in full costume accompanied on the piano. There are also concerts of opera arias and Neapolitan songs at other times of the year.

Outside the City Gates

The historic centre of Florence is home to the densest concentration of art treasures and sights in the world, but it's surprisingly small. This makes exploring beyond the central area, delineated by the eight surviving city gates, easy to achieve by bus or with a short walk. North of the Arno, the old city walls were pulled down in the 1870s to make way for *viali* (avenues) – now traffic-clogged multi-lane arteries.

South of the river, large sections of the 13th-century city walls still survive, and the tree-lined avenues that form an umbrella round this side of the city are picturesque. Here you'll find the best walks, views and sights; gently meandering lanes take you within minutes into gorgeous countryside.

Best cultural venues
Large-scale opera productions at
Teatro dell'Opera (*p164*).

Best gelateria
Hard-to-beat ice-cream, well
worth the bus ride out of town, at
Gelateria Badiani (*p163*).

Best green space
Giardino delle Rose (*p159*):
Giuseppe Poggi's garden has
panoramic views.

Best museums
Fascinating collection of arms,
armour and whatnots at Museo
Stibbert (*p159*).

Best lunch spots
Relax on the terrace in quiet San
Niccolò at Fuori Porta (*p162*).
Enjoy authentic Neapolitan pizza
at Vico del Carmine (*p162*).

Best nightspots
Head to Auditorium FLOG (*p163*)
and Tenax (*p164*) for live music,
international DJs and special
events.

Best sights
Soak up the finest Romanesque
architecture and picture-perfect
views at San Miniato al Monte
(*p161*) and Piazzale Michelangelo
(*p160*).

To the north-west is the green oasis of the **Parco delle Cascine**, a public park backed by woods. Backing onto it is the modern **Teatro dell'Opera**.

Coming back along viale Fratelli Rosselli, is the massive pentagonal stone **Fortezza da Basso**. Just north of the fortress lies Florence's decorative **Chiesa Russa Ortodossa** (Russian Orthodox church). From here, head to via dello Statuto and catch a bus north-west to visit the eccentric **Museo Stibbert**. Heading south-east towards piazza Beccaria is the atmospheric **Cimitero degli Inglesi**. East is the **Stadio Artemo Franchi** at Campo di Marte.

South of the Arno, steep lanes lined with high walls and impenetrable gates that protect beautiful villas rise sharply from the riverbank. From the city centre, the *coste* (steep, uphill streets) and long flights of mossy steps make short but testing walks up to fine vantage points on the hills.

The most famous viewpoint in Florence is probably from **piazzale Michelangelo**, a large, open square providing vistas over the entire city. From here it's a short walk to the exquisite **San Miniato al Monte**, one of Florence's oldest churches.

Sights & museums

Chiesa Russa Ortodossa

Via Leone X 12, Fortezza (055 490148, www.chiesarussafirenze. org) Visits and guided tours by appt.

With its five polychrome onion domes completed in 1904, this church is a reminder that the city was once popular with wealthy Russians (Dostoyevsky, Tchaikovsky and Gorky among them) as a retreat from the harsh winters back home.

❤ Giardino delle Rose

Viale Giuseppe Poggi 2 (055 2625323). Bus 12, 13. Open May-Sept 9am-8pm. Mar, Apr & Oct 9am-6pm. Nov-Feb 9am-5pm. Admission free.

Created in 1865 by architect Giuseppe Poggi, today the garden contains around 1,000 varieties of plants and over 350 species of roses. Sandwiched between viale Poggi, via di San Salvatore and via dei Bastioni, it covers about one hectare of land with panoramic views of the city. The garden is also home to nine bronzes and two plaster sculptures bequeathed by the widow of Belgian artist Jean-Michel Folon (1934-2005) to the city after a 2005 exhibition at nearby Forte di Belvedere (*see p181*).

Museo del Calcio

Viale Palazzeschi 20, Coverciano (055 600526, www.museodelcalcio. it). Bus 17 to the Viale Volta Terminus. Open 9am-1pm, 3-7pm Mon-Fri. 9am-1pm Sat. Closed Aug. Admission (incl audio guide) €5; €3 6-14s; free under-6s.

Soccer fans will be enthralled by Florence's football museum, housed in a converted barn adjoining Casa Italia in Coverciano. 'Casa Italia' is the nickname for the central training grounds of the Italian national football team and technical headquarters of the Italian Football Association. Exhibits in the museum range from the actual World Cups won by Italy to a vast collection of football-related postage stamps, as well as the shirts of Italian and international footballers. The huge multimedia databank provides entertaining photos and video footage from 1898 to the present day.

❤ Museo Stibbert

Via Stibbert 26, Rifredi (055 486049, www.museostibbert.it). Bus 4. Open 10am-2pm Mon-Wed; 10am-6pm Fri-Sun (last entry 1hr before closing). Closed Thur. Admission €8; €6 reductions.

A fascinating but bizarre collection that belonged to Frederick Stibbert (1838-1906), a brother-in-arms to Garibaldi, is housed here. Stibbert was born to an English father and Italian mother, who left him her 14th-century house. He bought the neighbouring mansion and joined the two to house his 50,000 artefacts. Crammed into the 64 rooms are Napoleon's coronation robes (Stibbert was a fan), a hand-painted harpsichord, arms and armour, shoe buckles, snuff boxes, chalices, crucifixes and even an attributed Botticelli. The rambling garden has a lily pond, stables, a neoclassical folly by Poggi, and ancient Greek and Egyptian-inspired temples.

➜ Getting around

Exploring the area immediately beyond the eight surviving city gates is easy by foot. For any sights lying further afield, the ATAF bus network has regular services to the suburbs.

Parco delle Cascine

Entrance nr ponte della Vittoria (055 2768806, parcodellecascine. comune.fi.it). Bus 17C, Tram T1.
Stretching west of the city on the right river bank with its 160 hectares (395 acres) of woods, lawns and sports facilities, the Cascine is the city's lung. It's at its busiest on Tuesday mornings when a large market is held, and on Sundays with parties playing football and families picnicking. Playgrounds dot the park; in-line skates can be hired, and a tourist information point and visitor centre is open at weekends in the former stables.

The first major changes to the park for decades have been made with the building of the T1 Tramvia (tramway). Trees were cut down, avenues converted to tracks and traffic diverted to make way for it. A dedicated bridge over the Arno was also built. There was a fierce debate over whether this complied with the terms of the Medici bequest of the park to the city.

In summer, the Cascine is used as a venue for events and gigs. It's safe enough when summer events are held, but be aware that the area is seamy at night, with prostitutes touting for business along the park's main roads and adjoining *viali*.

♥ Piazzale Michelangelo

Between viale Galileo and viale Michelangelo. **Open** *always.* **Admission** *free.* **Map** *p8*
Perched on the hill directly above piazza Poggi, Piazzale Michelangelo is considered the city's balcony. Despite the view being slightly inferior to that from the Forte di Belvedere (*see p181*) further west, the *piazzale* has the added value of being readily accessible at all times. As a consequence, its stone balustrade is perennially crowded with tourists. The spacious

piazza is also slowly but steadily being reclaimed from its former disgraceful status as a parking area for events ranging from summer festivals to New Year's Eve concerts.

Laid out in 1869 by Giuseppe Poggi, Piazzale Michelangelo is dominated by a bronze replica of Michelangelo's *David*. Now at the V&A in London, the plaster cast of the original *David* (*see p119* Accademia) that was used to make it was gifted in 1857 by the Grand Duke of Tuscany to Queen Victoria, who reportedly found the nude outrageous and had his private parts promptly covered with a fig leaf.

You can reach the *piazzale* with a pleasant but taxing hike from the Ponte Vecchio, along via San Niccolò to Porta San Miniato, up via del Monte alle Croci and left up the flight of stone steps winding between villas – or alternatively, up the rococo staircase Poggi designed to link Piazzale Michelangelo with the *piazza* in his name below. The lazy alternative is buses 12 and 13, which take the scenic route in opposite directions round Poggi's *viali*. In any case, wait for the sunset for picture-perfect photos.

Stadio Artemio Franchi

Viale Manfredo Fanti 14, Campo di Marte (For football: 055 503011, www.acffiorentina.it. For concerts: 055 667566, www.bitconcerti.it). Bus 7, 11, 17. Ticket prices vary.
Pier Luigi Nervi's football stadium near Campo di Marte station was built in 1930-32 and enlarged for the 1990 World Cup. It has an average capacity of around 45,000. Besides hosting the ACF Fiorentina home matches, the stadium moonlights as a music venue for Italian and international big-name gigs.

💜 San Miniato al Monte

*Via delle Porte Sante 34 (055 2342731, www.sanminiatoal monte.it). Bus 12, 13. **Open** Summer 9.30am-1pm, 3-8pm Mon-Sat; 8.15am-8pm Sun. Winter 9.30am-1pm, 3-7pm Mon-Sat; 8.15am-7pm Sun. **Admission** free. **Map** p8*

On a fine day, the view over Florence from San Miniato is nothing short of breathtaking.

Miniato (Minias) was an Armenian deacon and a member of the early Christian community in Florence. Martyred around AD 250, according to legend he picked up his own decapitated head and walked uphill from the banks of the Arno to here, where he finally expired and was later buried by his companions. There has been a chapel on this site since at least the fourth century, later replaced with a Benedictine monastery built in the early 11th century on the orders of reforming Bishop Hildebrand.

The Romanesque church façade is delicately inlaid with geometric figures in white Carrara and green Verde di Prato marble, and its 13th-century mosaic of *Christ Enthroned between the Madonna and St Minias* echoes the larger, more detailed one in the apse. The copper eagle surmounting the façade is the symbol of the Calimala (wool merchants) Guild which administered the convent from 1288. The original bell tower collapsed in 1499, and Baccio d'Agnolo's 1518 replacement was never quite completed.

The split-level interior is one of Tuscany's loveliest; its walls a patchwork of faded frescoes and its marble pavement beautifully inlaid with the signs of the zodiac and stylised lions and lambs. The serene 11th-century crypt is divided into seven small aisles by 38 slender columns. By the staircase to the right you can see red *sinopia* drawings for a *fresco* painting.

In the middle of the main nave is a chapel tabernacle. It was commissioned by Piero di Cosimo de' Medici and attributed either to Bernardo Rossellino or Michelozzo. The elaborate barrel vault is by Luca della Robbia, and the altarpiece by Agnolo Gaddi.

In the sacristy, a cycle of frescoes by Spinello Aretino (1387-88, but heavily restored in 1840) on the life of St Benedict was the first undertaking of the Olivetan monks after they took over the abbey in 1373.

Cappella del Cardinale del Portogallo

Villa La Petraia

Via della Petraia 40, Castello (055 452691, www.polomusealetoscana. beniculturali.it). Closed 2nd & 3rd Mon of mth. **Admission** *free.*

Sitting on a little hill, the villa and grounds, which were acquired by the Medici family in 1530, stand apart from the surrounding industrial mess. Originally a tower belonging to Brunelleschi's family, the villa and its fabulous formal terraced gardens by Il Tribolo are among those immortalised by Giusto Utens in his famous 14 lunettes, which since 2014 are attractively displayed here following a thorough restoration. It is one of the Medici villas included in the UNESCO list of World Heritage Sites.

Restaurants & wine bars

Da Ruggero €€

Via Senese 89r (055 220542). Bus 11, 36, 37. **Open** *noon-2.30pm, 7.30-10.30pm Mon, Thur-Sun. Closed Aug. Trattoria*

This rustic *trattoria*, a short walk south of Porta Romana, is one of Florence's best-kept secrets. Family-run by the Corsis for over 30 years, it serves a menu of traditional dishes that changes with the seasons, but always includes a hearty soup or two and an excellent spicy *spaghetti alla carrettiera* (literally, cart-driver's spaghetti). Among the roast meats, try the tasty pigeon or go for the exemplary *bollito misto* (classic beef and veal stew) served with tangy, parsley-fresh *salsa verde*.

❤ Fuori Porta €€

Via Monte alle Croci 10r, San Niccolò (055 2342483, www. fuoriporta.it). Bus D. **Open** *12.30pm-12.30am daily. Closed 2wks Aug. Wine bar*

One of Florence's best-stocked wine bars, Fuori Porta is situated in the lovely San Niccolò neighbourhood at Porta San Miniato and has a charming terrace overlooking the old city gate. It's a relaxed spot for a glass and a snack at lunch; evenings are buzzier. At any time, there are between 500 and 650 labels on the list, with about 50 available by the glass and 250cl carafe, which rotate roughly every week. Tuscan and Piedmontese reds dominate, but other Italian regions are also well represented; there are formidable lists of *grappa* and Scotch too. The wine bar is also known for its excellent pastas, *carpaccio* and salads; the classic snack here is delicious *crostini*. Make reservations before 9pm for dinner or expect to queue.

❤ Vico del Carmine €€

Via Pisana 40r (055 2336862). **Open** *7.30pm-12.30am Mon-Sat; 12.30-2pm, 7.30pm-12.30am Sun. Pizzeria*

Just a stone's throw from Porta San Frediano, this restaurant and *pizzeria* is done out as a typical street in old Naples (complete with washing lines strung across a balcony). Almost always full and noisy, it often loses points for brusque service and higher than average prices. Yet the quality of the food keeps pizza-lovers piling in. Baked in an authentic wood-burning oven and with ingredients that are strictly sourced from the Campania region (as are most of the wines), the pizzas have light, puffy crusts and miraculously un-soggy bases. Highly recommended is the remarkable '*a chiummenzana*: the folded-over crust is stuffed with ricotta while the base is topped with smoked scamorza cheese and cherry tomatoes. Less remarkable (but perfectly decent) are the pasta and fish choices.

Cafés, bars & gelaterie

Caffè Pasticceria Serafini

*Via Gioberti 168r (055 2476214,
www.pasticceriaserafini.it).* **Open**
7am-8.45pm Mon-Sat. Café
This bakery, café and bar close to
piazza Beccaria is a local favourite,
and what most of the locals drink
here is the *fornacino*, a creamy,
delicious coffee with chocolate
that defies description, or belief.
Equally unbelievable are the
aperitivi, which include not just
superior quality olives, *crostini*,
pizzas and nibbles, but more
substantial dishes such as gnocchi
with prawns and various side
dishes – all yours for the taking
with a €6 glass of wine. It gets
crowded, so get here early.

♥ Gelateria Badiani

*Viale dei Mille 20, Campo
di Marte (055 578682, www.
gelateriabadiani.it). Bus 17.* **Open**
*summer 7am-1am daily. Winter
7am-1am Fri, Sat; 7am-midnight
Sun-Thur. Closed Mon, winter only.*
Gelateria
This hugely popular gelateria,
located near the Stadio Artemio
Franchi (*see p160*), offers a terrific
selection of flavours including
monthly specials based on
seasonal fruit – think figs or fresh
strawberries – or novelty flavours
such as salted caramel, pistachio
pesto or black sesame. However, its
pride and joy is Buontalenti, a well-
guarded secret mix of just cream,
milk, sugar and egg yolks. The
ice-cream is named after Bernardo
Buontalenti (1531-1608), the Medici
court architect, who was in charge
of staging theatrical performances
and fireworks for his patrons. He
treated guests to a special frozen
dessert made from fruit, honey,
zabaglione, plus snow and ice from
specially- built ice houses in the
Boboli and Cascine gardens. At €2
for a *piccolo* (small cup), it's also a
bargain compared to city-centre
gelaterie. Gorgeous cakes, coffee
and, at lunchtime, a small selection
of savouries complete the picture.

Entertainment

♥ Auditorium FLOG

*Via M Mercati 24b, Outside the City
Gates (055 487145, www.flog.it). Bus
4, 14, 20.* **Open** *times vary Tue-Sat.
Closed June-Aug. Tickets €7-€20.*
No cards. *Live music*
At FLOG, music runs from rock to
Tex-Mex rockabilly, reggae and ska,
and there's usually a DJ after the
bands. Dance parties and theatrical
shows take place early in the week,
and the venue hosts the world
music festival Musica dei Popoli
and Azione Gay e Lesbica parties.

Glue Alternative Concept Space

*Viale Manfredo Fanti 20, Campo
Di Marte, Outside the City Gates
(www.gluefirenze. com). Bus 10, 17.*
Open *8pm-12.30am Fri, 10pm-2am
Sat. €10 membership.* **Admission
free.** *Live music*
Glue is a members-only music
haven, but pay for an annual
membership card and you'll have
access to all concerts and special
events, including cinema nights
and exhibitions. It's a prime space
to see young, budding Florentine
bands as well as more established,
primarily Italian acts.

Nelson Mandela Forum

*Piazza Enrico Berlinguer, Viale
Paoli 3, Outside the City Gates (055
678841, www.mandelaforum.it).
Bus 10, 17, 20. Tickets prices vary.*
No cards. *Live music*
This 7,000-capacity hall is where
Florence houses major touring
artists – Italian stars like singer
Emma Marone and international
acts such as Cirque du Soleil
and Mika.

OUTSIDE THE CITY GATES

Teatro Obihall

Via Fabrizio de André, nr lungarno A Moro 3, Outside the City Gates (055 6504112, www.obihall.it). Bus 14. Tickets prices vary. Live music

This 4,000-capacity venue hosts mainstream acts from Italy and abroad – PJ Harvey and Macy Gray have played here. There are upper balcony seats, but the main standing hall downstairs has better sound.

❤ Teatro dell'Opera

Piazzale Vittorio Gui 1, Outside the City Gates (055 2779309, www.operadifirenze.it). Bus C1, C2, D. Tram T1. Box Office *10am-6pm Tue-Fri, 10am-1pm Sat, 2hrs prior to shows.* Season *year-round.* Theatre/concert hall

The contemporary music hall designed by Paolo Desideri at the mouth of the Cascine Park has been in use since May 2014. At 1,800 seats, the stage area is twice as big as most opera theatres, proving exciting possibilities for elaborate sets. The theatre's performing year is divided roughly into three parts: October to April is the main concert and opera season; the **Maggio Musicale Fiorentino** festival then runs for two months from late April to late June with a mix of opera, ballet, concerts and recitals; finally, the summer season is held outdoors between June and July in the Ammannati courtyard of **Palazzo Pitti** (*see p167*). The spectacular 2,000-seat open-air venue on the roof hosts music acts such as Mika and Kraftwerk.

❤ Tenax

Via Pratese 46, Peretola, Outside the City Gates (055 308160, www.tenax.org). Bus 29, 30. Open *10pm-4am Sat. Closed mid May-Sept. Ticket prices vary.* Club

The most influential and international of the Florentine clubs is the warehouse-style Tenax in Peretola. Far enough outside the centre to make a night out an adventure, but not too far to be impractical without a car, it's best known as a live venue for hip international bands and for its DJ exchanges. When it's closed in the summer, Tenax also organises one-off events, often in the Stazione Leopolda. Big-name DJ Alex Neri's Nobody's Perfect on Saturday is the hottest night in the city by a long shot, heaving with house, big beat, progressive and drum 'n' bass.

Viper Club

Via Pistoiese, 50145, Outside the City Gates. (055 019 5922, www.viperclub.eu). Open *hours vary according to events. Bus 35, 56. Tickets prices vary.* Live music

Viper is increasingly known for its themed parties put on by branded outfits, such as Hot Shot – '90 in da House! (you read that correctly), a frequent throwback evening paying tribute to the gadgets, trends, tunes and television shows of the 1990s – mostly from across the Atlantic. These events are usually expertly marketed but often involve lengthy queues outside – and since getting to Viper is a bit of a haul, your time is better spent on a more musically-oriented night. Viper is one of Florence's best places to catch the latest sounds, whether live – the likes of Black Mountain, Marracash and Italian pop sensation Levante – or in storming DJ sets from international names.

Visarno Arena

Viale Manfredo Fanti 4, Campo di Marte, Outside the City Gates (055 503011). Bus 7, 17, 20. Tickets prices vary. No cards. Live music

This converted former racetrack in the Parco delle Cascine has become a major hub for open-air summer concerts and music festivals, hosting everyone from Massive Attack and Sting to Radiohead and Aerosmith.

Florence
Essentials

Accommodation

While room rates remain among the highest in Italy, the positive side to accommodation in Florence is the sheer variety of options. Whether your bed of choice lies in a boutique hotel with a sharp design edge or a cosy B&B on the top floor of an ancient *palazzo*, chances are that you'll find something appealing.

Location, location, location

While everyone may dream of staying in the **Duomo** area, this location, with its iconic views and the convenience of being able to drop your shopping bags and change your top on a whim, comes at a price. **Santa Maria Novella** has a diverse range of hotels, ranging from seedy one-star holes in side streets to the design gems overlooking the main square. **San Lorenzo** is where you'll find the widest choice of budget accommodation, with just as affordable eating options on your doorstep, but the neighbourhood can be noisy. **San Marco** is probably the most peaceful neighbourhood and offers some exciting options in historic *palazzi*, but its nightlife and dining scene can be on the quiet side. **Santa Croce** has some classy hotels and B&Bs interspersed with a high concentration of genuine residents. Meanwhile, **The Oltrarno** is better

---

In the know
Price categories

Our price categories are based on hotels' standard prices (not including seasonal offers or discounts) for one night in a double room with en suite shower/bath. Breakfast is included unless otherwise stated. Given the potential for off-season discounts, it's always worth trying to negotiate a better deal.

Luxury	€300+
Expensive	€200-€300
Moderate	€100-€200
Budget	up to €100

known for its nightlife than for its hotels, but some new exciting properties have entered the scene – just make sure your room doesn't overlook a busy street or a piazza where revelries continue into the small hours. Finally, staying outside the city gates can be an attractive option if you don't mind the bus commute. However, until the tramway lines are completed it's wise to avoid the traffic chaos of the area west of town.

When to go

If you're staying in the centre of the city during the long hot summer, a private terrace or balcony – or some kind of outside space – can make a big difference. Easter and the spring holiday weekends (for dates, *see p183*) can be both busy and expensive, but late September and most of October combine pleasant temperatures with thinner crowds. November and March may be rainy, and Florence in winter can be cold by Italian standards.

Prices and ratings

Accommodation prices can fluctuate a great deal depending on the time of year, last-minute vacancies and online special offers. Peak season for Florence's hotels runs roughly from Easter (the busiest weekend of the year) until October. It also covers Christmas, New Year, Italian public holidays and the Pitti fashion fairs in January and June. Hotel rooms at these times are at their most expensive and much in demand, so book well in advance.

On the other hand, low season (roughly November to February) offers great potential for accommodation bargains, especially among the upper-end establishments; budget hotels and B&Bs are less likely to lower their rates significantly. If you are willing to take your chances and are travelling off-season, it's worth doing the rounds to see what kind of bargain you can negotiate.

Suite Dreams

Fancy an alternative to a conventional hotel?

Most significant in recent years has been the huge increase in the number of B&Bs, *affittacamere* (rooms to rent including those found on sites such as Airbnb, Booking.com, Wimdu.com and Holidaylettings.co.uk). Renting a room or a flat is an enticing option, but always check amenities, cancellation policies, check-in and -out times and any hidden extras before booking. Also available are *residenze d'epoca* (listed buildings with no more than 12 rooms), but as these categories lie outside the star rating system, it can be difficult to judge what you're likely to get. They range from spartan, gloomy rooms with threadbare towels and no breakfast (yes, B&Bs with no breakfast) to homely pads furnished with antiques where you start the day with warm brioches. Good online resources include www.bedandbreakfast.it, www.bbitalia.it and www.caffelletto.it.

Case per ferie are religious institutions that offer a number of beds. The majority are cheap, but they're often single-sex and operate curfews; try www.monasterystays.com for listings. If you are young (or young at heart) and prefer camping or staying in a hostel, www.hostelworld.com is your go-to website.

Details of hotels, *affittacamere* (rooms to rent), apartments, campsites and hostels in Florence and its province can all be found online through www.firenzeturismo.it. Unaccountably, prices and website links are not provided.

One sour note for both hoteliers and travellers is an accommodation tax (*tassa di soggiorno*) ranging from €1.50 (for one-star hotels) to €5 (for five-star hotels) per person per night, up to a maximum of seven consecutive nights.

Hotels are officially given a star rating from one to five by the tourist board, but the rating is an indication of the facilities on offer rather than the standards. There can be enormous disparity within any given category, so it pays to do your research.

Hotels are required by law to display official maximum room rates in each room; if you feel you've been taken for a ride, there's an office for complaints.

Luxury

Four Seasons Hotel

Borgo Pinti 99, San Marco (055 26261, www.fourseasons.com/florence). **Map** *p117 R4.*

In Palazzo della Gherardesca, which has one of the largest privately owned gardens in Florence, this fabulous hotel is the result of a multi-million-euro restoration project. As well as the luxurious rooms, there are all the five-star facilities you'd expect, from the big spa to an outdoor pool. The rooms and suites are located in two buildings – the original *palazzo* and the Conventino – across four acres of garden, surrounded by winding paths, fountains and outdoor seating. If the hotel is out of your price range, the gardens are now open to the public, so you can come for a coffee or cocktail; you won't have access to the original frescoes, friezes and hand-painted reliefs that decorate the suites, mind you.

Gallery Hotel Art

Vicolo dell'Oro 5, Duomo & Around (055 27263, www.lungarnocollection.com). **Map** *p73 K9.*

Florence's original hip hotel opened in 1999, back when its East-meets-West design aesthetic was refreshingly different from the norm. Located in a tiny piazza near the Ponte Vecchio, the place has a cosy library with squashy sofas, thoughtfully supplied with cashmere throws and mountains of arty books to browse. The stylish Fusion Bar serves *aperitivi*, brunches, light lunches and dinners. The public rooms on the ground floor often double as show-space for contemporary artists and photographers. The bedrooms are super comfortable, and the bathrooms are a dream.

Hotel Brunelleschi

Piazza Santa Elisabetta 3, Duomo & Around (055 27370, www. hotelbrunelleschi.it). **Map** *p73 L7.*

It's hard to believe that the hotel's Byzantine tower was once a prison – easier to credit is that this is the city's oldest standing structure. The luxurious rooms are spread through the circular tower and reconstructed medieval church, retaining original features. Part of the restaurant is in the tower, and two penthouse suites enjoy 360º city views. There's even a private museum in the basement, along with an original Roman caldarium (plunge bath) that was found embedded in the foundations. Comfortable, welcoming and with great service, this place also gets a mention in both *The Da Vinci Code* and *Inferno*.

Palazzo Magnani Feroni

Borgo San Frediano 5, Oltrarno (055 2399544, www.palazzomagnaniferoni. com). **Map** *p142 F9.*

Expect top-class service and facilities, with prices to match, at this grand *palazzo* just south of the river. All but one of the ten big suites have separate sitting rooms elegantly furnished with sofas, armchairs and antiques. The most charming room of all is actually the smallest: a romantic junior suite with floor-to-ceiling frescoes and a little private garden. The fabulous roof terrace – complete with a bar serving light meals – offers views of the whole city.

Portrait Firenze

Lungarno Acciaiuoli 4, Duomo & Around (055 27268000, www. lungarnocollection.com). **Map** *p73 K9.*

The latest addition to the Ferragamo-owned Lungarno Collection of luxury boutique hotels is gathering praise across the board for its stunning location overlooking the Ponte Vecchio, its sleek designer interiors in muted hues with gold touches and its 37 huge rooms (including a spectacular penthouse suite), each featuring a fully-equipped kitchenette, which are particularly popular with families. The latest technology is integrated seamlessly and unobtrusively throughout the premises, and an excellent breakfast is served until 11am.

Westin Excelsior

*Piazza Ognissanti 3, Santa Maria Novella (055 27151, www.westinflorence. com). **Map** p97 E7.*

While it still offers an element of old-world luxury, the Westin Excelsior has introduced some contemporary touches. There's now a fitness area, plus two 'Westin Workout' rooms that have been equipped for the health-conscious guest. In addition, the restaurant offers a special menu of low-calorie dishes. All this, however, exists within a very traditional framework: the doormen are dressed in maroon and grey livery, and the grand public rooms have polished marble floors, neoclassical columns, painted wooden ceilings and stained glass. The 171 rooms and suites are sumptuously appointed; some boast terraces with views over the river to the rooftops of the Oltrarno.

Expensive
Antica Torre Tornabuoni Uno

*Via de' Tornabuoni 1, Santa Maria Novella (055 2658161, www. tornabuoni1.com). **Map** p97 J8.*

The roof terrace of this 12-room hotel, which occupies the upper storeys of an ancient tower overlooking piazza Santa Trinita, has arguably the most spectacular view of any hotel in Florence. Breakfast and drinks are served here in summer with a backdrop of just about every monument in the city. In cooler weather, the glassed-in loggia is almost as good. While undeniably comfortable, the bedrooms (several of which have private terraces) are not terribly inspiring; however, the views that they enjoy certainly are. Aside from the terrace, there are no public spaces.

Garibaldi Blu

*Piazza Santa Maria Novella 21, Santa Maria Novella (055 277300, www. hotelgaribaldiblu.com). **Map** p97 H6.*

Well placed near the train station and just a short walk from the main sights and the via Tornabuoni shopping

district, this boutique hotel provides a post-modern setting with a sombre palette of denim, grey and antique rose hues. Quirky palm trees made from recycled tyres rise alongside Pietra Serena Renaissance columns, while life-size Marvel superheroes loom on landings and in corridors. Twenty-two individually decorated rooms and suites mix original 19th-century frescoes and 1970s furniture. Shell out that little bit extra for a front room with a view of the lovely church façade. Some facilities, such as the conference and breakfast rooms, are shared with an adjoining sister establishment.

Grand Hotel Minerva

*Piazza Santa Maria Novella 16, Santa Maria Novella (055 27230, www. grandhotelminerva.com). **Map** p97 H6.*

Once an annex hosting guests to the adjacent convent, the Minerva has been a hotel since the mid 19th century, but is determinedly 21st century, with bright, modern colours and a young, dynamic team of staff. It's one of the nicest hotels in this category; it's also close to the train station. Many of the appealing rooms have sunny views over piazza Santa Maria Novella (it can get noisy in summer), while extras include in-room electric kettles, a kids' package of videos and games, and a shiatsu massage on request. Pet owners get a special deal (a room with a terrace and a wooden floor, cat litter and pet food) as do women travelling alone (room upgrades, special bath goodies, magazines, free room service). There's a small pool and a bar on the panoramic roof garden.

Hotel Davanzati

*Via Porta Rossa 5, Duomo & Around (055 286666, www.hoteldavanzati.it). **Map** p73 L8.*

The friendly owners know a thing or two about being good hosts: they invite guests to socialise over complimentary drinks and nibbles every day at 6.30pm, and provide free laptops and iPads with daily newspapers, streamed HD films and, of course, free Wi-Fi. Beamed ceilings, fragments of frescoes and chunks of exposed brickwork peep here and there, but the 19 rooms are pleasantly functional, spotlessly clean and offer a rare variety of combinations including family and interconnecting rooms. If you can handle the steep flight of 26 steps to the lift (the staff will help with the luggage) and unless you're hell bent on modern design, it's hard to find any drawbacks to this family-run gem set right next to the historic Palazzo Davanzati.

Hotel L'Orologio

Piazza Santa Maria Novella 24, Santa Maria Novella (055 277380, www. hotelorologioflorence.com). **Map** *p97 H5.*

If you like timepieces, you'll love this rather mad hotel – as the name implies, it's dedicated to great watches. Each of the five floors is themed around one brand – Patek Philippe, Rolex, but oddly no Timex – and each bedroom is themed around one vintage model; the public spaces (a grand foyer and pleasantly intimate drawing-room off it) are full of related art, antiques and furniture. A smart corridor leading to the plush and comfortable bar features a modern sundial on the floor. Breakfast is served on the fourth floor, which provides wonderful views across the city.

Soprarno Suites

Via Maggio 35, Oltrarno (055 0468718, www.soprarnosuites.com). **Map** *p142 H10.*

Located on the first and second floor of a 16th-century building at the heart of Florence's left bank quarter, Soprarno is a stylish B&B offering ten unique deluxe and superior rooms. The eclectic decor blends original frescoes with custom-made furniture and reflects the owners' passion for design and vintage pieces, ranging from printer's cabinets and clawfoot baths to neon signs. There's a pleasantly relaxed feel to the place, with plenty of books and magazines, vinyl records, an honesty bar and complimentary Wi-Fi. Guests are also welcome to use the first-floor kitchen-library-dining room where breakfast is served.

Mid-range
Art Atelier

Via dell'Amorino 20, San Lorenzo (055 283777, www.hotelartatelier.com). **Map** *p110 J5.*

Modern by Florentine standards, this 19th-century building exudes good taste and refinement. The rooms, many of them with vaulted ceilings and original features, use an intriguing mix of materials and decorating techniques – Carrara marble, stone, ceramics, frescoes and wall paintings – to create unusual spaces that are on the austere side, but not without charm, and there's an 'Art Atelier' space where exhibitions are held. Breakfast and service are very good, and the location is excellent – the Cappelle Medicee are within 100m, and the key sites in easy reach.

Il Guelfo Bianco

Via Cavour 29, San Marco (055 288330, www.ilguelfobianco.it). **Map** *p117 M4.*

Inhabiting two adjacent 15th-century townhouses, this pleasant, efficiently run hotel lies just north of the Duomo. The 40 bedrooms and one self-catering apartment (sleeping four) have been thoughtfully decorated in traditional style; the more capacious rooms allow for an additional two beds, making them a good choice for families. The walls throughout are hung with the owner's impressive contemporary art collection. The rooms that front on to via Cavour have been soundproofed, but those at the back are still noticeably quieter. Two attractive courtyards offer respite from the city noise; one is used for breakfast in warm weather.

Hotel dei Macchiaioli

Via Cavour 21, San Marco (055 213154, www.hoteldeimacchiaioli.com). **Map** *p117 M4.*

Opened in 2010, this well-placed boutique hotel will appeal to fans of the I Macchiaioli group of Tuscan artists.

This was their base for more than two decades in the mid 19th century. Palazzo Morrocchi, as it was then known, was filled with unusual frescoes by the group of artists, and many of them are still visible. The outstanding work is by Annibale Gatti – it covers the entire wooden ceiling of the main hall that looks out on to via Cavour. The rooms, all of them on the first floor, are old-fashioned and comfortable, and as charming as the staff.

Hotel Morandi alla Crocetta
Via Laura 50, San Marco (055 234 4748, www.hotelmorandi.it). **Map p117 P4.**
This hotel transports you back in time from the moment you enter the beautifully tiled entrance hall. With lovely Persian rugs on warm parquet floors, old-fashioned bedspreads in red and gold, and a sense of peace and calm that permeates the entire space. No wonder: the hotel is located in the former 16th-century convent of the Crocetta. Traces of the convent can be found in many of the rooms, with fresco fragments, vaulted ceilings and brick arches adding real individuality. Some rooms have terraces.

La Scaletta
Via de' Guicciardini 13, Oltrarno (055 283028, www.hotellascaletta.it). **Map p142 J10.**
A change of management in 2005 swept away the figurative cobwebs of the old-style Scaletta, housed in a grand 15th-century *palazzo* between the Ponte Vecchio and Palazzo Pitti, in favour of cleaner – even stylish – lines. The 11 buttermilk-painted bedrooms have elegant matching curtains and bedspreads, modern wrought-iron bedheads and nice old wardrobes. Most are quiet; three rooms overlook the Giardino di Boboli, while those on noisy via Guicciardini have effective double glazing. All rooms now have bathrooms. There are no fewer than three roof gardens/terraces that offer breathtaking views of Boboli and the city skyline; one has a bar that's open in the evenings.

Torre Guelfa
Borgo SS Apostoli 8, Duomo & Around (055 2396338, www.hoteltorreguelfa.com). **Map p73 K9.**
This popular hotel literally started at the top and worked its way down; the original rooms were all on the top floor, but the hotel now occupies the whole of the 14th-century *palazzo*, which incorporates the tallest privately owned tower in Florence. Evening drinks come with stunning views at the tower-top bar. Breakfast is served in a sunny, glassed-in loggia on the third floor, where there's also an elegant sitting room (with Wi-Fi access) with a painted box ceiling. Bedrooms are decorated in pastel colours with wrought-iron beds (including several four-posters); some are huge. Number 15 is a romantic little den with its own roof garden – you'll need to book at least six months in advance for this. The 12 rooms on the first floor are cheaper and simpler; those facing the street are quite dark.

Budget
Black 5 Townhouse
Via Giuseppe Verdi 5, Santa Croce (335 6368862, www.black5florencesuite.it). **Map p128 O8.**
From the outside, the curiously named Black 5 Townhouse looks like any other unprepossessing Florentine block. But once inside, the snazzy black and mirrored elevator gives a hint of things to come: animal skins on the floor, Pollock-esque art on the walls, and muted greys punctuated by bold splashes of colour. It's young, fresh and engaging, with each of the ten rooms spanning myriad gorgeous colours and styles – some have Pop Art wall coverings, others gloriously rich fabric headboards against lime green walls, and all come with wooden caisson ceilings, period brickwork and a whirlpool bath. Views are either over a central courtyard or the main road. The attic breakfast room opens on to a sweet little terrace with great views across the rooftops to Palazzo Vecchio and the Duomo.

Casa Pucci

Via Santa Monaca 8, Oltrarno (055 216560, www.casapucci.it). **Map** *p142 F10.*

Signora Pucci's ground-floor apartment, not far from buzzy piazza Santo Spirito, occupies part of an ex-convent dating from the 15th century. Three of the five rooms lead off a cool, plant-filled courtyard garden where a huge rustic table is laid in the mornings for summer breakfasts. The whole place has a nice, lived-in feel, from the big kitchen (which guests are free to use) to the spacious, homely rooms furnished with family antiques and paintings. Romantics should go for room no.5 with its four-poster bed and stone fireplace. A faithful clientele of return guests – plus amazingly low prices – means that you need to book well ahead.

Casa Schlatter

Viale dei Mille 14, Campo di Marte, Outside the City Gates (347 1180215, www.casaschlatter-florence.com). Bus 10, 17.

This characterful three-roomed B&B, just outside the city walls, was once the home and studio of idiosyncratic Swiss painter and sculptor Carlo Adolfo Schlatter. The conversion has been a wonderfully sympathetic one; the artist's work fills every available space and surface in the house, turning it into a strange but fascinating 19th-century museum that will ensure you get an eyeful of genuine weirdness at every turn, from bronze giant squids and gravestones to elegant canvases set on brilliant rose-coloured walls and unusual antique objects in the rooms. Schlatter's great-granddaughter Alessandra cooks amazing made-to-order savoury dishes and cakes for breakfast (which isn't included, but is great value at €7.50), serving them in a lovely garden.

Casci

Via Cavour 13, San Lorenzo (055 211686, www.hotelcasci.com). **Map** *p110 M4.*

The super-helpful Lombardi family runs this friendly pensione, which occupies a 15th-century *palazzo* just north of the Duomo, where opera composer Giacomo Rossini lived from 1851 to 1855. The open-plan bar and breakfast area has frescoed ceilings and shelves stocked with guidebooks; the 24 bedrooms are comfortable and come with up-to-date bathrooms. Rooms at the back look on to a beautiful garden; two sizeable family rooms sleep up to five. It's closed for three weeks in January.

Pensione Bencistà

Via Benedetto da Maiano 4, Fiesole, Outside the City Gates (055 59163, www. bencista.com). Bus 7.

Housed in a former convent and run as a pensione by the Simoni family since 1925, Bencistà has a fabulous setting on the hillside just below Fiesole. Public rooms are furnished with antiques; one has a fireplace and shelves stuffed with old books. Bedrooms are off a warren of passageways and staircases. No two are alike – those at the front enjoy unrivalled city views, as does the flower-filled terrace. The restaurant overlooks the city and serves homely, traditional food; half-board rates are available.

Scoti

Via de' Tornabuoni 7, Santa Maria Novella (055 292128, www.hotelscoti. com). **Map** *p97 J8.*

If you want to secure a room in the wonderful Scoti, housed on the second floor of a 15th-century palazzo, book well ahead: it's popular with visitors worldwide. The lofty bedrooms are simple but bright and sunny and all are en suite; the frescoed salon has retained its air of faded glory. Breakfast (charged extra) is served around a big communal table or in the rooms.

Getting Around

ARRIVING & LEAVING

By air

Amerigo Vespucci Airport at Peretola is by far the easiest way to reach Florence, but only CityJet and British Airways from London City Airport and Vueling from London Gatwick and Luton fly here. Pisa's **Galileo Galilei Airport** is a train or coach journey away from Florence, but it has frequent flights to and from the UK, and Delta operates a seasonal service to New York. A third choice is Bologna's **Guglielmo Marconi Airport**.

Florence Airport, Peretola (Amerigo Vespucci) 055 3061300, www.aeroporto.firenze.it.

About 5km (3 miles) west of central Florence, Amerigo Vespucci is linked to the city by **Volainbus** (800 373760, www.fsbusitalia.it), a bus shuttle service that runs half-hourly 5am-midnight, costs €6 (€10 return) and stops in the Busitalia station at via Santa Caterina da Siena 15. Buy tickets on the bus, at the airport bar or wherever bus tickets are sold. Tickets must be stamped on board. Bus season ticketholders don't have to buy an extra ticket. The new T2 tramway (*see opposite*) will run from the airport to the city centre and is expected to become operational early in 2018. A taxi to Florence costs from €22 (*see p176*) and takes 15-20 mins. For coaches to Pisa Airport, *see right*.

Pisa International Airport (Galileo Galilei) 050 849300, www.pisa-airport.com.

Direct trains to Florence no longer run all the way from the airport; you first need to reach Pisa Centrale by a shuttle bus costing €1.30 each way (in the process of being replaced by a faster but more expensive shuttle train). The train to Florence's Santa Maria Novella (SMN) station from Pisa Centrale takes about an hour and tickets are €8.40 each way.

A coach service from Pisa Airport to Florence SMN train station is run by **Autostradale** (050 6138469, www.autostradale.it). It leaves from outside the arrivals area in Pisa and from piazzale Montelungo in Florence (walk all the way down platform 16 inside the train station). Tickets can be bought from the kiosk in the airport, from Autostradale stewards at the terminus or online and cost €7.50 one way or €13.50 return. The journey takes 70 mins.

To get to Florence by car, take the Firenze–Pisa–Livorno road, which goes to the west of the city.

Bologna Airport (Guglielmo Marconi) 051 6479615, www.bologna-airport.it.

Aerobus (www.aerobus.bo.it) stops outside Terminal A (arrivals) and leaves for Bologna train station every 11 mins 5.30am-midnight. Tickets cost €6 from the machine in the terminal building and must be validated on board. The trip takes about 20 mins in total. A taxi costs about €15 (€18 at night).

From Bologna Centrale, trains to Florence are frequent and take 35-60 mins; prices vary. A downside of flying to Bologna is that you may find some trains to Florence fully booked, unless you've bought a ticket in advance.

The **Appennino Shuttle** (055 585271, www.appenninoshuttle.it) operates direct buses every couple of hours between Bologna Airport and piazzale Montelungo (near the Fortezza da Basso) in Florence. Tickets are €20 online, €25 on board and the journey is around 80 mins, but allow plenty of time for possible delays due to motorway traffic.

Travelling by car, the journey to Florence takes about 70 mins, south on the A1 motorway.

By rail

Train tickets can be bought online, from the ticket desks, from vending machines in the station, from www.trenitalia.com, or from selected travel agents.

Before boarding any train, stamp (*convalidare*) your ticket and any supplements in the yellow machines at the head of the platforms; failure to do so could mean a €50 fine.

The main station is Santa Maria Novella in the city centre. Some services go to **Campo di Marte** station to the north-east of the city. For train information call 892021 (24hrs daily) or visit www.trenitalia.com. Information on disabled access is available at the disabled assistance desk on platform 5 at Santa Maria Novella or by calling the national line 199 303060 (open 7am-9pm daily and English is spoken).

Campo di Marte *Via Mannelli, Outside the City Gates.*
Florence's main station when SMN is closed at night. Many long-distance trains stop here. The ticket office is open 6.20am-9pm daily.
Santa Maria Novella *Piazza della Stazione, Santa Maria Novella.* **Open** *4.15am-1.30am daily. Information office 7am-9pm daily. Ticket office 5am-10pm daily.* **Map** *p110 H4.*
Taxis serve Florence's Santa Maria Novella station on a 24-hr basis; many city buses also stop there. It's a five- to ten-minute walk into central Florence.

By road

Budget national and international coach travel is making a comeback. In Florence, you'll probably arrive using one of the following operators:
Eurolines/Baltour *(0861 1991900, www.eurolines.it) stopping at the Busitalia bus station in via Santa Caterina da Siena 15.*
Flixbus *(02 94759208, www.flixbus. it) stopping in piazzale Montelungo (viale Filippo Strozzi by the Fortezza da Basso, Outside the City Gates).*

Bus services

Public bus company ATAF *(800 424500, 199 104245 from mobiles, www. ataf.net).* **Open** *6.45am-8pm Mon-Sat.*
The ATAF infopoint (Santa Maria Novella station ticket hall, counters 8-9) has English-speaking staff, sells a variety of bus tickets, and has a free booklet with details of major routes and fares. The official app is Ataf 2.0.

Fares & tickets

It's cheaper to buy tickets before boarding buses, but you can now also get them on board from the driver at €2 for 90 mins. Tickets are available from the ATAF desk (*see above*), a few machines, *tabacchi* (tobacconists), news stands and any bars displaying an ATAF sticker. When you board, stamp the ticket in one of the validation machines. Bus tickets are also valid for trams (*see p176*). Be aware that plain-clothes inspectors regularly board buses for spot checks; anyone without a valid ticket is fined €50, payable on the spot or within 15 days at the main information office or in post offices.
90 min ticket *(biglietto 90 minuti)* €1.20; *valid for 90 mins of travel on all city area buses.*
Multiple ticket *(biglietto multiplo)* €4.70; *4 tickets, each valid for 90 mins.*
AGILE electronic cards *€10/€20/€30 with 10/21/35 x 90-min tickets respectively (swipe once over validating machine).*
24-hr ticket *(biglietto ventiquattro ore)* €5; *one-day pass that must be stamped at the start of the first journey.*
Daily family *€6; valid for up to 4 family members to midnight on the day of stamping.*
3-day ticket *(biglietto tre giorni)* €12.
7-day ticket *(biglietto sette giorni)* €18.
Monthly and yearly passes are also available.
Most ATAF routes run from 5.30am to midnight with a frequency of 10-30 mins. The orange and white *fermate* (bus stops) list the main stops

along the route. Each of the stops has its name indicated at the top.

Disabled travellers

Most buses across Florence are now of the newer design (grey and green) and are fully wheelchair accessible via an electric platform at the rear door. The older orange buses are sadly not.

Useful tourist routes

7 from piazza San Marco to Fiesole.

10 to and from Settignano.

12, **13** circular routes via Santa Maria Novella station, piazza della Libertà, piazzale Michelangelo and San Miniato. ATAF also runs a network of electric buses, which covers four central routes: **C1**, **C2**, **C3** and **D**. Normal bus tickets or season tickets are valid. These routes are detailed in ATAF's booklet and at www.ataf.net.

Tram services

The T1 **Tramvia** line from central Florence to Scandicci is up and running. Two more lines are due to be operational in 2018; T2 will serve the airport, while T3 will reach the Careggi hospital north of the city centre. For further information, visit www.gestramvia.it.

TAXIS

Licensed cabs are white with yellow graphics, with a code name of a place plus ID number on the door; 'Londra 6', for example. If you have problems, make a note of this code. You can only get a cab at a rank or by phone. Ranks are indicated by a blue sign with TAXI written in white, but this is no guarantee that any cars will be waiting. Try piazza della Repubblica, piazza della Stazione, piazza San Marco and piazza Santa Croce.

Fares & surcharges

Taxis in Florence are expensive. When the taxi arrives, the meter should read €3.30 during the day, €5.30 on Sun and on public hols, and €6.60 at night. The fare increases at a rate of €0.91/km. Lone women pay 10% less after 9pm, but only if they request the discount when booking. There is a daytime minimum fare of €5; €7 minimum on Sun and public hols; and a nighttime minimum fare of €8.30. Taxis between the airport and anywhere in the city centre have a fixed tariff of €22 in the day, €25.30 at night, plus €1 per piece of luggage.

Phone cabs

Try to book a cab at least a few hours before you need it. When your call is answered, give the address where you want to be picked up, specifying if the street number is *nero* or *rosso* (for an explanation, *see p179*). If a cab is available, you'll be given its code and a time; for example, '*Londra 6 in tre minuti*'. If not, a message or operator will tell you to call back.

Taxi numbers 055 4390; 055 4798; 055 4242; 055 4499.

DRIVING

The centre of Florence is easily walkable and the electric bus service is a good back-up so it's usually best to leave cars at home, particularly given the permanent and expanding Traffic-Free Zones (ZTL), which include the old city centre. Only residents or permit-holders can enter 7.30am-8pm, Mon-Fri; 7.30am-4pm Sat. This is usually extended in the summer to exclude cars from the centre in the evenings Thur-Sun.

Speed limits are currently 50kmph (30mph), or 45kmph (26mph) on motorbikes and mopeds, on urban roads; 70kmph (43mph) on urban highways; 90kmph (56mph) on secondary extra-urban roads (*superstrada*); 110kmph (68mph) on dual carriageways and 130kmph (80mph) on the motorway (*autostrada*).

Superstrada are free roads and have blue signs and a name beginning SS. *Autostrada* are toll roads and are indicated by green signs.

In a traffic emergency call 055 3285 (055 328 3333 for less urgent situations). For general traffic or parking information, call 055055 (8am-8pm Mon-Sat).

Breakdown services
Automobile Club d'Italia (ACI)
Viale Amendola 36, Outside the City Gates (055 24861/ 24hr emergencies 803 116 or 800 000 116, www.aci.it).
Bus 8, 12, 13, 14, 31. **Open** 8.30am-1pm, 3-5.30pm Mon-Fri.

The ACI charges reasonable rates and will tell you what to do in case of a breakdown. Members of associated organisations such as the AA, RAC or AAA may be entitled to free basic repairs or preferential rates.

Car hire
Avis, Europcar, Hertz and all the usual suspects operate from a car rental hub in via Palagio degli Spini near the airport (shuttle bus available from the airport car park).

Renting an electric car is a very practical option as you can drive them throughout most of the city centre. One conveniently central company offering electric car hire is **ELP** (055 2399231, www.citycarrent.org).

Car pounds
If your car's not where you left it, chances are it's been towed. Call 055 4224142 with the car's registration number to confirm. The central car pound, Depositeria SaS (www.serviziallastrada.it; open 8am-8pm Mon-Fri, 8am-7pm Sat; closed Sun), is in via Allende, behind the Novoli fruit and veg market (bus 23 or 57). The car owner must take proof of ownership and ID to regain possession.

If your car is stolen and found, it will be taken to the Ufficio Depositeria Comunale in via Benedetto Dei 2a (055 3283951). The office is open 8am-12.45pm Mon-Fri, and Thur to 6pm.

Parking
Parking in Florence is a major problem and is severely restricted – most main streets are no-parking zones. Parking is forbidden where you see *passo carrabile* (access at all times) and *sosta vietata* (no parking) signs. Beware of white lines, they can mean either free parking, or reserved parking for residents only (check vertical signage to confirm). Blue lines denote pay-parking; there will be either meters or an attendant to issue timed tickets, which you should return to them when you get back. Disabled spaces are marked by yellow stripes and require a permit. *Zona rimozione* (tow-away area) signs are valid for the length of the street, while temporary tow zones are marked at each end. Signs tell you when street cleaning takes place – your car will be towed if parked on a street being cleaned.

The safest place to leave a car is in one of the underground car parks (*parcheggi*), such as **Parterre** and **Piazza Stazione**, which both have surveillance cameras.

CYCLING

Moped & bike hire
Mille e Una Bici (www.bicifirenze.it) is a council-supported scheme to encourage the use of bikes. There are hire points all around the city including at the three main train stations, piazza Ghiberti, Parterre and Stazione Leopolda. Bike hire costs either €2/hr or €10/day.

The company below also rent out bikes. To hire a scooter or moped (*motorino*), you need a credit card, ID and cash deposit. Helmets must be worn on all mopeds.

Florence by Bike
Via San Zanobi 54r, San Lorenzo (055 488992, www.florencebybike.it). **Open** 9am-1pm, 3.30-7.30pm Mon-Fri; (9am-7pm Sat; 9am-5pm Sun. Shorter hours in winter. **Map** p110 L2.
Bike hire costs either €3/hr or €14/day. Guided tours are also available, and the majority of staff speak good English.

WALKING

Our street maps cover most of the centre, and a good street map is available free from tourist offices. For an overview map, *see p8*.

Resources A-Z

ACCIDENT & EMERGENCY

Emergency numbers
Ambulance *Ambulanza* **118**.
City traffic police *Vigili Urbani* **055 3285** (emergency).
Emergency services & state police
Polizia di Stato **113**.
Fire service *Vigili del Fuoco* **115**.
Police *Carabinieri* (English-speaking helpline) **112**.

A&E departments
If you need urgent medical care, it's best to go to the *pronto soccorso* (casualty) department of one of the hospitals listed below; they're open 24 hrs daily. Alternatively, call 118 for an ambulance (*ambulanza*).

To find a doctor on call in your area (emergencies only), phone 118. For a night (8pm-8am) or all-day Sun emergency home visit, call the **Guardia Medica** for your area (quartiere 1: 055 6938980; Oltrarno: 055 215616).
Ospedale di Careggi Largo
Brambilla 3, Outside the City Gates (055 794 111, www.aou-careggi.toscana.it).
Bus 2, 8, 14C. The main hospital and the best place to go to for most emergencies.
Ospedale Meyer *Viale Pieraccini 24, Outside the City Gates (055 56621, www. meyer.it). Bus 14C. Children's hospital.*
Ospedale Palagi Viale *Michelangelo 41, Outside the City Gates (055 65771). Bus 12, 13. Open 8am-8pm daily. For eye emergencies.*
Santa Maria Nuova *Piazza Santa Maria Nuova 1, San Marco (055 69381). Map p97 N6. The most central hospital in Florence. There's also a 24-hr pharmacy directly outside.*
If you need a translator to help out at the hospital, contact:
AVO (Association of Hospital Volunteers) *Via G Carducci 8, Outside the City Gates (24hrs 055 2344567, www.avofirenze.it). Open Office hours 10am-midday, 4-8pm Mon-Fri; closed Aug. AVO has a group of volunteer interpreters who help out with explanations to doctors and hospital staff in 22 languages. They also give support and advice.*

Travel Advice
For up-to-date information on travel to a specific country – including the latest on safety and security, health issues, local laws and customs – contact your government's department of foreign affairs. Most have websites with useful advice for would-be travellers.

Australia
www.smartraveller.gov.au

Republic of Ireland
foreignaffairs.gov.ie

Canada
www.voyage.gc.ca

UK
www.fco.gov.uk/travel

New Zealand
www.safetravel.govt.nz

USA
www.state.gov/travel

ADDRESSES

Addresses in Florence are numbered and colour-coded. Residential addresses are 'black' numbers (*nero*), while most commercial addresses are 'red' (*rosso*).

ATTITUDE & ETIQUETTE

In churches, women are expected to cover their shoulders and not wear anything skimpy. Shorts and vests are out for everyone.

Queues are a foreign concept, but in a crowded shop, customers know who is before them and who's after, and usually respect the order. In shops, say *buongiorno* or *buona sera* on entering and leaving, and bear in mind that it's generally considered rude to walk in, look around and leave without asking for what you are looking for or at least greeting the shop assistant.

When addressing anyone except children, it's important to use the appropriate title: *signora* for women, *signorina* for young women, and *signore* for men.

DISABLED

Disabled facilities in Florence are improving. Recent laws stipulate that all new public offices, bars, restaurants and hotels must be equipped with full disabled facilities. Currently, the standard of access still varies greatly, though most museums are wheelchair-accessible, with lifts, ramps on steps and toilets for the disabled.

Pavement corners in the centre of town are now sloped to allow for wheelchair access. New buses are equipped with ramps and a wheelchair area. Trains that allow space for wheelchairs in the carriages and have disabled toilets have a wheelchair logo on the outside, but there is no wheelchair access up the steep steps on the south side of the station: use the east or north entrance, or call the information office for assistance (*see p185*). Taxis take wheelchairs, but tell them when you book.

There are free disabled parking bays all over Florence, and disabled drivers with the sticker have access to pedestrian areas of the city. There are wheelchair-accessible toilets at Florence and Pisa airports and Santa Maria Novella station, as well as in many of Florence's main sights and at several public toilets.

The Tourist Board produces a booklet (also in English, available in print from tourist offices or as a PDF downloadable from www.firenzeturismo.it) with disabled-aware descriptions of venues across Florence Province. The official council website (www.comune.fi.it) also has useful sightseeing itineraries suitable for disabled visitors.

Wheelchair hire is free of charge both from the Misericordia (055 212222) and the Fratellanza Militare (055 26021). If they don't have any available, they can refer to paid hire services.

EMBASSIES & CONSULATES

There are no embassies in Florence. However, there are some consular offices, which offer limited services.

Australian Embassy *Via Antonio Bosio 5, Rome (06 852721, www.italy.embassy.gov.au).*

British Embassy *Via Venti Settembre 80A, Rome (06 4220 0001, www.gov.uk/government/world/italy).*

Canadian Embassy *Via Zara 30, Rome (06 854442911, www.italy.gc.ca).*

Irish Embassy *Piazza Campitelli 3, Ghetto, Rome (06 6979121, www.embassyofireland.it).*

New Zealand Embassy *Via Clitunno 44, Rome (06 8537501/ www.nzembassy.com/italy).*

South African Honorary Consulate *Piazza dei Salterelli 1, Duomo & Around (055 281863, lnx.sudafrica.it/en).* No office. Call to make an appointment.

US Consulate *Lungarno Amerigo Vespucci 38, Outside the City Gates (055 266951, it.usembassy.gov). Bus D.* **Open** *9am-12.30pm Mon-Fri.* In case of emergency call the above phone

number; a message refers you to the current emergency number.
For details of all other embassies, see embassy.goabroad.com.

HEALTH

Emergency healthcare is available for all travellers through the Italian national health system. EU citizens are entitled to most treatment for free, though many specialised medicines, examinations and tests will be charged for. To get treatment, you'll need a European Health Insurance Card (EHIC). The card will only cover partial costs of medicines. In non-emergency situations, citizens from countries with a reciprocal agreement with Italy (e.g. Australia) should go to the state health centre, **Azienda Sanitaria di Firenze** (ASF, www.asf.toscana.it) on the second floor of borgo Ognissanti 20 (open 9am-1pm Mon-Fri). Other non-EU visitors are charged for health care. All foreign visitors are strongly advised to take out private health insurance before travelling.

For hospital treatment, go to one of the casualty departments listed above (*see p178* Accident & emergency). If you want to see a GP, go to the **ASL** (Azienda Sanitaria Locale, local health unit) for the district where you are staying, taking your EHIC with you. The ASLs are listed in the phone book and they usually open 9am-1pm and 2-7pm Mon-Fri.

Dentists

The following dentists speak English. Always call ahead for an appointment.
Dr Marcello Luccioli *Via de' Serragli 21, Oltrarno (055 294847).* **Open** *3-6.30pm Mon, Tue, Thur. Map p142 F10.*

Dr Alessandro Cosi *Via Quintino Sella 4, Outside the City Gates (055 214238/ 335 332055 mobile). Bus 14.* **Open** *9am-1pm, 3-7pm Mon-Fri.*

Doctors & clinics

A comprehensive list of English-speaking doctors and medical facilities in Florence, by specialisation, can be provided by the American Consulate (*see opposite*).
Clinica Dermatologica *Ospedale Palagi, viale Michelangelo 41, Outside the City Gates (055 6939654). Bus 12, 13.* **Open** *8am-noon Mon, Wed, Fri; 8-11am Tue, Thur. Map p73. Clinica Dermatologica carries out Examinations, tests, treatment and counselling for all sexually transmitted diseases, including HIV and AIDS. Some services are free, while others are state-subsidised. Some staff speak English.*

Dr Stephen Kerr *Piazza del Mercato Nuovo, Duomo & Around (055 288055/335 8361682, www.dr-kerr. com).* **Open** *Surgery by appointment 9am-3pm Mon-Fri. Drop-in clinic 3-5pm Mon-Fri. Map p73 K8. This friendly, knowledgeable English GP practises privately in Florence. Standard charge for a consultation in his surgery is €60.*

Medical Service *Via Roma 4, Duomo & Around (24hr line 055 475411, www. medicalservice.firenze.it).* **Open** *Clinic 11am-noon, 1-3pm Mon-Sat; 5-6pm Mon-Fri. Map p73 L7. A private medical service that organises home visits. Catering particularly to foreigners, it promises to send an English-speaking GP or specialist out to you in the city of Florence within an hour for a fee of €70-€200. Clinic visit €50-€60.*

Pharmacies

Pharmacies (*farmacia*), which are identified by a red or green cross hanging outside, function semi-officially as mini-clinics, with staff able to give informal medical advice and suggest non-prescription medicines. Normal opening hours are 8.30am-1pm and 4-8pm Mon-Fri and 8.30am-1pm Sat, but many central pharmacies are open all day. Prescriptions are required for most medicines. If you require regular medication, make sure you know their chemical (generic) rather than brand name, as they may be available in Italy only under a different name.

ID

In Italy, you're required by law to carry photo ID at all times. You'll be asked to produce it if you're stopped by traffic police (who will demand your driving licence, which you must have on you whenever you are in charge of a motor vehicle). ID will also be required when you check into a hotel.

INSURANCE

EU nationals are entitled to reciprocal medical care in Italy, provided they are in possession of a European Health Insurance Card (EHIC; *see p180*).

Despite this provision, short-term visitors from all countries are advised to get private travel insurance to cover a broad number of eventualities (from injury to theft). Non-EU citizens should always ensure that they take out comprehensive medical insurance with a reputable company before leaving home.

Visitors should also take out adequate property insurance before setting off for Italy. If you rent a car, motorcycle or moped, make sure that you pay the extra for full insurance and sign the collision damage waiver before taking off in the vehicle. It's also worth checking your home insurance first, as it may already cover you.

LEFT LUGGAGE

There's a left luggage point in Santa Maria Novella train station open 6am-11pm daily on platform 16 (055 9337749, www.kipoint.it). The minimum charge is €6 for the first five hrs.

LGBT

IREOS-Queer Community Service *Center Via de' Serragli 3, Oltrarno (055 216907, www.ireos.org).*

Open 6-8pm Mon-Thur, Sat. **Map** *p142 G9.* Ireos hosts social open houses and offers HIV testing, referrals for psychological counselling and self-help groups. It also organises hikes and outings and has free internet access most evenings and Sat mornings. See website for details.

Queer Nation Holidays *Via del Moro 95r, Santa Maria Novella (055 2654587, www.qnholidays.it).* **Open** *9.30am-6pm Mon-Fri; 9am-1pm Sat.* **Map** *p97 J6.* This tour operator and travel agent can organise individual and group travel. It can also make referrals to other gay and lesbian organisations.

LOST PROPERTY

Property found throughout the city (including ATAF buses) is sent to the municipal *Ufficio Oggetti Trovati* (Lost & Found Office), Via Veracini 5/5, Outside the City Gates (055 334802). Bus 17. Open 9am-12.30pm Mon, Wed, Fri; 2.30-4pm Tue, Thur. A fee upwards of €3.50 is charged for the service.

The Amerigo Vespucci Airport uploads a photographic record of found objects on its website www.aeroporto.firenze.it. For more information email oggettismarriti@aeroporto.firenze.it.

MONEY

Italy is in the euro (€) zone. There are euro banknotes for €5, €10, €20, €50, €100, €200 and €500, and coins worth €1 and €2, plus 1¢, 2¢, 5¢, 10¢, 20¢ and 50¢ (cents). Credit cards are widely accepted, though AmEx and Diners Club slightly less so than Visa and MasterCard. Travellers' cheques can still be changed at all banks and bureaux de change but are only accepted as payment (in any major currency) by larger shops, hotels and restaurants.

Banks & ATMs

Expect long queues in banks even for simple transactions, and don't be surprised if the bank wants to photocopy your passport or driving licence as proof of ID. Many banks no longer give cash advances on credit cards, so check for the signs, or ask before queuing. Branches of most banks are found around piazza della Repubblica.

In Italy, ATMs are known as *Bancomat*, which is also the colloquial name for debit cards. Select English as the operating language and, if possible, use ATMs located outside a post office (*postamat*) or a bank branch and do so during banking hours (*see p182 Opening hours*), so there is assistance available if needed.

Bureaux de change

Changing your money in a bank usually gets you a better rate than in a private bureau de change (*cambio*) and will often be better than in your home country. However, if you need to change money out of banking hours, there's no shortage of bureaux de change (*cambi*). Commission rates vary considerably: Always take ID for any financial transaction.

InterChange *Via Por Santa Maria 35r, Duomo & Around (055 214500, www.interchange.eu).* **Open** *10am-8pm daily.* **Map** *p97 L9.* One of the few exchange offices open on Sun. No commission for cash withdrawal via MasterCard or Visa.

Credit cards

Italians have an enduring fondness for cash, but nearly all hotels of two stars and above, as well as most shops and restaurants (though still surprisingly few museums), accept at least some of the major credit cards.

Lost/stolen

Most lines are freephone (800) numbers, have English-speaking staff and are open 24 hrs daily.
American Express card *emergencies* 06 72282.
Diners Club 800 393939.
CartaSì 800 151616.
MasterCard 800 870866.
Visa 800 819014.

Tax

Sales tax (IVA) is applied to all purchases and services at 4%, 10% and 22% in an ascending scale of luxury, but is almost always included in the price stated. At some luxury hotels, tax will be added on to the quoted rates, but prices will be clearly stated as *escluso* IVA.

By law, all non-EU residents are entitled to an IVA refund on purchases of €155 and over at shops participating in the 'Tax-free shopping' scheme, identified by a purple sticker. On presentation of your passport, they will give you a 'cheque' that can be cashed at the airport desk on your way home at the Tax Free Cash Refund desk at the airport. You'll need to show your passport and the unused goods, and there's a three-month time limit. IVA paid on hotel bills cannot be reclaimed.

OPENING HOURS

Bank opening hours are generally 8.20am-1.20pm and 2.35-3.35pm Mon-Fri. All banks are closed on public holidays.

Most **post offices** open 8.15am-1.30pm, closing an hour earlier on Sat; the main post office stays open 8.15am-7pm Mon-Sat (*see right*).

Food shops generally open early in the morning and close for lunch 1pm-3.30pm (some stay closed till 5pm); then open again until 7.30pm. They are generally closed on Wed afternoons (Sat afternoons in summer).
Other shops tend to open later in the morning and are closed on Mon mornings. Many shops now stay open all day (*orario continuato*).

POLICE

In an emergency, go to the tourist aid police or the nearest *carabinieri* post or police station (*questura*); we have listed central ones below, but others are found in the phone book. Staff will either speak English or be able to find someone who does. If you have had something stolen, tell them you want to report a *furto*.

A statement (*denuncia*) will be taken, which you'll need for an insurance claim. Lost or stolen passports should also be reported to your embassy or consulate. (*See p178* Accident & emergency.)

Comando Provinciale Carabinieri *Borgo Ognissanti 48, Santa Maria Novella (055 2061, 055 27661).* **Open** 24hrs daily. **Map** p97 F6. A *carabinieri* post near the town centre; the best place to report the loss or theft of personal property.

Questura di Firenze Ufficio Denuncie *Via Zara 2, San Lorenzo (055 49771).* **Open** 24hrs daily. **Map** p110 N1. To report a crime, go to the Ufficio Denuncie, where you will be asked to fill in a form.

Police *Via Pietrapiana 50r, Santa Croce (055 203911).* **Open** 8.30am-12.30pm Mon, Wed, Fri; 3-4.30pm Thur. **Map** p128 P7. Interpreters are on hand to help report thefts, lost property and any other problems.

POSTAL SERVICES

Stamps (*francobolli*) can be bought at *tabacchi* or post offices. Most post boxes are red and have two slots, Per la Città (for Florence) and Tutte le Altre Destinazioni (everywhere else).

A letter takes about five days to reach the UK, eight to the US. There are now two classes of post (*posta prioritaria*) called Posta1 and Posta4, which generally fulfil the next-day or four-day delivery promise in Italy. A small letter or postcard weighing 20g or less sent to addresses in Italy costs €2.80 by Posta1 and 95¢ by Posta4.

Postamail Internazionale to any EU country costs €1 (estimated delivery 8 days); to the US, it'll cost €2.20 (16 days); sending mail further afield will cost €2.90 (22 days). A faster but more expensive option is Postapriority Internazionale: €3.50 and 3 days to the UK, €4.50 and 6 days to North America, €5.50 and 8 days to Australia.

Heavier mail is charged according to weight. For guaranteed fast delivery, use a courier or the SDA Italian post office courier service.

The Italian post call centre number is 803160. Officially Italian only, though you may strike lucky.

Post offices

Local post offices (*ufficio postale*) in each district generally open 8.15am-1.30pm Mon-Fri; 8.15am-12.30pm Sat. The main post office (Posta Centrale) has longer opening hours and a range of additional services.

Posta Centrale *Via Pellicceria 3, Duomo & Around (055 2736481).* **Open** 8.15am-7pm Mon-Fri; 8.15am-12.30pm Sat. **Map** p73 K8. This is Florence's main post office.

Poste restante

Poste restante (general delivery) letters (in Italian, *fermoposta*) should be sent to the main post office (*see above*), addressed to Fermoposta and the code and address of the post office you wish to pick up your mail from. You need a passport to collect mail and you may have to pay a small charge if sent from outside Italy (if sent from Italy a charge of €3 is added to the postage). Mail can also be sent to any Mail Boxes Etc. (MBE) branches.

PUBLIC HOLIDAYS

On public holidays (*giorni festivi*) virtually all shops, banks and businesses are shut, though most bars and restaurants stay open so you will be able to eat and drink. Public holidays are as follows:

New Year's Day (*Capodanno*) 1 Jan
Epiphany (*La Befana*) 6 Jan
Easter Day (*Pasqua*)
Easter Monday (*Lunedì di Pasqua*)
Liberation Day (*Venticinque Aprile/ Liberazione*) 25 Apr
Labour Day (*Primo Maggio*) 1 May
Republic Day (*Festa della Repubblica*) 2 June
Florence Saint's Day (*San Giovanni*) 24 June

Feast of the Assumption
(Ferragosto) 15 Aug
All Saints' *(Tutti i Santi)* 1 Nov
Immaculate Conception *(Festa dell'Immacolata)* 8 Dec
Christmas Day *(Natale)* 25 Dec
Boxing Day *(Santo Stefano)* 26 Dec

There is limited public transport on 1 May and Christmas afternoon. Holidays falling on a Sat or Sun are not celebrated the following Mon, but if a holiday falls on a Thur or Tue, many locals also take the intervening day off and make a long weekend of it; such a weekend is called a *ponte* (bridge). Beware of the *rientro* or homecoming, when the roads are horrendously busy.

Many people also disappear for a large chunk of Aug, when *chiuso per ferie* (closed for holidays) signs appear in shops and restaurants detailing dates of closure. These closures are co-ordinated on a rota system by the city council, so there should be something open in each area at any given time.

SAFETY & SECURITY

Crime has slightly decreased in Tuscany in recent years. Serious street crime is rare, and Florence remains a relatively safe city to walk in. Take care at night, when lone women in particular should stick to the main well-lit streets. For visitors to the city, the main risk comes from the numerous pickpockets and bag-snatchers. Buses, shops, bars and other crowded areas are petty criminals' hunting grounds. As you would in any major city, take common-sense precautions:

• Don't keep wallets in back pockets. This is a pickpocket's favourite swipe, especially on buses and public transport.
• Wear shoulder bags diagonally and facing away from the road to minimise the risk of *scippi* – bag-snatching from mopeds, which is still common in the city.
• Never leave bags on tables or the backs of chairs in bars.
• Keep an eye on your valuables while trying on clothes and shoes.
• Watch out for 'baby-gangs' of children or teenagers who hang around the tourist spots and create a distraction by flapping a newspaper or card while trying to slip their hands into bags or pockets. If you are approached, keep walking, keep calm and hang on to your valuables.

For emergency numbers, *see p178*. For information on the police, *see p182*.

SMOKING

A law banning smoking in all public places came into force in 2005 and is scrupulously respected and enforced. This includes bars, restaurants and clubs, although there is a clause that allows some venues to set aside a smoking room, as long as it is separated by double doors and adequately ventilated and filtered. Owners who allow customers to smoke are fined heavily; the smoker can also be fined. Cigarettes are on sale at *tabacchi* and *bar-tabacchi*; both are recognisable by the blue/black and white sign outside.

TELEPHONES & INTERNET

Dialling & codes
The international code for Italy is 39. To dial in from other countries, preface it with the exit code: 00 in the UK and 011 in the US. All normal Florence numbers begin with the area code 055. This must always be used in full, even when you are calling from within the same area, and when dialling internationally. Italian mobile phone numbers begin with 3 (no zero).

To make an international call from Florence, dial 00, then the country code (Australia 61; Canada 1; Irish Republic 353; New Zealand 64; United Kingdom 44; United States 1), followed by the area code (for calls to the UK, omit the initial zero) and individual number. The same pattern works to mobile phones.

All numbers beginning 800 are free lines (*numero verde*). Phone numbers starting with 3 are mobile numbers; those with 199 codes are charged at local rates; 167 numbers are billed at premium rates.

Mobile phones

Basic pay-as-you-go mobiles can be bought from many phone shops and some post offices from around €20, including the SIM card and €5 of calls. Top-up cards are available from all *bar-tabacchi* and some newsstands; either call the number given on the card, or, if the bar has the electronic top-up facility, tap in your phone number and the amount requested will be credited automatically. One top-up has to be made at least every 11 mths to keep the number active. If your device is unlocked, SIM cards can also be bought without having to buy a phone; prices vary.

Operator services

To make a reverse-charge (collect) call, dial 170 for the international operator in Italy. To be connected to the operator in the country you want to call, dial 172 followed by a country code (so 172 00 44 for the UK and 172 00 1 for the US) and you'll be connected directly to an operator in that country.

Wi-Fi

Many restaurants, cafes and hotels offer free Wi-Fi. The city of Florence also offers 500Mb (or 2 hrs, whichever limit you hit first) free internet traffic per user per day in many popular tourist locations across town. Just watch out for the *FirenzeWiFi* network to pop up in your hotspot list, click *Free Internet* from your browser and you're ready to surf. SIM cards with data plans may be purchased from the main mobile operators (*see above*).

TIME

Italy is one hour ahead of London, six ahead of New York and eight behind Sydney. Clocks go forward an hour on the last Sun in Mar and back on the last Sun in Oct, in line with other EU countries.

TIPPING

The 10-15% tip customary in many countries is considered generous in Florence. Locals sometimes leave a few coins on the counter when buying drinks at the bar and, depending on the standard of the restaurant, will drop €1-€5 for the service after a meal. That said, some larger restaurants are now starting to add a 10-15% service charge on the bill automatically. Tips are not expected in small restaurants, although they are always appreciated. Taxi drivers will be surprised if you do more than add a euro or two.

TOILETS

Always visit the restrooms whenever you stop at a bar, restaurant or museum because public toilets are few and far between and cost around €1 to use. Locate the nearest public facilities (including wheelchair-accessible toilets) with the official *Firenze Turismo* app (*see p186*). Of course you can do as the locals do and, for about the same price, purchase a small bottle of water or gulp an espresso from a bar and use the establishment's facilities instead – just make sure the toilet is available before placing your order!

TOURIST INFORMATION

To be sent an information pack in advance of your visit, get in touch with ENIT, the Italian tourist board (UK: 020 7408 1254, www.italia.it; US: 212 245 5618, www.italiantourism.com). Tell staff where and when you're travelling, and whether or not you have any special interests.

In Florence, the tourist information service is operated jointly by the Tourism departments of Comune di Firenze and Città Metropolitana. The official website www.firenzeturismo. it has a useful download area with informative maps and brochures in PDF format. The helpful, multilingual staff do their best to supply reliable information: not easy, since museums and galleries tend to change their hours without telling them. There's no central information service for the Tuscany region; you have to contact the APT in each area. There is a head office in each provincial capital, then local offices in various towns within the province. Details are given in the Day Trips chapter.

Tourist information offices
Via Cavour 1r, San Lorenzo (055 290832). **Open** *Summer 8.15am-7.15pm Mon-Sat; 8.30am-1.30pm Sun. Winter 8.15am-7.15pm Mon-Sat.* **Map** *p110 L5.*

Parco delle Cascine Visitor Centre *piazzale delle Cascine, Outside the City Gates (055 365707).* **Open** *10am-4pm Fri, 10am-5pm Sat-Sun.*

Infopoint Bigallo *piazza San Giovanni 1, Duomo & Around (055 288496).* **Open** *9am-7pm Mon-Sat; 9am-2pm Sun.* **Map** *p73 L6.*

Piazza della Stazione 4a *Santa Maria Novella (055 212245).* **Open** *9am-7pm Mon-Sat; 9am-2pm Sun.* **Map** *p97 H4.*

Run by the City of Florence, these offices provide maps and info. There are also offices in Florence and Pisa airports. Tourist information offices cannot provide hotel booking services. *See p166* Accommodation for more details.

Useful apps
Useful apps that you may want to install on your device before your visit include:
ATAF 2.0 Official app of the bus and tram network. Free.
Firenze Turismo Official app of the Tourist Board. Map-based search of museums, restaurants, facilities, services, accessibility and events. Free.
Florence Heritage Combining historical and contemporary Florence with 12 suggested itineraries. Free.
Inferno Florence Guide Written by editors of local events website The Florentine this app is for Dan Brown fans. Follow in the footsteps of Inferno with a map of locations, 31 listening points around the city, original photos and more. £2.99
Uffizi: The Official Guide Aimed to help you make the most of your Uffizi experience with a guide to exhibition rooms, key artworks, artists and an interactive map allowing virtual access to each room. £3.99

VISAS & IMMIGRATION

Non-EU and UK citizens require full passports to travel to Italy. EU citizens are permitted unrestricted access to Italy to travel; citizens of the USA, Canada, Australia and New Zealand should check about visa requirements at an Italian embassy or consulate in their own country before setting off for Italy.

WEIGHTS & MEASURES

Italy uses only the metric system; remember that all speed limits are in kilometres (km): 1km = 0.62 miles; 1 mile = 1.6km. Petrol, like other liquids, is measured in litres: 1 UK gallon = 4.54l; 1 US gallon = 3.79l. A kilogram (kg) is equivalent to 2.2lbs (1lb = 0.45kg). Food is often sold in *etti* (sometimes written hg); 1 *etto* = 100g (3.52oz). In delicatessens, ask for multiples of *etti* (un *etto*, due *etti*, etc).

Vocabulary

Pronunciation

Vowels

a   as in **a**pple
e   like a in **a**ge (closed e), or **e** in s**e**ll (open e)
i   like **ea** in **ea**st
o   as in h**o**tel (closed o) or in h**o**t (open o)
u   like **oo** in b**oo**t

Consonants

c   before a, o or u: like the **c** in **c**at; **before e or i: like the ch in check**
ch   like the **c** in **c**at
g   before a, o or u: like the **g** in **g**et; **before e or i: like the j in jig**
gh   like the **g** in **g**et
gl   followed by 'i': like **lll** in mi**lli**on
gn   like **ny** in ca**ny**on
qu   as in **qu**ick
r   is always rolled
s   has two sounds, as in **s**oap or ro**s**e
sc   followed by 'e' or 'i': like the **sh** in **sh**ame
sch   like the **sc** in **sc**out
z   has two sounds, like **ts** and **dz**
Double consonants are sounded more emphatically.

Useful words & phrases

hello and goodbye (informal) ciao; **good morning, good day** buongiorno; **good afternoon, good evening** buona sera; **I don't understand** non capisco/non ho capito; **do you speak English?** parla inglese?; **please** per favore; **thank you** grazie; **you're welcome** prego; **when does it open?** quando apre?; **where is...?** dov'è...?; **excuse me** scusi (polite), scusa (informal); **open** aperto; **closed** chiuso; **entrance** entrata; **exit** uscita; **left** sinistra; **right** destra; **car** macchina; **bus** autobus; **train** treno; **bus stop** fermata dell'autobus; **ticket/s** biglietto/i; **I would like a ticket to...** vorrei un biglietto per...; **postcard** cartolina; **stamp** francobollo; **glass** bicchiere; **coffee** caffè; **tea** tè; **water** acqua; **wine** vino; **beer** birra; **the bill** il conto; **single/twin/double**

bedroom camera singola/a due letti/matrimoniale; **booking** prenotazione; **May I see the menu?** Posso vedere il menù?; **The bill, please.** Il conto, per favore.

Days of the week

Monday lunedì
Tuesday martedì
Wednesday mercoledì
Thursday giovedì
Friday venerdì
Saturday sabato
Sunday domenica
yesterday ieri
today oggi
tomorrow domani
morning mattina
afternoon pomeriggio
evening sera
night notte
weekend fine settimana, weekend

Numbers & money

0 zero; **1** uno; **2** due; **3** tre; **4** quattro; **5** cinque; **6** sei; **7** sette; **8** otto; **9** nove; **10** dieci; **11** undici; **12** dodici; **13** tredici; **14** quattordici; **15** quindici; **16** sedici; **17** diciassette; **18** diciotto; **19** diciannove; **20** venti; **21** ventuno; **22** ventidue; **30** trenta; **40** quaranta; **50** cinquanta; **60** sessanta; **70** settanta; **80** ottanta; **90** novanta; **100** cento; **1,000** mille; **2,000** duemila; **100,000** centomila; **1,000,000** un milione.

How much does it cost/is it? Quanto costa?/quant'è?
Do you have any change? Ha da cambiare?
Can you give me a discount? Mi può fare uno sconto?
Do you accept credit cards? Si accettano le carte di credito?
Can I pay in pounds/dollars/travellers' cheques? Posso pagare in sterline/dollari/con i travellers?
Can I have a receipt? Posso avere una ricevuta?

Index